The Letter of

JUDE

A Wake-up Call to Christians in the
Twenty-first Century

Guy Manuell

THE LETTER OF JUDE:
A Wake-up Call to Christians in the Twenty-first Century

Printed in the United States of America
ISBN 979-8-89633-032-5 (sc)
ISBN 979-8-89633-034-9 (e)

This book is printed on acid-free paper.

Because of the dynamic nature of the Internet, any web addresses or
links contained in this book may have changed since publication and
may no longer be valid. The views expressed in this work are solely those
of the author and do not necessarily reflect the views of the publisher,
and the publisher hereby disclaims any responsibility for them.

2025.02.17

Page Solutions - Prowriters Network
124 Rock Crystal Ln,
Lakeside Park,
KY 41017A
United States

PAGE
SOLUTIONS
PROWRITERS NETWORK

'Biblical exegesis and theology are not disciplines solely for academic scholars. In this commentary on Jude, Guy Manuell shows how someone active in church life and a businessman, can apply himself to commenting on the Greek text of a New Testament book. This he does with competence and freshness, and is able to apply it in a manner often missing in commentaries. He is able to show how relevant the book of Jude is for the contemporary church. Wide reading has enriched his study, and now his commentary is going to be a stimulus to others as they approach Jude.'

Dr. Allan M. Harman
Research Professor of Old Testament,
Presbyterian   Theological   College,
Melbourne, Australia

'This deeply researched and briskly argued study does not limit itself to describing Jude's meaning for its first-century readers. It is equally concerned with calling attention to "a cancer that is ravaging the body of Christ" today. Making creative comparison between ills addressed in Jude and problems evident in Paul's Corinth, Guy Manuell furnishes an exposition of Jude that enlightens, provokes, encourages, challenges, and most of all instructs. It interprets a pastoral letter with pastoral insight yet scholarly grasp of Jude's language, historical setting, and contemporary interpretation. I recommend it highly for those who teach and preach in the church, as well as for any others who are willing to see the desperate decadence of our times (including, often, in churches) and the glory of God's call to repentance and godly living through the true faith in the
Lord Jesus Christ whom Jude exalts, serves, and pungently proclaims.' **Dr. Robert W. Yarbrough**

Contents

Preface

My interest in *Jude* began with a desire to translate a book of the New Testament (NT). *Jude* seemed an achievable task, given its small size! That effort led to an appreciation of its relevance to the situation prevalent in the Christian church in the twenty-first century. The outcome is this commentary. It is designed to assist theological students and Christian pastors and ministers who wish to supplement their knowledge of *Jude*. This commentary is also designed for well-informed lay people who want to understand the Bible without having to delve into every intricate detail of the Greek language or ancient documents concerning the letter. Hopefully, some seminary teachers will find it of value in updating their knowledge of *Jude* and considering issues never before discussed.

It attempts to provide a clear explanation of the Greek text of *Jude*. If this letter is properly understood, it should compel twenty-first-century Christians to contemplate how they might address some of the practical problems facing the modern church as they contend for the faith once for all time entrusted to the saints (*Jude* 3).

This book also provides an analysis comparing *Jude* with 1 Corinthians in terms of their comparable literary styles, and the errors found by Jude and the apostle Paul in the churches to which they wrote. It suggests the possible identification of Jude's 'Intruders' as men with previous (Christian) experience in the Corinthian church. Such a connection between the two letters has never previously been examined as far as can be ascertained.

Jude is placed in his historical context: a Jewish author in the second half of the first century ad,[1] who wishes to warn members

---

[1] . This text uses BC and AD to denote years, in preference to the currently politically correct BCE/CE nomenclature used by historians. It is Christ who has changed the measurement of world time, not racial, ethnic, or political sensitivities.

of the early Jesus movement against Intruders in their midst and prevent those believers' deviation from the fundamental tenets of 'the faith'. This commentary uses what Schreiner describes as 'a historical approach,' whereby he states, 'I believe that the goal of interpretation is to pursue the author's intention.'[2] This naturally leads to the question as to whether some of Jude's sources for his inspiration were themselves orthodox then, and acceptable now. For reasons argued in the text, they were and are. Therefore, even though a small book in size (only twenty-five verses), *Jude* speaks as authoritatively as any other book in the NT.

Jude reminds us of Paul's warning to Timothy: 'For the time will come when they will not endure sound doctrine; but wanting to have their ears tickled, they will accumulate for themselves teachers in accordance with their own desires.' (2 Tim. 4:3).

It is all very well writing a commentary that analyses an ancient text to determine what it intended to say and to whom. But *Jude* is a book in the NT that is God's Word to us today. Some commentaries on *Jude* provide in-depth analysis in a historical context but have far less to say about the implications of the letter for modern Christians. This commentary seeks to bring *Jude* alive in the twenty-first century and make its message clear to the modern church. It is a message of vital importance to those in a supposedly Christian community (particularly in the West) in which the fundamentals of Christian doctrine ('the faith') are persistently questioned and disavowed much more than they are defended.

---

[2]. T. R. Schreiner, *1, 2 Peter, Jude*, The New American Commentary (Nashville, TN: Broadman and Holman, 2003), 404 n. 5. Schreiner specifically condemns works that do not have this aim.

Regrettably, the present church in Western society has reached this outcome more comprehensively than many Christians would have imagined possible one hundred years ago. Even many of those now calling themselves 'evangelical' have abandoned any pretence of adhering to biblical doctrines. This was brilliantly revealed by Francis Schaeffer, who observed that 'the great evangelical disaster [is] the failure of the evangelical world to stand for truth as truth. There is only one word for this—namely *accommo-*

dation: the evangelical church has accommodated to the world spirit of the age.'[3] Jude would be horrified by what he would see and hear today in many 'Christian' churches and would have to start writing all over again!

In his condemnation of the Intruders, Jude's language is stronger than that of anyone else in the NT, except, perhaps, for Jesus himself. With today's obsession about political correctness in everything said or written, so that no one suffers any distress or takes any offence, Jude's tone may seem rather strong to some. However, it is a breath of fresh air when someone speaks biblical truth plainly. In the words of T. H. Huxley, 'The necessity of making things plain to uninstructed people was one of the very best means of clearing up the obscure corners in one's own mind.'[4] Jude had no doubt that the Intruders of whom he wrote faced certain doom because of their actions and words.

Schaeffer concludes that 'Evangelicals today are facing a watershed concerning the nature of biblical inspiration and authority.'[5] His description of a watershed is quoted below because it is a profound illustration of what has happened, and is still happening, to the Western Church:

> Not far from where we live in Switzerland is a high ridge of rock with a valley on both sides. One time I was there when there was snow on the ground along that ridge. The snow was lying there unbroken, a seeming unity. However, that unity was an illusion, for it lay along a great divide; it lay along a watershed. One portion of the snow when it melted would flow into one valley. The snow which laid close beside would flow into another valley when it melted.

---

[3] . F. A. Schaeffer, *The Great Evangelical Disaster* (Westchester, IL: Crossway Books, 1984), 37.

[4] . T. H. Huxley, in *The Oxford Dictionary of Quotations* (Oxford: Oxford University Press, 1999), 397:16.

[5] . Schaeffer, *Evangelical Disaster*, 44.

Now it just so happens on the particular ridge that the melting snow which flows down one side of that ridge goes down into a valley, into a small river, and then down into the Rhine River. The Rhine then flows on through Germany and the *The Letter of Jude*

water ends up in the cold waters of the North Sea. The water from the snow that started out so close along that watershed on the other side of the ridge, when this snow melts, drops off sharply down the ridge into the Rhone Valley. This water flows into Lac Leman—or as it is known in the English-speaking world, Lake Geneva—and then goes down below that into the Rhone River which flows through France and into the warm waters of the Mediterranean.

The snow lies along that watershed, unbroken, as a seeming unity. But when it melts, where it ends in its destinations is literally a thousand miles apart. That is a watershed. That is what a watershed is. A watershed divides. A clear line can be drawn between what seems at first to be the same or at least very close, but in reality, ends in very different situations. In a watershed there is a line.[6]

Jude helps us to avoid the error of falling down the wrong side of the watershed that is the line between biblical truth and error. Jude's letter calls faithful men and women to forswear silence and to speak boldly of the plain truth of the Bible's revelation of Christ as Lord as well as his demands on the lives of his followers. *Jude* is 'a graphic and striking description of the apostasy. What was a little cloud the size of a man's hand in Jude's day, is in our day, a storm of hurricane proportions.'[7]

---

[6] . Schaeffer, *Evangelical Disaster*, 43–44.

[7] . J. V. McGee, *The General Epistle of Jude* in *Thru the Bible with J. Vernon McGee* (Pasadena, CA: Thru the Bible Radio, 1983), 5:851.

It would be exceedingly difficult to contemplate writing about the Letter of Jude without having many expert commentaries at one's elbow. They explore subtle nuances of the original language, provide voluminous historical sources and references to other commentators—skills beyond my capacity. However, it also needs to be said that their work contains much technical detail that is probably beyond the interest of those readers for whom this book is intended.

There are many highly technical commentaries and journal articles about *Jude* that explore nuances in the Greek text, the interpretation of a range of ancient manuscripts of *Jude*, a vari-

ety of original sources in the ancient world for various words or phrases appearing in the letter, plus other technical issues regarding the text. As a matter of policy, many of these sources are not used unless they bear specifically on the biblical text under consideration. This is for several reasons. First, much of this material engages the Greek text in a manner that is far too technical for this volume's intended readers. Secondly, significant parts of these comments are either anachronistic or simply incorrect in the light of more recent scholarship. Thirdly, there is no point in providing every possible explanation available, knowing beforehand that they are either incorrect or implausible.

There is a silent contribution to this book from the myriad of Christians throughout the past twenty centuries who have successfully contended for the faith once for all time entrusted to the saints, and who have made it possible for the gospel of our Lord Jesus Christ to be alive and trustworthy today. Without their perseverance, the gospel would have disappeared.

I express gratitude to Ruth Weatherlake and the librarians of the Leon Morris Library at Ridley College, Melbourne for their willing assistance. All omissions and errors are, of course, my responsibility.

Most of all, I acknowledge the gracious hand of the Triune God—Father, Son and Holy Spirit—who has guided me on this journey (Psalm 48:14).

Guy Manuell
Curlewis, Australia
November 2021

Issues of Clarification

The following notes provide guidance on the style and format of this book. ***Greek Text***

The Greek text used in this book is the United Bible Societies' *Greek New Testament,* 5th edition, 2014.

Transliteration

When Greek words first appear in the commentary they are spelt in Greek, followed by an English transliteration in italics. Unless there is a need to refer to the Greek text, subsequent appearances of those Greek words generally appear in the transliterated form, for ease of reading. A copy of the Greek text of *Jude*, together with a table of the English transliteration of Greek letters, appears at the end of the book.

References to Other Sources

This commentary provides my own reflections on *Jude*. However, where comments have originated from other sources, appropriate acknowledgement is given. Biblical quotations are from the New American Standard Bible 1995[8] (NASB), unless otherwise stated. ***Other Matters***

Peter Davids' terminology 'the early Jesus movement' is used when referring to earliest Christianity.[9]

References to the Letter of Jude are in italics (*Jude*) and references to its author are not.

---

[8] . *New American Standard Bible* (La Habra, CA: Foundation Press Publications, 1995)

[9] . P. H. Davids, *The Letters of 2 Peter and Jude*, The Pillar New Testament Commentary (Grand Rapids, MI: Wm. B. Eerdmans Publishing Company, 2006), 3.

Introduction

Judea in the First Century ad[10]

The Letter of Jude was written to some first-century ad followers of Jesus, who lived in Palestine. The early Jesus movement had its centre in Jerusalem until the destruction of the city by the Romans in ad 70. Before analysing this letter, a broad description of the eastern Mediterranean world in the first century assists in understanding its historical context. The geographical area of relevance to *Jude* ranges across the Roman Empire from (in modern terms) Greece, Turkey, Palestine, and on to Egypt. Judea was caught in the middle of this vast territory, with its major city, Jerusalem, one of the empire's most important cities at the eastern end of the Mediterranean. This was the case from before Jesus' birth until beyond the destruction of Jerusalem in ad 70. The Greco-Roman (Hellenistic) culture of the Roman Empire contributed importantly to the problems discussed in *Jude* and, therefore, the way Jude sought to resolve them for his readers.[11] Neyrey correctly emphasises the critical need for twenty-first century readers to abandon their modern thought patterns and read the letter by 'appreciating the symbolic and social world of a people not only separated from us by two thousand years but also by a radically different culture.'[12]

---

[10]. For detailed facts contained in this section, see L. G. Perdue and W. Carter, *Israel and Empire: A Postcolonial History of Israel and Early Judaism* (London: Bloomsbury T. and T. Clark, 2015), 217–291; E. M. Smallwood, *The Jews Under Roman Rule* (Leiden: E. J. Brill, 1976), 144–80. A broad overview of the subject is found in M. Goodman, *Rome and Jerusalem: The Clash of Ancient Civilizations* (New York: Vintage Books, 2007).

[11]. See P. Garnsey and R. Saller, *The Roman Empire: Economy, Society and Culture* (Berkeley, CA: California University Press, 1987) for a general overview of the Roman Empire in the first century.

[12]. J. H. Neyrey, *2 Peter, Jude* (New York: Doubleday, 1993), 3. Neyrey 'employs

In 63 bc, the Roman general Pompey defeated Mithridates VI of Pontus, ended the Hasmonean state and brought Palestine into the Roman Empire. Pompey sacked Jerusalem and established Hasmonean prince Hyrcanus II as Ethnarch and High Priest but he was denied the title of king. A later appointment by Julius Caesar was Antipater the Idumaean, also known as Antipas, as the first Roman Procurator. Herod the Great, Antipater's son, was designated 'King of the Jews' by the Roman Senate in 40 bc but he was unable to gain military control of the region until 37 bc. During his reign the last representatives of the Hasmoneans were eliminated. Granted almost unlimited autonomy in the country's internal affairs, Herod became one of the most powerful monarchs in the eastern part of the Roman Empire. A great admirer of Hellenistic culture, he launched a massive construction programme, which included the cities of Caesarea and Sebaste and the fortresses at Herodium and Masada. He also remodelled the Jerusalem Temple into one of the most magnificent buildings of its time. But despite his many achievements, Herod's dependence on Rome's favour prevented him from winning the trust and support of his Jewish subjects.

Herod the Great died in 4 bc and his kingdom was divided mostly among three of his sons, who became 'tetrarchs' (rulers of a quarter part—even though, in this case, they were rulers of thirds). One of these tetrarchies was Judea, corresponding to the territory of the historic Judea, plus Samaria and Idumea. Herod's son, Herod Archelaus, ruled Judea so badly that he was dismissed in ad 6 by Roman emperor Augustus after an appeal from his own population. He was replaced by several Roman prefects over Judea. The most famous of these was Pontius Pilate, who ruled from ad 26 to 36 and was widely hated for his despotic acts towards the Jews. Caiaphas had been appointed High Priest of Herod's Temple in ad 18 by the prefect Lucius Vitellius. Favour with Rome allowed Herod's grandson, Herod Agrippa i, to rule briefly over Judea (ad 41–44), but his early death again left the governorship of Judea in the hands of Roman prefects. The Jewish historian Flavius Josephus[4] graphically

a new and perhaps unfamiliar method for reading these documents, namely, the use of the social sciences for interpretation of ancient documents.'
4. Flavius Josephus, *The Antiquities of the Jews*, trans. L. H. Feldman, Loeb Clas-
depicts the unwise and often heinous acts of this string of Roman prefects.

Another of Herod the Great's sons, Herod Antipas, ruled as tetrarch of Galilee and Perea from 4 bc to ad 39 before he was dismissed by Roman emperor Caligula. The third tetrarch, Herod's son Philip, ruled over the north-eastern part of his father's kingdom (the northern Transjordan) from 4 bc to ad 34.

Between ad 41–44, Judea regained its nominal autonomy, when Herod Agrippa i was made 'King of the Jews' by Roman emperor Claudius, thus in a sense restoring the Herodian dynasty, but the region remained under complete Roman domination. Following Agrippa's death in ad 44, the province returned to direct Roman control, incorporating Agrippa's personal territories of Galilee and Perea, under several prefects. Nevertheless, Agrippa's son, Agrippa ii, was designated 'King of the Jews' in ad 48. Because Agrippa ii maintained loyalty to the empire, he retained his kingdom until he died near the end of the first century, when Judea returned to complete Roman control. He was the seventh and last of the Herodians.

Growing anger against increased Roman suppression of Jewish life resulted in sporadic violence that escalated into a fullscale revolt in ad 66. Superior Roman forces, led by Titus, were finally victorious, razing Jerusalem to the ground (ad 70) and defeating the last Jewish outpost at Masada (ad 73), the virtually impregnable fortress built by Herod the Great. From ad 70 to 135 Judea's rebelliousness required a governing Roman legate capable of commanding legions.

As a Roman province, Judea's revenue was of little importance to the Roman treasury. The region had little agricultural or mineral wealth. However, by the first century ad, Egypt had become the breadbasket of the empire and huge volumes of grain were exported from Egypt to other parts of the empire around the Mediterranean. Much of this grain was transported by ship, but a not insignificant proportion was transported by land. This is what made Judea so important to the empire. Judea comprised the land and coastal sea routes between Egypt and the eastern

---

sical Library (London: Heinemann, 1969). Books XIX and XX are relevant to this period.

Mediterranean. Being a critical supply route, the Romans were determined to maintain control of the region, despite its own lack of resources and the persistent intransigence of the local population towards Roman rule.

The people of Judea were generally of low prosperity, being either small (family) business owners (like carpenters or fishermen), artisans, farmers, or hired labourers. There are examples of these occupations in the Gospels. It is quite inappropriate to regard these individuals' state of existence as that of ignorant peasants. It is possible to overemphasise Jesus' background as more impoverished than it was (and many commentators have). [13] However, Roman taxes would have hindered the accumulation of wealth. Jewish cultural customs made life difficult for single women and widows. Therefore, there was little impetus to increase the demand for goods or services above what was necessary for a modest existence. Also, the region was dotted with many small villages (like Nazareth and Capernaum) so this also hindered the development of the economy. Nevertheless, Jesus could not have credibly told stories about rich and wealthy people if they did not exist. Passages like Luke 12:16–21 and Matt. 25:14–28 suggest that there were some very wealthy people too, as there are in many societies today. Such people would have employed large numbers of low-paid workers (see Matt. 20:1–12). The Gospels also describe the wealth of Jewish tax collectors, working under the Roman occupation, through their rapacious activities (Luke 19:1–8).

---

[13] . To some extent, this represents a common prejudice in modern society that those who succeed from difficult or poor backgrounds have earnt more entitlement to praise than those who accomplished the same achievements having come from a more privileged environment. This is a human viewpoint that has no justification from the gospel.

4

Overall, the population of Judea welcomed anything that would improve their economic lot and lighten the burden of Roman rule. It is hardly surprising that Jesus attracted large crowds in rural areas, where the people thought that deliverance from their present physical difficulties was on Jesus' agenda. The incident in John 6:15 after the feeding of the five thousand demonstrates the misinterpretation of Jesus' message by the common people and their desperation for an improvement in their economic and political situation.

The greatest benefit that Rome gave to the then-known world around the Mediterranean was *Pax Romana*: a general aura of peace that enabled relatively safe travel over long distances, enabling Paul and his companions to travel from Jerusalem to Asia Minor (modern Turkey), Greece and even Rome. In due course, members of the early Jesus movement would travel to the ends of the then-known world to spread the gospel, which could not have spread as rapidly as it did without the overarching benefit of the peace imposed by Rome. The other important aspect of this benign order was communication. Letters and messages could be transmitted across the empire relatively quickly by the standards of the day, as seen in Acts and Paul's letters. This meant that communities of the Jesus movement could keep in touch with one another with relative speed and ease. Indeed, it was just such a timely communication that not only alerted Jude to the problem about which he wrote but also enabled him to respond promptly.

It is not possible to paint a broad canvas of Judea in the first century without commenting on the state of Judaism as it affected those who came to believe in Jesus. The Gospels make it clear that Jesus was dissatisfied with a religion that had the trappings of Old Testament (OT) ritual and procedure but lacked the true spirit of both faithful devotion and obedience to Yahweh (YHWH) (Matt. 23:27). In Judea, the early Jesus movement would have been regarded as one among many Jewish sects that were trying to revive the faith of their ancestors. However, it must be emphasised that Jesus' followers regarded themselves as unique in a theological sense among these other Jewish revivalist groups by their acceptance of Jesus as Messiah. They were people anxiously looking forward to the return of Jesus while trying to cope with a world and cultures (primarily Roman and Greek) entirely at odds with their beliefs. This situation has its own parallels in the modern world, where Christians are faced with increasingly hostile cultural environments.

'The Hellenistic influence, which shows itself *inter alia* in the profusion of Greek loan-words to be found in the Rabbinic literature, depended not on politics but on culture. For this very reason, therefore, it had a stronger impact than the Roman influence.'[14] There is ample evidence of communication between Jews in Rome and Jerusalem after Judea became a Roman province (Acts 28:21) and '[a]s early as the time of Hyrcanus ii (76–67 bc and 63–40 bc) we find Athenians in Jerusalem, the coming and going between the two cities being occasioned as much by official as by private affairs.'[15] The lingua franca of the first century was Greek, hence the reason for writing the earliest Christian documents in a language that was comprehended in the farthest reaches of the empire around the Mediterranean Sea. Paul would have spoken in Greek to his Gentile (and probably most Jewish) hearers outside Judea, enabling the gospel of Jesus to spread rapidly by oral communication. There can be no doubt that Jesus and his disciples spoke Greek, as evidenced by John 12:20–22. The description of 'Greeks' in this incident does not necessarily mean that the inquirers were natives of Greece. It indicates that they were Gentiles (perhaps converts to Judaism), and it is most likely that they did not speak Aramaean, so the conversation between them and Philip—and, subsequently, between them and Jesus—would have occurred in Greek. The very fact that John describes these people as 'Greeks' speaks strongly in favour of this linguistic reality.

It would be necessary for the early members of the Jesus movement to come to grips with the implications of the gospel for their social and personal assimilation into Hellenistic culture and the political situation in which they found themselves. *Jude*

---

[14] . J. Jeremias, *Jerusalem in the Time of Jesus* (London: SCM Press, 1969), 64.

[15] . Jeremias, *Jerusalem in the Time of Jesus*, 64.

reminds its readers that allegiance to Christ and his gospel must always overrule every other opposing consideration. This is particularly relevant today when so many competing influences (e.g., materialism, politics, culture, relationships, status, family) vie for every person's supreme loyalty. The Letter of Jude is as relevant today as it ever was.

The Author

The dating of the letter (see below) is an important determinant of the identity of its author. If it is a *second-century* document, the author cannot have been one of the four Judases mentioned in the NT:

1. Judas Barsabbas (Acts 15:22);[16]
2. the apostle Judas, son of James (Luke 6:16; John 14:22; Acts 1:13);
3. Judas called Iscariot,[17] who was one of the Twelve and who betrayed Jesus (Luke 6:16);
4. Judas, the brother of Jesus.

The fourth Judas (above) is mentioned in Matt. 13:55 and Mark 6:3 as a brother of Jesus, together with James, who became the leader of the early Jesus movement in Jerusalem, Joses (an abbreviation of his father's name, Joseph) and Simon. Another possibility is that the letter is pseudepigraphical [18] or pseudonymous.[19] But questions easily arise: Why would anyone choose the name Jude (Judas)? Why not use James or Peter or the name of one of Jesus' better-known disciples? These possibilities

---

[16] . E. E. Ellis, *Prophecy and Hermeneutic in the Early Church* (Grand Rapids, MI: Wm. B. Eerdmans Publishing Company, 1978), 226–230.

[17] . Iscariot refers to his birthplace of Kerioth in southern Judah. He was the only one of the Twelve who was not a Galilean.

[18] . Jewish writings ascribed to various biblical patriarchs, prophets, or teachers, but composed c. 200 BC to AD 200.

[19] . A text whose claimed authorship is represented by a separate author, or a work whose real author attributes it to a person in the past.

have been rejected by most modern commentators but still have their adherents.[20]

Since his Greek name is Judas (his Hebrew name would have been Judah), why is the writer of this letter called 'Jude'? The most likely reason is to distinguish him from the betrayer. The only ancient comment on this point is from Hilary of Arles, who postulated that 'Jude does his utmost to make sure that nobody confuses him with Judas Iscariot, which is why he confesses that he is Christ's servant and James' brother.'[13] The writer of *Jude* is clearly not the apostle, Judas son of James, and the writer of *Jude* does not call himself an apostle (v. 17). Could the writer of *Jude* be a brother of Jesus? This is now the widely held view.[14]

It is helpful to take account of the writer's self-description as 'slave of Jesus Christ'[15] and 'brother of Jacob' (James). In the first century, Judah (Judas/Jude) was as common a Hebrew name as Alan is today in Western culture. If this writer simply called himself Jude, no one would know who he was or with what authority he could write a letter like this. He needed some identification, such as his place of birth or the name of his Jewish tribe. This writer chooses to identify himself (in an explicit manner understood by the early Jesus movement) by naming his famous brother, Jacob (James). It is likely that James is mentioned to support the contents of Jude's letter: it is as if Jude is alleging that James would have written the same things had he the opportunity. 'Among the patristic authors, Jude is more often referred to as an "apostle" than as "brother of James" or "brother of the Lord". But by any of these appellations, he is designated as an authoritative

---

[20] . Adherents include J. N. D. Kelly, *A Commentary on the Epistles of Peter and of Jude*, Black's New Testament Commentary (London: Adam and Charles Black, 1969), 242; B. Reicke, *The Epistles of James, Peter and Jude*, The Anchor Bible (New York: Doubleday, 1964), 190–191. See the list in R. J. Bauckham, *Jude and the Relatives of Jesus in the Early Church* (London: T. and T. Clark, 1990), 174 of others who hold these views. For a rejection of these views, see Schreiner, *1, 2 Peter, Jude*, 406; C. E. B. Cranfield, *1 and 2 Peter and Jude*, Torch Bible Commentaries (London: SCM Press, 1960), 146–148; D. Guthrie, *New Testament Introduction* (Downers Grove,

IL: Inter-Varsity Press, 1970), 905–908; P. H. Davids, *2 Peter and Jude: A Handbook on the Greek Text*, Baylor Handbook on the Greek New Testament (Waco, TX: Baylor University Press, 2011), xviii–xix.

13. G. L. Bray, 'James, 1–2 Peter, 1–3 John, Jude' in *Ancient Christian Commentary on Scripture* (Downers Grove, IL: Inter-Varsity Press), 2000, 11:246. (This work is abbreviated ACCS throughout the rest of these notes.) This is supported by S. J. Kistemaker, *Exposition of the Epistles of Peter and the Epistle of Jude, New Testament Commentary* (Grand Rapids, MI: Baker Books, 1987); J. MacArthur, *2 Peter and Jude*, The MacArthur New Testament Commentary (Chicago: Moody Publishers, 2005), 142. Hilary of Arles (c. 401–449) was Archbishop of Arles and leader of the Semi-Pelagian Party. Hilary incurred the wrath of Pope Leo I when he removed a bishop from his see and appointed a new bishop. Leo demoted Hilary from a metropolitan see to a bishopric to assert papal power over the church in Gaul.

14. See also comments below on v. 1.

15. See comprehensive comments on v. 1 regarding this matter.

figure.'[21]

Given the virgin birth of Jesus (Matt. 1:25), his brothers[22] and sisters[23] described in the Gospels were the children of Joseph and Mary, obviously younger than him.[24] James was clearly the oldest of these, and Judas was younger than James,[25] although Matthew and Mark differ in their order of two of the brothers. Jude identifies himself at the outset of his letter as 'brother of James'. There was only one prominent James in the early Jesus movement: the brother of Jesus. James was the eldest of Jesus' younger brothers. The brothers of Jesus were widely known in the movement, even as far away as Corinth (1 Cor. 9:5), and at least two were married and entitled to the right to have 'a believing wife' accompany them. It would, therefore, be most surprising if Jude were not well known within the early Jesus movement in Palestine. Although interesting in his generalisations about life in

[21] . J. Hultin, 'Jude's Citation of 1 Enoch,' in *The Function of 'Canonical' and 'Non-Canonical' Religious Texts*, ed. J. H. Charlesworth and L. M. McDonald (London: T. and T. Clark, 2010), 120 n. 2.

[22] . Matt. 12:46–47; 13:55; Mark 6:3; John 2:12; 7:3, 5, 10.

[23] . Matt. 13:56; Mark 6:3.

[24] . The suggestion by Clement of Alexandria that Jude was a son of Joseph by a previous marriage is rejected as fanciful speculation.

[25] . Accepting the convention that siblings would be listed according to their age.

first-century Palestine, Neyrey sometimes goes too far in his speculative assumptions about the social context in which Jude found himself.[26]

Early Christian writers made the following comments about Jude's heritage:

> **Clement of Alexandria:** Jude was the brother of the sons of Joseph, but despite his relationship to the Lord, he did not say that he was Jesus' brother. What did he say? He called himself Jude, the servant of Jesus Christ; that is, of the Lord, and the brother of James, who was the Lord's brother. (*Adumbrations*)[27]
>
> **Eusebius of Caesarea:** When Roman emperor Domitian ordered that those of the race of David be slain, an ancient story holds that some of the heretics accused the grandchildren of Jude (the brother of the Saviour, according to the flesh), on the grounds that they really were of the family of David and were related to Christ Himself. Hegesippus makes this quite clear. (*History of the Church* 3.19)[23] Hegesippus further says that other descendants of one of the so-called brothers of the Lord, Jude by name, lived until the reign of Trajan (ad 98–117), after giving testimony of their faith in Christ in the time of Domitian (ad 81–96). (*History of the Church* 3.32)[24]
>
> **Oecumenius:** This apostle, after calling himself the servant of Jesus Christ, went on to add that he was the brother of James, because James was so highly regarded in the church that Jude was bound to benefit from so close an association with him. Note that he refers to his correspondents as those who have been 'called', because it was not they who decided to follow Jesus, but God who

---

[26] . Neyrey, *2 Peter, Jude*, 32–41.

[27] . *ACCS*, 245. Clement of Alexandria (c. 150–215) was a highly-educated Christian convert from paganism, head of the catechetical school in Alexandria, and pioneer of Christian scholarship. His major works, *Protrepticus*, *Paedagogus*, and the *Stromata* bring Christian doctrine face-to-face with the

reached out to call them to his service. (*Commentary on Jude*)[25]

It is interesting that the first and last of the seven books of the Bible often known as the 'catholic epistles'[26] (James; 1 and 2 Peter;

---

ideas and achievements of his time.

23. *ACCS*, 245. Eusebius of Caesarea (c. 260/263–340) was Bishop of Caesarea, partisan of Emperor Constantine, and first historian of the Christian church. He argued that the truth of the gospel had been foreshadowed in pagan writings but had to defend his own doctrine against suspicion of Arian sympathies.

24. *ACCS*, 245. See also C. Bigg, *A Critical and Exegetical Commentary on the Epistles of St Peter and St Jude*, The International Critical Commentary (New York: C. Scribner's Sons, 1901), 317–318.

25. *ACCS*, 246. Oecumenius (sixth century) was called the Rhetor or the Philosopher and wrote the earliest extant Greek commentary on Revelation. Scholia by Oecumenius on some of John Chrysostom's commentaries on the Pauline Epistles are still extant.

26. This is using 'catholic' in its proper meaning of 'universal'; i.e. such letters were supposed to be addressed to members of the Jesus movement in general, rather than to a specific assembly. They are claimed to be more like sermons for general distribution. The term has nothing to do with Catholicism, and it does not mean that the letter should be associated with the Roman Catholic Church.

1, 2 and 3 John; Jude) are the letters of James and Jude, the brothers of Jesus—the eldest and the younger(est?).

By the time of writing this letter, Jude had undergone a radical transformation in his thinking. John 7:5 describes the unbelief of Jesus' brothers. It is possibly not until after the resurrection that Jesus' brothers recognised his divinity (1 Cor. 15:7). Acts 1:14 records that Jesus' mother, Mary, and his brothers were in an upstairs room with the disciples after Jesus' ascension. By the time this letter was penned, Jude had recognised Jesus for who he really was: the Son of God, God himself. How ironic that Jesus would have known at least two Judases well. One was a disciple who followed Jesus from early on in his ministry but eventually betrayed him. The other was a brother who misunderstood early on but later believed. There are important lessons here. Christians should not be too quick to condemn or reject those who do not grasp the gospel quickly or readily. It may well be that Jude penned verse 22 from personal reflection on his own earlier beliefs.

Jesus had the same experience in John 6:66. Judas Iscariot was just an extreme example of a not uncommon tendency over the centuries. We all know people who have professed strong faith in Christ only to fall by the wayside during life's journey. This is an aspect of the parable of the sower (Matt. 13:24–33). There is also an example in Paul's letters. In his personal letter to Philemon, Paul commends Demas, along with other Christians, including Luke (Phlm. 24). However, when writing to Timothy (2 Tim. 4:10), Paul announces that 'Demas, having loved this present world, has deserted me and gone to Thessalonica'. Time can change things in a person's faith—for good or ill.

Much of the discussion about Jude's claim to authorship revolves around the text and style of the letter. Cruder forms of doubt come in the style of 'How could a Jewish peasant from Galilee be able to write in such a manner in Greek?' Bauckham considers that very issue:

> [A]uthenticity appears not only possible but very probable. The work has all the marks of a fairly early work of Palestinian Jewish Christian provenance—in its use of the Hebrew Bible, haggadic traditions and apocryphal works of Palestinian origin, its strongly apocalyptic character, its skilful pesher–type exegesis, its imminent eschatological expectation and strong orientation towards the parousia, its concern with a controversy about antinomian teaching rather than about doctrine.[28]

Given all the evidence, the conclusion is that the author of *Jude* is Judah (otherwise called Judas or Jude), the half-brother[29] of Jesus

---

[28] . Bauckham, *Relatives of Jesus*, 177.

[29] . It is not being pedantic to note that, if Jesus' virgin birth is given credence, all his siblings were technically half-brothers and half-sisters whose parents were Joseph and Mary.

and brother of James, the leader of the Jerusalem assembly. For the past century, nearly all commentators have accepted this identification of the author of this letter. G. L. Green concludes that 'Jude, as others during his period, most likely made use of the services of a secretary when he composed the letter.'[30] That, clearly, is pure speculation.

The Relationship of *Jude* to 2 Peter

Most commentaries on *Jude* are paired with a commentary on 2 Peter because much of *Jude* (fifteen verses out of twenty-five) is also found in 2 Peter, a longer letter.[31] This is because one letter's contents have contributed to the text of the other.[32] As discussed below, there now seems no doubt that *Jude* preceded 2 Peter. For that reason, this commentary concentrates on *Jude* alone. In writing first, Jude should be given attention in his own right. That much of his letter found its way into 2 Peter ought to tell of its perceived worth by later readers, even an apostle, although it should be noted that 2 Peter 2:17b is the only identical clause with *Jude* (v. 13b). Peter's use of Jude's text addressed a different issue involving false teaching. Therefore, close attention should be paid to what Jude writes—and why he writes what he does. Each book needs to be considered on its own merits to understand the different problems addressed in each. Schreiner provides a helpful analysis of the parallels between the two books.[33]

If the author of 2 Peter was the apostle himself, the date of his death would set an outer limit to the date when *Jude* was composed. When did that occur? Using J. A. T. Robinson,[34]

[30] . G. L. Green, *Jude and 2 Peter*, Baker Exegetical Commentary on the New Testament (Grand Rapids, MI: Baker Academic, 2008), 8.

[31] . Bauckham, Bigg, Cranfield, Davids, E. M. G. Green, G. L. Green, Mayor and Wand, inter alia, have written joint commentaries on Jude and 2 Peter. See Bibliography for details.

[32] . Another possibility is that some of Jude and 2 Peter originated in another (unknown) document. That possibility is rejected, but it is accepted by Reicke, *Epistles of James, Peter and Jude*, 189–190.

[33] . Schreiner, *1, 2 Peter, Jude*, 416–417.

[34] . J. A. T. Robinson, *Redating the New Testament* (London: SCM Press, 1976).

Bauckham indicates the death of Peter occurred in ad 64 or 65. The authorship of 2 Peter remains a struggle with incomplete historical evidence, one which will probably never reach a firm conclusion. Bauckham is certain that 2 Peter is pseudepigraphical [35] and this influences his conclusions about dating *Jude*. Fifteen years earlier, E. M. G. Green closely examined the arguments for and against the apostle's authorship of 2 Peter, [36] concluding that it was written by Jesus' disciple, Simon Peter. Davids, however, provides a more nuanced verdict. While willing to confirm the strength of Bauckham's arguments, he is unwilling to concede that the letter was definitely not written by Peter.[37] My conclusion is that Green's and Davids' analyses support authorship of 2 Peter by the apostle himself. If this is correct, and *Jude* precedes 2 Peter, this has critical implications for the dating of *Jude*.

Date and Place of the Letter

The dating of *Jude* is one of the most difficult tasks in examining the letter. Most commentators now accept that *Jude* preceded 2 Peter.[38] However, several commentators opt for a later date of composition, ranging from the late first century to the middle of the second century.[38] Part of their explanation lies in their interpretation of two passages in *Jude* (vv. 3, 17) that could be construed as indicating a later date than the one proposed. As discussed below, neither verse implies either an early or late date for *Jude* but does nothing to distract from the conclusion of an early date. More than a century ago, Bigg concluded that 'the easier inference is that Jude followed Peter'.[39] He hoped that this might make dating and analysing the letter easier but he was

---

[35] . R. J. Bauckham, *Jude, 2 Peter*, Word Biblical Commentary (Waco, TX: Word Books, 1983), 161–162. This view is shared by Cranfield, *Jude*, 146 and, for this reason, he dates Jude around AD 80.

[36] . E. M. G. Green, *2 Peter and Jude*, Tyndale New Testament Commentaries (Grand Rapids, MI: Wm. B. Eerdmans Publishing Company, 1968), 13–35.

[37] . Davids, *2 Peter, Jude*, 149; see also 123–30, 148–149, 159–160.

[38] . See Kelly, *Epistles of Peter and of Jude*, 234; Bauckham, *Jude, 2 Peter*, 8; Davids, *2 Peter, Jude*, 12; J. B. Mayor, *The Epistle of St Jude and the Second*

wrong.[40] Much of the difficulty in dating *Jude* is removed if it is accepted that its author was the brother of Jesus *and the author of 2 Peter was the apostle himself.* Second Peter might be dated around ad 62–63, near the end of the apostle's life.[41]

Another relevant issue is the possible relationship between *Jude* and 1 Corinthians (see 'Rhetorical Analysis: *Jude* and 1 Corinthians' below). Should that be the case, the dating of 1 Corinthians is also relevant to the dating of *Jude*, given the argument that *Jude* was written later than 1 Corinthians. Morris dates 1 Corinthians as 'somewhere about the mid-fifties'.[42] Moffatt's estimate is 'not earlier than 55 and not later than 57'.[43]

Watson's research into the literary style of *Jude*, discussed below, strongly suggests that *Jude* preceded 2 Peter.[44] If *Jude* pre-

---

Epistle of St Peter (London: Macmillan, 1907), xxi–xxv.

38. This implicitly rejects authorship of 2 Peter by the apostle. Bauckham, Relatives of Jesus, 168–169 provides a wide range of dates for Jude from many commentators, ranging from ad 54 to 160.

39. Bigg, *Jude*, 315–18, 323; R. C. H. Lenski, *The Interpretation of the Epistles of St Peter, St John and St Jude* (Minneapolis, MN: Augsburg Publishing House, 1966), 243, 597 also argues for this position.

40. Throughout this commentary this basic assumption by Bigg continually compromises his analysis of Jude.

41. Petrine authorship of 2 Peter is advocated by inter alia E. H. Plumptre, *The General Epistles of St Peter and St Jude*, Cambridge Bible for Schools and Colleges (Cambridge: Cambridge University Press, 1879), 79–81; E. M. G. Green, *2 Peter and Jude*, 22–23; Guthrie, Introduction, 925–926.

42. L. L. Morris, *The First Epistle of Paul to the Corinthians*, Tyndale New Testament Series (Leicester, UK: Inter-Varsity Press, 1983), 29.

43. J. Moffatt, *The First Epistle of Paul to the Corinthians*, The Moffatt New Testament Commentary (London: Hodder and Stoughton, 1947), xv.

44. D. F. Watson, *Invention, Arrangement and Style: Rhetorical Criticism of Jude and 2 Peter*, SBL Dissertation Series 104 (Atlanta, GA: Scholars Press), 1988.

ceded 2 Peter, that puts an outer boundary on the date of Jude's authorship around ad 60–61. If *Jude* follows the events described in 1 Corinthians, it must have been written later than ad 57.

The reference in verse 3 to 'the faith once for all time entrusted to the saints' has been suggested by some to indicate the beginning of a formal statement of orthodox doctrine that could only have emerged near the end of the first century or, possibly, in the second century.[39] This is the core of the argument to place *Jude* among the catholic epistles and give it a date later than ad 70. This issue is also considered in comments on verse 3 below. This interpretation uses a theory to give these words a particular meaning that cannot be sustained. Jude's Greek text cannot justify the attribution of a late date to the letter and 'late date' arguments emerge primarily because of forcing historicity into Jude's language when there is no evidence of its presence.

In verse 17, Jude's use of τῶν ῥημάτων...τῶν ἀποστόλων (*tōn rhēmatōn...tōn apostolōn*—the words of the apostles) has raised much comment about the dating of the letter. The readers are encouraged to *remember* (μνήσθητε—*mnēsthēte*) what the apostles said. Some commentators have interpreted the use of 'remember' as evidence of a later date of composition. It would hardly be surprising for Jude to exhort his readers to remember something that they had been told a year before, for example. The text makes clear that the readers have received prior instruction from 'the apostles', but there is no suggestion in the Greek text to indicate how long ago this had occurred. Similarly, there is no evidence as to whether these apostles were dead or alive when Jude wrote—that is mere speculation. The nature and identity of those called 'apostles' in the first century is discussed more fully in comments on verse 17; it can be noted here that it is a term of some breadth. It will be shown in the commentary that the references to 'remember' and 'apostles' (v. 17) cannot be indicators of the date of the letter (early or late).

It is important to note Mayor's comment that ὅτι ἔλεγον ὑμῖν (*hoti elegon humin*— that they said to you) "imply that *the warning was spoken, not written*, and that it was often repeated."[40] This is an important clue to the dating of *Jude*. Jude is writing to people to

---

[39] . For example, H. Windisch, 'Die Katholischen Briefe,' in *Handbuch num Neuen Testament* 15, ed. H. Preisker (Tübingen: J. C. B. Mohr, 1951); K. H. Schelkle, 'Spätapostolische Briefe als frühkatholisches Zeugnis,' *Neutestamentliche Aufsätze fur J Schmidt*, ed. J. Blinzler, O. Kuss and F. Mussner (Regensburg: Verlag Friedrich Pustet, 1963), 225–332. This view is particularly strong among German theologians. See Bauckham, *Jude, 2 Peter*, 3, and Davids, *2 Peter, Jude*, 23, for refutation of this point.

[40] . Mayor, *Jude*, 46 (emphasis added).

whom the apostles spoke personally, indicating an early date. Jude reminds his readers that the apostles' words were said to them.

As with any line of inquiry that relies on uncertain data, so the dating of *Jude* must be assessed using certain assumptions. Their validity is the foundation on which the analysis is constructed. The following assumptions are used:

- Jude was a brother of Jesus.
- Peter the apostle was the author of 2 Peter around AD 60–63 and died around AD 64–65.
- Jude preceded 2 Peter.
- Jude is dated later than 1 Corinthians, which was penned around AD 55 to 57.

This suggests that Jude wrote his letter around ad 57 to 61, which would have given Peter time to read and use it in his second letter. This places the date of *Jude* close to the time of Paul's later correspondence.

For reasons discussed below concerning the language used in *Jude*, a location in Palestine is favoured as the place of composition. Further support for a Palestinian origin is the fact that Jude (and James) would have been best known in that region, with their identities (particularly James) adding further credence to the letter.

Another argument for Palestine as the place of composition is Jude's linguistic style (examined below). Additionally, evidence is presented of the sophistic nature of Jude's style of argument, which also suggests that the places of *both* writing and reception would have been cities where Greek literary styles were taught and understood by better-educated people. Davids concludes that:

> it is harder to imagine an author who lived outside of Palestine consulting sources in Hebrew or Aramaic or an author born outside of Palestine allowing Semitisms or Semitic enhancements to creep into his Greek (unless, like Paul, they had done significant study in Palestine). As we will see, there is considerable evidence that our

author did have contact with Hebrew or Aramaic source material.[41]

Where Jude resided is unknown, but it was probably Jerusalem.

The Reason for the Letter

Some people, thinking themselves to be followers of Jesus (described as *'the Intruders'*),[42] had infiltrated a congregation(s) that knew Jude and was known by him. Kistemaker goes so far as to allege that 'they were itinerant teachers who were bent on destroying the church of Jesus Christ.'[43] *Jude* provides no support for this proposition. The need for Jude's letter was an urgent response to what he perceived to be an immediate danger to these believers. Jude writes in the strongest terms, warning against this infiltration and encouraging his readers to resist their influence by holding firm to 'the faith'.[44] The primary purpose of this letter is to *motivate the readers to action* (cf. Heb. 13:22). Jude needed to confront errant behaviour that had both theoretical and practical implications for his readers. This matter is addressed more comprehensively in comments on verse 3. Martin's analysis follows:

> Jude does not use Paul's language, which prefers terms like 'the gospel' (Phil. 1:7, 27; Rom. 2:2–16; 16:25 (if authentic); 1 Cor. 15:1–2); 'the faith' (Phil. 1:27; Col.

---

[41] . Davids, *2 Peter, Jude*, 13, 22.

[42] . This description reflects the more recent considerations of R. A. Reese, *2 Peter and Jude*, The Two Horizons New Testament Commentary Series (Grand Rapids, MI: Wm. B. Eerdmans Publishing Company, 2007); P. H. Davids, *A Theology of James, Peter and Jude*, Biblical Theology of the New Testament (Grand Rapids, MI: Zondervan Publishing House, 2014), 252, who recognise that Jude never claimed that the Intruders taught anything or were perceived as preachers or teachers.

[43] . S. J. Kistemaker, *Exposition of the Epistles of Peter and the Epistle of Jude*, New Testament Commentary (Grand Rapids, MI: Baker Books, 1987), 373.

[44] . See V. C. Pfitzner, 'Paul and the Agon Motif,' *Novum Testamentum* Supplement 16 (Leiden: E. J. Brill, 1967) and comments on v. 3.

2:6–7; cf. Eph. 4:5; 1 Tim. 6:20–21); 'the truth' (Col. 1:5; cf. 2 Thess. 2:13; 2 Tim. 2:18, 25; 4:4); 'the apostolic traditions' (1 Cor. 11:2; 15:1–2; Gal. 1:9; Col. 2:6; 1 Thess. 4:1; cf. 2 Thess. 2:15). Other allusions to a corpus of distinctive doctrine, held to be a sacred deposit from God, are 'the apostles' teaching' (Acts 2:42); 'the standard of teaching' (Rom. 6:17); 'the words of faith and good doctrine' (1 Tim. 4:6); 'the pattern of sound words' (2 Tim. 1:13); and 'sound teaching' (2 Tim. 4:3; Ti. 1:9).

These diverse references give the impression of a web of saving truth and moral guidelines which provided for early believers the 'way' by which their new life in Christ was to be understood and practised. (Note the contrast in v. 11: the way of Cain.)[45]

One question that must be addressed is why virtually all commentators have called these interlopers 'false teachers'. The main reason lies in the 'Jude text' in 2 Pet. 2:1. It is clearly the case that, from the information available in *Jude*, the Intruders *did not* commit theological or doctrinal errors, nor did they oppose the leadership of the Jesus movement. *But the Intruders did contravene the established morality of the Jesus movement and Jewish morality generally.* This is an example where actions spoke louder than words. It was not necessary for these people to proclaim orally a 'new' gospel or to argue with the accepted teaching of the apostles to be regarded as unacceptable participants in the early Jesus movement. Their behaviour said it all. They acted in a manner which was quite contrary to Jesus' and Paul's teaching about appropriate behaviour for Jesus' followers. Paul's views were not disputed by the apostles (see Acts 15).

To reflect the seriousness of the matter, *Jude* provides several warnings from ancient times using examples of wrongdoers in the OT and other Jewish sacred writings. Jude is confident that the

---

[45] . R. P. Martin, 'The Theology of Jude, 1 Peter, and 2 Peter' in *The Theology of the Letters of James, Peter and Jude*, eds A. Chester and R. P. Martin (Cambridge: Cambridge University Press, 1994), 76.

fate of these Intruders was prophesied long ago and that it was inevitable that they were doomed for destruction.

While most commentators are content to view the letter as an appeal to fellow believers to protect themselves from bad influences, other reasons for its production have been advanced. Neyrey considered the letter to be an 'honour challenge':

> Jude claims a certain honour by virtue of blood relations with James (and Jesus); his official status is that of 'servant' of Jesus. But 'certain men' are obviously challenging this status. This letter contains the author's riposte, a defence both of the honour of Jesus which is slighted (vv. 4, 8) and of the honour ascribed to Jude which is challenged.[46]

This simply debases the letter to a missive of purely personal spite, rather than a pastoral response to serious error. It is an instance where Neyrey lets his 'social science' commentary overtake the textual facts.

Neyrey's reasoning is supported by Brosend, who goes even further in condemning Jude by suggesting that he was 'taking things personally'. [47] Brosend provides two possible interpretations of the reason for the letter. The first begins with the (traditional) view that Jude is defending the faith, but Brosend then accuses Jude of using a 'rhetoric of excess'.[48] The second interpretation takes this even further:

> The entire letter of Jude is an ad hominem attack unworthy of the faith in whose name it was written. It is mean-spirited, improperly personal, and evidence of little more than the author's knowledge of the very worst characterisations in the biblical and extra-canonical

---

[46] . Neyrey, *2 Peter, Jude*, 52.

[47] . W. F. Brosend II, 'The Letter of Jude: A Rhetoric of Excess or an Excess of Rhetoric?,' *Interpretation* 60:3 (2006): 292–305. Similar conclusions are contained in W. F. Brosend II, *James and Jude*, The New Cambridge Bible Commentary (Cambridge: Cambridge University Press, 2006), 183–187.

[48] . Brosend, *Rhetoric*, 303.

> tradition…the letter of Jude, in this view, is a repugnant excess of rhetoric, and the best thing to do with it is what the Church, with the exception of Second Peter's attempt to baptise it, has always done—ignore it.[49]

Brosend appears to favour the second interpretation. In a scene in one of Gilbert and Sullivan's operettas, *Princess Ida* (sometimes called *Castle Adamant*), one character, Psyche, makes a critical remark about another. Cyril responds, 'That's rather strong!' But Psyche has the last word: 'The truth is always strong!' Whether or not Jude's language is 'equal parts rhetoric of excess and excess of rhetoric'[50] (it is not, given the issue at hand), what Jude said was true and that must be accepted. 'Indifference to error is a sign of false liberalism and humiliating weakness.'[51]

In a similar vein, Brosend misunderstands Jude's emphasis on purity (vv. 7, 11, 13, 15, 16, 18, 23), not as a desire for godliness (cf. v. 15), but as some issue for Jude's own self-enhancement:

> It is not immorality or sexual licence that is the crux of the matter, but the usurpation of place, in particular the attempt by the opponents to usurp Jude's place. The rhetoric of impurity serves to support the rhetoric of claiming and taking something other than one's rightful place, which is itself a form of pollution.[52]

---

[49] . Brosend, *Rhetoric*, 304.

[50] . Brosend, *Rhetoric*, 305.

[51] . N. M. Williams, *Commentary on the Epistle of Jude*, An American Commentary on the New Testament (Philadelphia, PA: American Baptist Publication Society, 1888), 7:8.

[52] . Brosend, *James and Jude*, 188. See D. Lockett, 'Purity and Polemic: A Reassessment of Jude's Theological World' in *Reading Jude With New Eyes: Methodological Reassessments of the Letter of Jude*, eds R. L. Webb and P. H. Davids (London: T. and T. Clark, 2008) for comments on Jude's references to purity and his distinction between the qualities of the Intruders ('impure') and his readers ('pure'). The article seems to ignore the fact that Jude's understanding of purity is primarily based on the requirements of the Hebrew Scriptures. Lockett writes, 'The bi-polar language of purity shapes the way readers view the world from God's perspective and thus enables readers to reinterpret their own life stories (as individuals and as a corporate whole) with respect to the false teachers. This language constructs a particular worldview

Put simply, both of Brosend's interpretations are rejected. There is no evidence that the Intruders were challenging Jude personally (they may not have even heard of him), nor is there any reason to regard the letter as Jude's personal attack on these men. The letter serves to condemn their behaviour and speech from a Christian, not a personal, perspective. Comments below (see vv. 22, 23) provide a refutation of Brosend's view.

Jude has often been viewed as a lengthy attack on unbelievers, with some words of encouragement at the end for believers. On the contrary, the main force of the letter is to encourage the readers to contend for the faith once for all time entrusted to the saints (v. 3), with how this can be accomplished (vv. 20–23). Verses 4–19 have the purpose of describing the errors and sins of the unbelieving Intruders, which must be recognised and then rejected by the readers.

The Intruders

It was reported to Jude that some men had infiltrated one or more communities of the early Jesus movement and were leading them away from 'the faith'. At the outset, they must have claimed to be followers of Jesus (and possibly thought they were) and did and said what was necessary to be accepted as new members of a congregation. However, it soon became apparent to some of the more mature believers that their claims as Jesus' followers were not matched by their deeds and, to some extent, their words. Jude spells out in detail why he considers their behaviour to be contrary to the gospel, and how such sin like theirs had been condemned in both the OT and Jewish prophetic writings like 1 Enoch (also known as the Book of Enoch). He warns that such behaviour can only result in divine judgement.

One question that must be addressed is why virtually all commentators have called these interlopers 'false teachers'. The main reason lies in the '*Jude* text' of 2 Peter 2:1, which mentions

---

providing a 'hermeneutic', as it were, for dealing with the ill-defined boundary between the audience and the false teachers.' The Hebrew Scriptures provided black and white boundaries for Jude's readers of which they only need to be reminded, rather than taught.

false teachers. A plain reading of *Jude* indicates that the Intruders' speech was ungodly (vv. 15-16) but there is no suggestion at all of false teaching; i.e., the propounding of new beliefs or doctrines.[53] *They were 'bad behavers' but not 'false teachers'. This misunderstanding of the nature of the Intruders seems unable to be eradicated from an understanding of what Jude was writing about.*[54]

The possibility that the Intruders experienced charismatic inspiration goes beyond what the letter says. A comprehensive list of the letter's descriptions of the Intruders does not lend itself to imputing charismatic revelation to the Intruders, unless the word 'charismatic' is used in its current sense of possessing a charming and persuasive personality. It is more likely that the Intruders had sophistic skills (discussed below); such skill in persuasion would have attracted a particular section of these congregations (more likely to be the wealthy and/or well-educated—cf. 1 Cor. 1:26) and drawn them away from the basic practices of 'the faith' (v. 3).

Various descriptions of the Intruders in *Jude* may be of assistance in determining why they were perceived as a threat. It was not by their words that these men acted contrary to the principles of the faith but, primarily, by their deeds. Some mature Christians in these congregations were sufficiently astute to

---

[53] . Bauckham's commentary described the Intruders as 'false teachers' and this description has persisted for 40 years. More recent examples of this persistent claim can be found throughout the contributions in *Reading Jude With New Eyes: Methodological Reassessments of the Letter of Jude*, eds R. L. Webb and P. H. Davids (London: T. and T. Clark, 2008).

[54] . Although A. M. Mbuvi. *Jude and 2 Peter*, A New Covenant Commentary (Eugene, OR: Cascade Books, 2015), 14 specifically notes that 'Over the years, the opponents in Jude have been conflated with the *pseudodidaskaloi* (false-teachers) in 2 Peter, even though nowhere in Jude are they referred to as false-teachers.' Despite citing Mbuvi, A. J. Köstenberger, *Handbook on Hebrews through Revelation* (Grand Rapids: Baker Academic, 2020), 206 persists on using the 'false teachers' nomenclature.

23

inform Jude of these activities; therefore, we have his letter to these believers, particularly warning those individuals who were being misled. The same situation still occurs in churches today where people do not have to say anything contrary to accepted doctrine; it is their behaviour that gives them away. So, there is a need for Christians to be on guard to counter them if they lead to disunity, factionalism, or immorality—key issues throughout the entire life of the church.

Jude describes them as 'dreamers', and that is considered in comments on verse 8 below. The symptoms of pride (vv. 12, 16) and sexual immorality (vv. 8, 13) of the Intruders in *Jude* are mirrored in 1 Cor. 5:2, 6; 6:12–20, respectively. The Intruders are self-seeking (v. 12), as were the shepherds of Ezekiel 34. Another relevant OT reference is Zechariah 10:2–3. They are also 'grumblers' who reject God's authority and 'follow after their own lusts' (v. 16). Finally, they cause divisions (v. 19), as occurred in Corinth.

Why does Jude see fit to include particular OT and Jewish events as examples of the sins of the Intruders? It is helpful to look beyond them specifically, concentrating on the *types of sin* that Jude describes. There are some characteristics reminiscent of Paul's warning in 2 Timothy 2:14–26 that are relevant in discerning the particular shortcomings in the lives of the biblical characters that attracted Jude's attention. The criticisms of the Intruders throughout *Jude* are listed below but examined in more detail at the appropriate verses.

Verse	Criticism
4	Licentiousness
	denying (the authority of) Jesus Christ
8	Dreamers
	defiling the flesh rejecting
	authority
	reviling heavenly majesties
10	reviling what they do not understand
	knowing things by instinct in the manner of wild animals

12	reefs in love feasts boldly carousing together
	looking after themselves waterless clouds,
	carried along by winds unfruitful trees—twice
	dead—uprooted
13	wild waves, tossing up their shame like foam
	wandering stars

Verse	**Criticism**
16	Grumblers
	Complainers following
	their own lusts speaking
	arrogantly
	flattering to gain advantage
19	causing divisions—factionalism worldly-minded
	devoid of the Spirit

The fundamental charges brought against the Intruders are their rebellion against God's authority, factionalism, and their various forms of immorality: sexual misbehaviour, impiety, greed, boasting and grumbling. Brosend has been able to classify these faults as encompassing all the so-called seven deadly sins.

> They are guilty of sloth ('dreamers', v. 8), lust ('pursued unnatural lust', v. 7); 'they indulge their own lusts', v. 16), anger ('bombastic speech', v. 16), pride ('reject authority', v. 8), envy ('grumblers and malcontents', v. 16), gluttony ('they feast with you without fear, feeding themselves', v. 12) and greed ('flattering people to their own advantage', v. 16 and 'for the sake of gain', v. 11). A perfect seven of the seven deadly sins on this scorecard.[55]

Where did the Intruders come from? There are no clues in *Jude* but it is possible to cautiously suggest something about their backgrounds. They infiltrated primarily Jewish communities. The ease with which they did this may have been assisted by the fact that they were themselves probably Jews or God-fearing

---

55 . Brosend, *Rhetoric*, 304.

Gentiles.[56] Clearly, they could not have been as well accepted as they were had they not assimilated into the community by means of language, custom and a ready familiarity with the teachings of the early Jesus movement. If they did not possess this initial knowledge, they could not have built upon it with their own errant behaviour and language. They called themselves followers of the Way, even though they did not behave in the manner expected of followers of Jesus.[63]

It was not as if false teaching by word or action was unknown in the early days of the Jesus movement. The NT is replete with examples of those who attempted to insert new themes or ideas into the gospel preached by Paul. Of course, Jesus warned that this would occur, described how they would be identified and spelt out their outcome (Matt. 15:17–20).

Given that the bulk of *Jude* concentrates on these Intruders, we should consider the widespread adverse influence of bad behaviour and false teaching on the early Jesus movement in general. Paul's letters and Acts provide a background to Jude's criticisms, as shown below.

---

[56]. Gentiles who had converted to Judaism.

[63]. An interesting point here is whether their offensive behaviour became apparent as soon as they arrived in a community, or whether it became evident only after their lifestyle gained a foothold among their followers.

NT Reference

Acts 20:29   savage wolves will come   4

in among you, not   10

sparing the flock   12

19

Romans   17   keep your eye on those 8 who cause dissensions and hindrances
16:17, 18   contrary to the teaching which you learned, and turn away from them
18   such men are slaves not of our Lord Christ but of their own
appetites and by their smooth and flattering speech they deceive the hearts
of the unsuspecting

NT Reference			**Jude**
1 Corinthians 1:17–2:14	1:17 for Christ did not send me to…preach the gospel in cleverness of speech	3	contend for the faith once entrusted to the saints
	1:27 God has chosen the foolish things of the world to shame the wise	18 4	mockers deny Jesus Christ
	1:29 no man should boast before God	16	speaking arrogantly
	2:4 and my message and my preaching were not in persuasive words of wisdom, but in demonstration of the Spirit and of power	13 19	wandering stars worldly-minded, devoid of the Spirit
	2:5 that your faith should not rest on the wisdom of men but on the power of God	16	speaking arrogantly
	2:12 now we have received, not the spirit of the world, but the Spirit who is from God	19	worldly-minded
	2:13 we also speak, not in words taught by human wisdom, but in those taught by the Spirit, combining spiritual thoughts with spiritual words	19	devoid of the Spirit

NT Reference	Jude

2:14 but a natural man 19 revile things they do not does not accept the understand things of the Spirit of God, for they are foolishness to him; and he cannot understand them, because they are spiritually appraised

1 Cor. 6:9–20   9 the unrighteous will not 4, 5,   ungodly persons inherit the kingdom of   15 God. Do not be deceived;   4, 7,   licentiousness and sexual neither fornicators, nor   8, 13,   immorality idolaters, nor adulterers,
16 nor effeminate, nor homosexuals

10 nor thieves, nor the 18   way of Cain, error of covetous, nor drunkards,   Balaam nor revi lers, nor
11   shepherding themselves.
swindlers, will inherit the 12,   following after their own kingdom of God   16,   lusts
18

13 the body is not for   4, 7,   licentiousness and sexual immorality, but for the   8, 13,   immorality Lord   16, 18 flee immorality   18

1 Cor. 8:1   knowledge makes   16   speak arrogantly arrogant, but love edifies

1 Cor. 11:18   when you come together   12   reefs in your love feasts as a church, I hear that   19   cause divisions divisions exist among you

1 Cor. 11:33– 34   33 so then, my brethren, 12   reefs in your love feasts, when you come together   shepherding themselves to eat, wait for one another 34 if anyone is hungry, let him eat at home, so that you will not come together for judgment

NT Reference				Jude
2 Cor. 11:12–13	12	boasting	16	speak arrogantly
	13	such men are false apostles, deceitful workers, disguising themselves as apostles of Christ	4	deny Jesus Christ
Eph. 4:14		we are no longer to be children, tossed here and there by waves, and carried about by every wind of doctrine, by the trickery of men, by craftiness in deceitful scheming	4	crept in unnoticed clouds
			12	without water, trees doubly dead
			13	wild waves tossing up foam of their shame
Phil. 3:19		whose end is destruction, whose god is their appetite, and whose glory is in their shame, who set their minds on earthly things	4	marked out for condemnation wild
			13	waves tossing up foam of their shame following
			16, 18	after their own lusts
			19	worldly-minded
Col. 2:4, 8, 18	4	deluding with persuasive argument	8	reject authority
	8	philosophy and empty deception, according to the traditions of men	12	clouds without water
	18	taking his stand on visions he has seen, inflated without cause by his fleshly mind	8	dreaming
1 Tim. 1:6		fruitless discussion	12	clouds without water
			13	trees doubly dead, wandering stars

NT Reference		Jude
Ti. 1:10–11	10 rebellious men, empty 4 and deceivers 8	talkers, deny Jesus Christ reject authority
	18	mockers
	19 11	cause divisions
	teaching things they 8 should not teach, for the 12 sake of sordid gain 16, 18	revile angels clouds without water lust for gain
Ti. 3:10	reject a factious man 12 after a first and second 19 warning	reefs in love feasts cause divisions

It is notable that the most frequent discussion of this type of trouble occurs in Paul's correspondence with Corinth. The presence in the Corinthian congregation of people from various ethnic origins (Jews, Romans, Greeks, and other Gentiles) and the lower orders of society has never been disputed by any of the commentators.

> Until relatively recently, the majority of interpreters stressed that the Pauline churches appealed to the lower classes. This argument, first made by Celsus, was largely adopted by others, and reinforced by Deissmann in this [twentieth] century.[57]

The more recent matter of debate has been the extent to which the early Jesus movement congregations (including Corinth) had members from the more educated and higher ranks of society than had previously been thought likely. Even in this context, Filson's conclusion is still valid. 'The apostolic church was more nearly a cross section of society than we have sometimes thought. The fact that the poor predominated must not obscure this truth; the poor have always outnumbered the wealthy.' This reality should be brought to bear when considering the composition of the Christian group in a city such as Antioch.

Little evidence is available to determine the identity of the

---

[57] . A. D. Clarke, *Secular and Christian Leadership in Corinth: A Socio-Historical and Exegetical Study of 1 Cor 1–6* (Leiden: E. J. Brill, 1993), 41.

Intruders in Jude. Nevertheless, some clues arise from the similarity in both the literary style of *Jude* and 1 Corinthians as well as their underlying subject matter. All the evidence suggests the *possibility* that the Intruders may have been former members of the Corinthian assembly or were influenced by them.

There has been a good deal of conjecture as to whether the Intruders were Gnostics. Given the earlier conclusion that *Jude* was written around the middle of the first century, this cannot be the case. Gnosticism was a second-century phenomenon. However, this does not mean that these Intruders did not exhibit many of the traits that would eventually be attributed to Gnosticism.

An appropriate conclusion is that (without realising it) Jude's Intruders were precursors of some aspects of Gnosticism but not its progenitors. There is no need to label the Intruders to understand their sin. The issue of Gnosticism is irrelevant when reading *Jude*.

The Readers

While it is appropriate to concentrate on the writer and his message, we must not lose sight of his audience. Who were Jude's initial readers? There is no precise information in Jude (or Acts) about their identity or location (other than to presume that they lived away from Jerusalem), but there are a few clues about their identity from the contents of the letter, which suggest that Jude's focus was primarily on believers with a strong familiarity with Judaism.

Jude not only recalls events recorded in the OT but also extends his examples to extra-biblical Jewish sources, especially the Book of Enoch (also known as 1 Enoch) and the Assumption of Moses (also known as the Testament of Moses). The breadth of Jude's examples suggest that his readers were primarily followers of Jesus (Jews and God-fearing Gentiles) who were well-versed in a range of Jewish literature; otherwise, they would have been unable to fully appreciate the examples quoted—there would have been no point in using them. The style of the letter (see below) is such that Jude expects his readers to be fully conversant with his Jewish scriptural examples, to accept their divine inspiration and spiritual significance for their own immediate circumstances, and to react immediately to their warnings. Jude's reference to James in verse 1 reflects the readers' knowledge of James' identity and their respect for him. Thus it seems more likely that they were located in Palestine, but away from Jerusalem.

It is relevant to note that Jude's letter was written in Greek (not Hebrew or Aramaic, as may have been the case for Jewish believers unfamiliar with Greek documents). There would have been no point in Jude going to the trouble he did in composing its rhetorical style if that form of communication would have fallen on ignorant ears. These (primarily Hellenistic?) Jewish readers (or hearers)—or at least the most influential ones— would, therefore, need to have some understanding of Hellenistic rhetorical styles and some sophistication in Greek language skills to appreciate Jude's style and vocabulary. G. L. Green raises an important question regarding the readers (and those influenced by the Intruders) when he asks, "should we assume that Jude was penned for those who were part of the social elite?" His question is critical to understanding both the nature of the Intruders and the style of the letter (cf. 1 Cor. 1:26). It is composed and directed to a specific audience. Kelly is incorrect in describing most readers as 'Gentile Christians', even if they did have a Hellenistic cultural understanding. While the style and language of Jude is consistent with his readers living in "highly Hellenised cities where we know that there were communities of the Jesus movement", we cannot discount the significant Jewish examples used by Jude. Cities like Antioch and Alexandria meet the description of highly Hellenised environments, centres of Greek learning inhabited by sophists, with large Jewish populations.

Walck offers a surprising conclusion when he states: "The Book of Jude, it can be assumed, was never of any interest to the Jewish community, but at the same time was of great interest to Christians for its trinitarian formulations, thus meeting the criteria for acceptance by Christians, despite its use of non-biblical sources."[58]

In summary, we should regard the likely recipients of Jude's letter as one or more Jesus movement groups in a larger, Hellenised city around that broad region of the eastern Mediterranean, with more likelihood attached to Palestine. The literary style of the letter implies that the initial recipients comprised the better-educated elements of those communities. Antioch was such a city.[59] That the addressees of Jude may have lived in Antioch is supported by Jobes,[60] Wand,[61] E. M. G. Green,[62] and Koester.[63]

If the Intruders were itinerant sophists, their presence around the north-eastern Mediterranean was not uncommon. These Intruders give every indication of belonging to this community. It is possible that there were earlier visitors to the community addressed by Jude who had expressed orthodox beliefs and behaviour. If so, that previous participation by (legitimate) strangers may have encouraged Jude's congregation(s) to have been more inclined to welcome these new visitors but, perhaps, also to be more susceptible to being fooled by them. However, Jude could not have written his letter unless there were mature believers among his readers who knew right from wrong: those who reported the Intruders to him. We cannot know what

---

[58] . L . W. Walck, 'Response to Jeremy Hultin's "Jude's Citation of 1 Enoch",' in *The Function of 'Canonical' and 'Non-Canonical' Religious Texts*, eds J. H. Charlesworth and L. M. McDonald (London: T. and T. Clark, 2010), 130.

[59] . B ecause the Letter of Jude found favour early in Egypt, Alexandria was suggested in J. J. Gunther, 'The Alexandrian Epistle of Jude,' *New Testament Studies* 30:4 (1984): 549–562. *Jude* was commented on by Clement of Alexandria. Syria is suggested in H. Koester, *Introduction to the New Testament: History and Literature of Early Christianity*, 2nd ed. (New York: Walter de Gruyter, 2000), 2:252.

[60] . K. H. Jobes, *Letters to the Church: A Survey of Hebrews and the General Epistles* (Grand Rapids, MI: Zondervan Publishing House, 2011), 242

[61] . J. W. C. Wand, *The General Epistles of St Peter and St Jude, Westminster Commentaries Series* (London: Methuen, 1934), 194.

[62] . E. M. G. Green, *2 Peter and Jude*, 56.

[63] . Koester, *Introduction to the New Testament*, 252.

proportion of this community came under the spell of the Intruders.

It needs to be recognised that many Intruders have infiltrated the modern church, particularly in seminaries and theological colleges. Just as the behaviour of their first-century counterparts revealed their true identity as marauding wolves, so the writings of current (liberal) false teachers in academia reveal them to be enemies of the gospel of Christ. A typical example is the particularly virulent attack on Jude as a whole, formulated by Aichele who is clearly disturbed by any attempt to impose traditional Christian doctrine on believers.

> As is very evident in the letter of Jude, paranoia may arise in response to human institutions and events, but ultimately it takes the form of the One God who sees and knows all, who is everywhere and yet invisible, and who demands perfect obedience even as he judges without any chance of appeal. Paranoia is universalising and monotheistic, and it desires one exclusive truth, such as the single correct Word of God offered by the biblical canon. It is in this sense of the word 'paranoia' that I call the letter of Jude a paranoid gospel. That the letter describes Christ as *despotēs* only makes this explic-it.[64]

First-Century Education

A predictable objection to the writer being a brother of Jesus is: how could a carpenter[65] from Nazareth obtain an education in Greek? Neyrey confirms this objection when he concludes that the language and structure of a letter like *Jude* 'are unlikely

---

[64] . G. Aichele, *The Letters of Jude and Second Peter: Paranoia and the Slaves of Christ* (Sheffield, UK: Sheffield Phoenix Press, 2012), 35. This is an illustration of Schaeffer's 'watershed' in contemporary Christian society. See comments on verse 4 regarding Jude's use of *despotēs*.

[65] . This assumes that Jude followed the normal Jewish practice of the time by following his father's (Joseph's) occupation, as Jesus did.

achievements of Jesus' blood relatives, who, like him, were landless artisans living in peasant villages.'[66] However, there are more compelling and rational explanations to the contrary than this crude analysis. There were opportunities to learn Greek in the Galilee region, as well as in Jerusalem. E. M. G. Green goes so far as to say, "The fairly good quality of his [Jude's] Greek should surprise only those who are unaware of the Hellenisation in first-century Palestine, *particularly Galilee*."[67] If Jude moved to Jerusalem after Christ's resurrection, he would still have been relatively young, having sufficient time to gain the appropriate linguistic knowledge and skill. It is relevant to note that the famous first-century historian Flavius Josephus was a Jew from Galilee with excellent Greek-language skills.

As noted above, many first-century Palestinian Jews were conversant in Greek, which was widely taught in Jerusalem. This was where Paul was raised as a young man and educated by Gamaliel (Acts 22:3); he would have learned Hebrew and Greek in that process. The location of Paul's education has been the subject of much investigation, led by van Unnik's comprehensive study.[68] A more recent examination by Hengel[69] analysed the tension between the diverse facts of Paul's preference for the Septuagint (LXX)[70] when quoting Scripture:

---

[66] . Neyrey, *2 Peter, Jude*, 31.

[67] . E. M. G. Green, *2 Peter and Jude*, 45. (Emphasis added). See also N. Turner, *Grammatical Insights into the New Testament* (Edinburgh: T. and T. Clark, 1965), 48, 146, 168, ch. 7. Turner, 48, goes so far as to say that 'Serious consideration should be given to the view that there was a biblical or Jewish kind of Greek spoken in Palestine during the first century. It would be the language of Jesus as well as of Mark and Luke and John.'

[68] . W. C. van Unnik, *Tarsus or Jerusalem: The City of Paul's Youth*, Sparsa Collecta 1, *Novum Testamentum* Supplement 29 (Leiden: E. J. Brill, 1973), 259–320.

[69] . M. Hengel, *The Pre-Christian Paul* (London: SCM Press, 1991).

[70] . The Septuagint (often abbreviated LXX) is the name given to the Greek translation of the Hebrew Scriptures. The Septuagint had its origin in Alexandria, Egypt and was translated from 300–200 BC. Widely used among Hellenistic Jews, this Greek translation was produced because many Jews spread throughout the Roman Empire were beginning to lose their Hebrew language. The process of translating the Hebrew to Greek also gave many non-Jews a glimpse into Judaism. According to an ancient document called the Letter of Aristeas, it is believed that seventy Jewish scholars were

his Greek-language skills, his familiarity with non-Jewish literature and his strict Jewish upbringing (to the extent of becoming a Pharisee under Gamaliel's training).

Although Hengel notes that there was "a good Greek school in Jerusalem",[71] he is unwilling to concede that Paul received a top-quality education in Greek philosophical thought. He is content to agree with Norden's conclusions 'that despite his [Paul's] sovereign contempt for beautiful form, the apostle often enough made use of the means of elegant rhetoric which are absent from the Gospels, but…not of such as he appropriated from the reading of Greek writers.'[72] Following Norden, Hengel assesses that "it seems to me most plausible to *suppose* that Paul learned the basic insights of his indubitable rhetorical art, which is not oriented on classical literary models, through practical application in the Greek-speaking synagogues in Jerusalem."[73] From this description of the education available in Jerusalem in the first century, it is clear that Jude would have had the opportunity to gain the literary skills and styles necessary for him to write this letter.

Language and Style of the Letter

Many scholars regard this letter as an 'epistolary sermon'. The contention is that Jude could have delivered what he said in this epistle as a homily (sermon) if he had been in his readers' presence. Instead, he cast it in the form of a letter since he could not address them directly. Other New Testament epistles

---

commissioned during the reign of Ptolemy Philadelphus to carry out the task of translation. 'Septuagint' means 'seventy' in Latin and the text is so named to credit these seventy scholars. For more information, see http://www.septuagint.net.

[71] . Hengel, *The Pre-Christian Paul*, 39, 58, 59.

[72] . E. Norden, *Die antike Kunstprosa vom VI Jahrhundert v Chr Bis in die Zeit der Renaissance* 2 in M. Hengel, *The Pre-Christian Paul* (London: SCM Press, 1991), 58.

[73] . Hengel, *The Pre-Christian Paul*, 58 (emphasis added).

that are really written homilies include James, Hebrews, and 1 John.[74]

Notwithstanding this view, there is widespread agreement among commentators that *Jude* is a genuine letter. It contains the appropriate introduction that is so common in Paul's letters. The usual style was 'from A to B', with a salutation. Jude follows that pattern, although his salutation is really a blessing. The shortness of the salutation may indicate that, whereas Paul's authority sometimes needed to be justified, Jude's position and reputation in the Jerusalem church were so well known that the authority of his letter would not be questioned by his readers. While all of Paul's letters in the NT inform us of the recipients, it is not necessary that Jude must do this. Paul's identification of his readers may have been to distinguish one letter from another or to clarify the original recipients' locations to inform readers of copies of his letters.

The text reveals that Jude knows to whom he is writing and they know him. The introductory part of first-century letters in the NT has been examined by O'Brien.[75] *Jude* fits easily into this framework, and the salutation is accompanied by a specific Christian greeting. The most obvious greeting for a first-century Jew was *shalom* (peace), and Jude includes this. He also adds mercy, and that unique Christian element, love. Jude does not give thanks for his readers, as Paul generally does.[76] However, it is unusual that Jude does not conclude his letter with a greeting, as do most NT letters, but with a doxology.

Having heard of the threat to sound behaviour (and, by implication, doctrine) from the arrival of some distorters of the truth, Jude appears to have penned his letter quickly. At first glance, it does not appear to have been composed with much attention to a logical structure, as it races back and forth between

---

[74] . T. L. Constable, *Notes on Jude 2021 Edition*, in https://www.planobiblechapel. org/tcon/notes/html/nt/jude/ jude.htm. (Accessed 21 Jun 2021).

[75] . P . T. O'Brien, 'Introductory Thanksgivings in the Letters of Paul', Supplement to *Novum Testamentum* 49 (Leiden: E. J. Brill, 1977).

[76] . Galatians is an exception because that letter is critical of its audience.

examples of those in error in ancient times and a description of the current offenders. It is as if Jude remembers some ancient wrongdoing and then says, 'See! These interlopers are just like that!' He uses this style five times, as per the following table:

Verse	Ancient Error	Verse	Contemporary Comparison
5	non-belief of Israelites leaving Egypt	8	rejecting authority
6	angels not keeping their own domain	8	reviling angelic majesties
7	Sodom and Gomorrah		defiling the flesh
9	archangel Michael and the dispute with Satan over the body of Moses	10	reviling things they do not understand
11	Cain, Balaam, and Korah	12–13	self-indulgence and challenging God's authority
14–15		16	prophecy of Enoch grumblers; arrogant, lustful behaviour
17–18	prophecy of Jesus' apostles	19	causing divisions, being worldly-minded

Although this table reflects the substance of Jude's comparisons, the analysis above gives little credit to the skill of the author. Jude is a skilfully crafted letter by a Jewish writer who displays a broad and sometimes unusual vocabulary. Bigg observes that "Jude's own writing is strong, dignified, and sonorous. The style and tone of the Epistle set before us a stern and unbending nature. There is no pathos in Jude, and he inclines always to a harsh view."[77] This may be so with respect to his opponents, but we will also see that Jude shows considerable care for his readers. As noted above, one of the starkest features of the letter is the vehemence of its language.

> Its style is vigorous and colourful; and the author, who deploys a rich vocabulary, writes smooth-flowing,

---

[77] . Bigg, *Jude*, 311.

> excellent Greek interspersed with occasional Semitisms. His background is Jewish-Christian, and he is well versed in the OT and its traditional, often legendary interpretation known as haggadah, and also in apocalyptic literature, which he freely exploits.[78]

Given the preference in modern society for restraint in written (and oral) expression, especially the avoidance of giving offence to anyone (no matter what the circumstances), Jude's strident language might seem 'over the top' and inappropriate for Christian use—especially in a book of the Bible!

In democratic environments (e.g., Australia, Canada, the United Kingdom or the United States) where Christians are facing increasing opposition to their beliefs from both government and society but (so far) have little fear of physical persecution, it is easy for them to forget that they are actually engaged in a spiritual war against Satan and his hordes. Jude was engaged in a war when he wrote this letter (cf. Rom. 7:23; 8:35–39). Paul was in a war when he penned his condemnation of opponents (Gal. 1:6, 9; 2:13; 3:1; 5:12). During the Cold War, President Ronald Reagan didn't describe Soviet Communist leaders as 'nasty chaps' but used more forceful language against those fierce opponents. Jude was doing the same thing. From an eternal perspective, lives were at stake.

This was not the time for sensitivity regarding offending the devil's workers, but a time to stand up strongly for the truth. We now live in a world where offending someone by intemperate language seems to be one of the greatest crimes of all. [79]

---

[78] . Kelly, *Epistles of Peter and of Jude*, 228.

[79] . This is particularly noticeable in Australia, where any attempt at rational debate about important issues (on many subjects) is thwarted by the left-wing intellectual elite, who accuse their opponents of 'offending people's feelings', simply to denounce and silence them by using anti-discrimination legislation. For example, there is still much debate in Australia about repealing that part of section 18C of the *Racial Discrimination Act 1975* (Cth), which makes it a criminal offence to say or do something to someone in a public place that 'is reasonably likely, in all the circumstances, to offend, insult' that person 'because of the race, colour or national or ethnic origin of the other person' (emphasis added). Intelligent debate about critical issues is becoming

Increasingly, governments in so-called Western democracies are enacting 'anti-hate' legislation that is deliberately designed to stifle free speech (oral and written), especially the voices of conservatives (including Christians) who advocate the retention of traditional values and rejection of left-wing, neo-Marxist doctrines that threaten the very fabric of Western civilisation. Christians must shake off any attempt by society to muzzle the message of the cross through the imposition of political correctness on their words or actions (1 Cor. 1:18–31; Acts 5:29).

While not advocating rude or improper behaviour, it is now time for Christians not to be fooled by political correctness that attempts to squash their beliefs and ideas under a blanket of 'decency' or, even worse, 'tolerance' (see John 14:6). It is time for Christians to speak out against Satan's power and influence in our world. Whereas Paul and the early Christians were liable to be flogged (or even killed), we in the West might suffer a tongue lashing, at worst, from our opponents. Christian brothers and sisters in the Third World often suffer persecution, famine, dispossession, and even death for their preparedness to speak the name of Jesus and defend the gospel. Islamic State Muslims have done these very things to Christians in northern Iraq and Syria. Believers in North Korea, China, Iran (and many other countries) live lives of quiet desperation as they try to exist with the constant threat of extreme persecution. Yet Western countries, in the main, sit idly by, doing (and saying!) little. The United Nations does nothing except mouth platitudes. There is little media recognition that the most persecuted people in these regions (in the world, in fact!) are Christians. In the twentieth century, more Christians were killed for their faith than were in the previous nineteen centuries combined. But the media will never disclose those facts.

---

impossible. It will not be long before the offence of the gospel (cf. Gal. 5:11) will cause someone to be charged with offending someone. Anti-discrimination legislation has already been used by same-sex 'marriage' advocates to bring charges against a Roman Catholic bishop in Tasmania who had the effrontery to publish a parish letter arguing that marriage should only be between a man and a woman.

How much more should comfortable (by comparison) Christians in the West be willing to face criticism (and even unpopularity!) for standing up and being heard for what is right. So, I am not perturbed by Jude's strident language; indeed, I would like to see more of it from Christian leaders today who, overall, remain fairly silent.

A new element in the examination of *Jude* was contributed by Watson, who examined the letter in the light of rhetorical criticism. Watson's methodology applied first-century rhetorical conventions to *Jude*, with surprising results. Earlier scholarship (e.g., Bigg), which had been more reliant on personal assumptions and preferences, was confirmed or rejected by Watson's rigorous analysis. Watson's conclusions from his comprehensive analysis of the literary structure and style of *Jude* are important in this regard:

> As far as rhetorical conventions are concerned, Jude's rhetoric conforms to its best principles.
>
> He chooses deliberative rhetoric which, of the three species of rhetoric, is best suited to move the audience to refrain from affiliation with the sectarians. Deliberative aims at persuasion and dissuasion, and its end is the advantageous and harmful. The heavy use of epideictic rhetoric supports the deliberation, helping to prove the proposition that the sectarians are ungodly, to decrease their ethos, and to elicit negative pathos; all with the intent of dissuading the audience from falling prey to their teaching and practice.
>
> It can be affirmed that the author of Jude is skilled in the rhetoric of his time. The origin of this skill, whether gained from daily interaction with verbal and written culture and/ or from formal training is impossible to determine. However, clearly to do justice to its content, the epistle must be interpreted in light of the conventions of Greco-Roman rhetoric. It must be viewed as a reasoned rhetorical attempt to counter a

specific exigence experienced by a particular audience.[80]

Rhetorical criticism[81] examines the relationship between the biblical text and its impact on its original audience in the text's historical setting, especially considering the purpose and effectiveness of the text (to teach, exhort, persuade, etc.) plus the stylistic techniques used to transmit the message. This analysis is assisted by the fact that Greco-Roman rhetoric was guided by its own textbooks from the first-century era.[82] Jude's use of rhetoric is examined in a subsequent section.

Watson's original interpretation created a helpful starting point for a new round of analysis concerning the literary structure of *Jude*. Schreiner's summary is that, while Watson's conclusion may overstate Jude's reliance on formal guidelines and a deliberate rhetorical structure, it does fit within that well-established pattern, even if he did not consciously intend to do so.[83] Although the letter was written in Greek, and this fact strongly influences analysis of the text, this should not obscure the fact that Jude was a Jew. His cultural background and the impact of Judaism throughout his life must also be taken into account when considering his letter, regardless of the language in which it was written.

Evident Jewish influences must also be incorporated into the analysis of Jude's style and structure, but *Jude* 'contains a peculiarly elaborate and interesting example of formal exegesis of Scripture in the style of the Qumran pesharim.'[84] Since Bauckham's reference to Jude's '*pesher*-type exegesis', subsequent scholarship has questioned his analysis 'concluding that, although Jude is not an example of *pesher*[85] exegesis, there

---

[80] . Watson, *Invention*, 78–79.

[81] . As defined in J. Muilenburg, 'Form Criticism and Beyond,' *Journal of Biblical Literature* 88:1 (1969): 1–18. See also Watson, *Invention*, 2.

[82] . Watson, *Invention*, 4–6.

[83] . Schreiner, *Jude*, 419–426 provides a detailed analysis of Watson's conclusions.

[84] . Bauckham, *Relatives of Jesus*, 179.

[85] . 'Pesher refers to a distinct type of ancient interpretation of biblical prophecy or to a text that represents that type of interpretation. The term is a Hebrew

are still some fruitful avenues of comparative research to explore regarding the epistle and the Qumran pesharim.'[86] Account also needs to be taken of the use of Jude's *pesher* technique in pseudepigraphical material. This technique derives from an apocalyptic interpretation of the text.

Even though only twenty-five verses in length, Jude contains fourteen words that are used but once in the NT:

Word in Jude	Verse	Greek Root of Word	English Meaning
ἀποδιορίζοντες	19	ἀποδιορίζω to divide	ἀπταίστους 24 ἀπταίστος stumbling
γογγυσταί	16	γογγυστῆς	grumbler
δεῖγμα	7	δεῖγμα	example
ἐκπορνεύσασαι	7	ἐκπορνεύω	to give up to sexual immorality
ἐπαγωνίζεσθαι	3	ἐπαγωνίζεσθαι	to contend
ἐπαφρίζοντα	13	ἐπαφρίζω	to foam up
μεμψίμοιροι	16	μεμψίμοιρος	fault-finder
παρεισέδυσαν	4	παρεισδύω	to slip in secretly
πλανῆται	13	πλανήτης	wandering
σπιλάδες	12	σπιλάς	blemish
ὑπέχουσαι	7	ὑπέχω	to suffer

---

word whose verbal root, pšh, means to 'loosen' or 'interpret'. This mode of interpretation is exemplified in the sectarian documents found at Qumran (e.g. the Habakkuk commentary (1QpHab)), in which the meaning of obscure ancient texts was interpreted to refer to the Qumran community itself by employing an array of specific techniques. This understanding of the ancient prophesies gave the community an unprecedented dignity and significance in their own eyes, as they perceived the telos of prophecy given centuries before.' Jobes, *Letters to the Church*, 254.

[86] . B . A. Jurgens, 'Is It Pesher? Readdressing the Relationship between the Epistle of Jude and the Qumran Pesharim,' *Journal of Biblical Literature* 136:2 (2017): 491–510, 492.

φθινοπωρινὰ	12	φθινοπωρινός	autumn
φυσικῶς	10	φυσικῶς	by instinct

Only four of the fourteen words above occur in the LXX. Three more words only occur once more in the NT, and each of them is found in 2 Peter. To some extent, the rarity of Jude's vocabulary is easily explained by the fact that several of his descriptions of the Intruders are unique in the NT, although the words appear regularly in non-biblical Greek documents. Few of his words are truly rare. Jude also uses words that are *double entendres*: these are discussed in comments on the relevant verses. Jude piles description upon description. Neyrey refers to Jude's use of triplets, 'which are evidence of a concern for coherence and texture in the discourse.'[87] His summary is helpful:[88]

v. 1   identification of the addressees:
         'beloved...called...kept' v.

2   benediction:
         'mercy and peace and love be multiplied'

v. 4   identification of the opponents:
         'proscribed...turn away...deny' vv.

5–7   precedents of sinners judged:
         Israel in wilderness, angels, Sodom v. 8

identification of the opponents:
         'defile...flout...insult'

v. 11   woe to three sinners judged:
         Cain, Balaam, Korah
         'gone the way of...abandoned themselves...destroyed' v.

12   metaphors of vanity:
         'rainless clouds...fruitless trees...doubly dead' v.

14   the judgment of the Lord:
         'coming...pass judgment...convict'

v. 16   identification of the opponents:

---

[87] . Neyrey, *2 Peter, Jude*, 24–25.
[88] . Neyrey, *2 Peter, Jude*, 28.

'disgruntled...murmurers...go the way of passion' v.

19   vices of the opponents:

'create division...physical...have no Spirit' vv.

20–21   virtues of the faithful:

'build yourselves up...praying...await' vv.

22–23   on dealing with the opponents:

'snatch...have mercy...hate'

v. 25   honourable attributes of God:

'glory, majesty, might and authority' v. 25

duration of God's honour:

'before all ages, now and forever'

It has been widely thought that Jewish writers of the (Greek) NT would most readily refer to the (Greek) LXX as a reference for their quotations from the OT. Jude does not follow this pattern. The reason may be that the rabbi in Nazareth used a Hebrew version of the OT, which would have imbued the young Jude with familiarity with that text. While Jude's use of the Hebrew Scriptures reflects his own familiarity with that text, it may also indicate that his readers were primarily Jews who may also have been more familiar with the Hebrew text than the LXX (notwithstanding their Hellenistic background). Wand suggests that the unusual use of Jewish apocalyptic literature may also reflect a primarily Jewish audience, as well as pointing towards Jude as the author.[89]

Following on from Watson's rhetorical analysis of the letter, Webb introduced the concept of 'story' as an integral part of the author's literary style.[90] He proposes that three stories are woven

---

[89] . W and, *Jude*, 189.

[90] . R. L. Webb, 'The Use of "Story" in the Letter of Jude: Rhetorical Strategies of Jude's Narrative Episodes,' *Journal for the Study of the New Testament* 31:1 (2008): 53–87. Webb defines 'story' as 'a synopsis of events (i.e. "this happened and then that happened"), and a plot as an explanation of the causal relationships between events (i.e. "this happened because that happened"),' following the style of M. H. Abrams, *A Glossary of Literary Terms*. 8th ed. (Boston: Thomson Wadsworth, 2005), 233.

into the letter: 'narrative episodes drawn from the Jewish scriptural tradition, the story of Jesus, and the story of the Christian community'.[91] Webb examines the historical force of these stories, discovering significant benefit from the individual stories as well as from the impact of their interrelationship. His article also draws out the significance of the Jewish scriptural passages chosen by Jude; again, both individually and in combination with each other.

Rhetorical Analysis: Jude and 1 Corinthians

Digressing from the Letter of Jude for a moment, it is important to examine the situation in the Corinthian church, because that is a much better documented[92] example of the circumstances so briefly described in *Jude*. The following analysis of the Corinthian church provides an important historical context for both the content and the literary style of *Jude* as well as the behaviour and attitudes of the Intruders. The core of this analysis is the use and/ or understanding of rhetoric by the upper levels of contemporary Corinthian society, Paul, Jude, the Intruders and the readers of *Jude*. Rhetoric in the first century was speaking (or writing) that was designed to persuade its hearers (or readers) to accept a particular point of view or take a particular course of action. In the first century, rhetoric was an essential part of Greco-Roman education and was widespread throughout the Roman Empire around the Mediterranean.

It is necessary to understand this important means of communicating ideas across the Roman Empire in the first century, particularly to people of influence, to appreciate the way *Jude* was composed. Rhetoric was especially practised by a group of public speakers called 'sophists'. Their name is derived from σοφία (*sophia*), meaning 'wisdom'. It is the derivation of the modern word 'sophisticated', which, ironically relevant to

---

[91] . W ebb, *Use of Story*, 53. Note the psychological aspects of Jude's rhetoric in 72–78, 80. See also comments in 72 about the impact on the readers of referring to Jesus.

[92] . In both 1 and 2 Corinthians themselves and academic studies.

this ancient context, has a current sense of 'worldly-wise' rather than genuinely wise. There is clear evidence of the teaching of sophistic techniques in major cities of the empire, such as Rome, Corinth, Athens, Alexandria and Antioch. Winter's examination of sophism in Alexandria and Corinth in relation to Christianity 'has shown that Athens had indeed a great deal to do with Jerusalem in this formative period for Judaism, and the Academy had certainly disturbed the concord of the [Christian] church through the sophistic movement and its promoters in Corinth.'[93] Although no evidence exists for its occurrence in Jerusalem, it would be most surprising if sophistic influences were not also at play in that great city of the Roman Empire.[94]

One of the principal tools of statesmanship in Rome and its colonies was the ability to persuade through oratory. The possession of this skill was considered a powerful status symbol in a status-obsessed society.[95] The Greco-Roman society of the first century lavished every gift on men who were well-educated and eloquent. Since the power of persuasion and leadership went hand in hand, oratory was a highly prized skill.[96] To assume positions of leadership and responsibility, it was essential to be among the wise, the well-born and the powerful[104] (cf. 1 Cor 1:26). Those who prized oratory most were the sophists. Because oratory was the most obvious means of gaining notice in public, those possessing rhetorical skills were able to gain both reputation and honour (and also money!) quite quickly. Sophists specialised in public oratory; the most famous were the first-century equivalent of today's pop stars.

A distinctive aspect of sophistic rhetoric was boasting. This attitude was prevalent in the Corinthian church, evidenced by Paul's constant rebukes against 'boasting' in 1 Cor. 1:26–31 and being 'puffed up' in 1 Cor. 4:6, 18, 19; 5:2; 8:1; 13:4.[105] Jude's criticisms of the Intruders centre on their professed superior

---

[93] . B . W. Winter, *Philo and Paul Among the Sophists* (Grand Rapids, MI: Wm. B. Eerdmans Publishing Company, 2002), 254.

[94] . See Hengel, *The Pre-Christian Paul*, 39, 58, 59.

[95] . See Clarke, *Secular and Christian Leadership*, 37, 38.

[96] . P. Marshall, 'Enmity in Corinth: Social Conventions in Paul's Relations with

spirituality, which must have been known through their boasting (v. 16). Another important aspect of rhetoric was to make one's opponent appear to be dishonourable. Jude uses this aspect of rhetoric in his letter, reflected in Mitchell's argument.

> Paul's response to the Corinthian situation…is an argument in which each of the topics of Corinthian debate…is subsumed under a discussion of what he considers to be the seminal problem at Corinth— factionalism—which is the innate cause and further result of these specific contentions.[106]

Her point is that '1 Corinthians is in fact a united and coherent appeal for unity and cessation of factionalism'.[107] *Jude* places

---

the Corinthians.' *Wissenschaftliche Untersuchungen zum Neuen Testament*, 2 Reihe 23 (1987), 383: 'It is difficult to grasp how pervasive and influential rhetoric was in Greco-Roman society…In classical education, speaking correctly, fluently and clearly involved thinking and behaving appropriately. Formal conventions were adhered to by the speaker and were expected by his audience. The eloquent and well-educated speaker won great honours and was esteemed as a leader of society.'

104. There are so many similarities between the ethics and morality of the societies of large cities in the first and twenty-first centuries!
105. W inter, *Philo and Paul*, 196–201, demonstrates the parallels between the boasting of the Corinthians and that of the sophists in secular society.
106. M. M. Mitchell, *Paul and the Rhetoric of Reconciliation: An Exegetical Investigation of the Language and Composition of 1 Corinthians* (Louisville: Westminster/John Knox Press, 1992), 1–2. 107. Mitchell, *Paul and Rhetoric*, 19.

emphasis on the need to avoid factionalism (vv. 11-13, 16).

Welborn's assessment is that Paul's concern involved the wealthy and powerful minority in the Corinthian church dominating the lower-class majority in just the same way as occurred in secular society.

> The point is simply that neither in 1 Corinthians nor in ancient literature in general is there evidence of the poor creating factions of their own. Rather, the tensions between rich and poor always present in στάσισ [*stasis*]

are exploited by rich aristocrats in their contest for control of the state.[97]

In the case of *Jude*, this attempt at domination is for control of the congregation. From the nature of eldership in 1 Peter we can conclude that elders were senior members of the congregation, both in age and experience as believers (the latter being more important according to 1 Pet. 5:5), worthy of respect and responsible for the well-being of the congregation (including teaching) in a caring and non-exploitative manner. This behaviour is flouted by the Intruders in *Jude*, where those seeking to influence/take over the congregation were exploitative.

Until the late 1960s, biblical criticism mainly comprised a number of variants of form criticism, which divides the Bible, books of the Bible, and sections within them into pericopes (stories), which are analysed to determine the type of literature to which they should be assigned (e.g., law, history, poetry, prose, etc.). The analyst then tries to determine what theologians have called the *Sitz im Leben*:[98] the historical setting in which the text was composed. Watson's analysis of *Jude's* rhetorical style was a new development. From his examination, Watson concluded that 'by a considerable margin, the priority of Jude [over 2 Peter] is strongly confirmed.'[110]

Perhaps surprisingly, there is also a good deal of commonality in the literary style of *Jude* and 1 Corinthians, particularly given the circumstances that each letter tried to address (discussed below). There have been a number of literary analyses of the Pauline Epistles influenced by the work of Betz on 2 Corinthians and Galatians.[99] Using Betz's methodology, ancient sources and

---

[97] . L. L. Welborn, *Politics and Rhetoric in the Corinthian Epistles* (Macon, GA: Mercer University Press, 1997), 28.

[98] . Literally, 'setting in life'; see http://en.wikipedia.org/wiki/Biblical_criticism for comments on different types of biblical criticism. (Accessed 21 Jun 2021.) 110. Watson, *Invention*, 189.

[99] . H. D. Betz, *Galatians: A Commentary on Paul's Letter to the Churches in Galatia* (Philadelphia, PA: Fortress Press, 1979); H. D. Betz, *2 Corinthians*

ancient Greco-Roman rhetorical handbooks, Mitchell examined Paul's first letter to the Corinthians and determined that its form, function and content fit within a literary style called 'deliberative rhetoric' (also called 'political rhetoric'), one of the three categories of rhetoric found in Aristotle's *Rhetorica*, 1.3.3.[100] It is the rhetoric of the assembly, and thus relevant to Paul's attempt to bring unity to the Christian community in Corinth. While others (Fiorenza[101] and Welborn[102]) have considered 1 Corinthians to contain some deliberative rhetoric, only Mitchell has completed the work necessary to identify the letter (as a whole) as a unified, consistent epistle that argues one theme throughout.

Mitchell's explanation clarifies this.

> [d]eliberative argumentation was characterised by four things: 1) a focus on future time as the subject of deliberation; 2) employment of a determined set of appeals or ends, the most distinctive of which is the advantageous (τὸ συμφέρον) (to sumferon); 3) proof by example (παράδειγμα) (*paradeigma*); and 4) appropriate subjects for deliberation, of which factionalism and concord are especially common. Because each of these four elements of deliberative rhetoric is found in 1 Corinthians, this is a clear indication that 1 Corinthians employs that rhetorical species in its argumentation.[103]

This is the same literary structure that appears in Jude to address a similar set of goals. There appears to have been no analysis of the similarity between the literary structures of *Jude* and 1 Corinthians.

---

8 and 9: A Commentary on Two Administrative Letters of the Apostle Paul (Philadelphia, PA: Fortress Press, 1985).

[100]. Mitchell, *Paul and Rhetoric*, ch. 1–2.

[101]. E. S. Fiorenza, 'Rhetorical Situation and Historical Reconstruction in 1 Corinthians,' *New Testament Studies* 33:3 (1987): 386–403.

[102]. L. L. Welborn, 'A Conciliatory Principle in 1 Cor. 4:6,' *Novum Testamentum* 29:4 (1987): 320–346.

[103]. Mitchell, *Paul and Rhetoric*, 23.

Mitchell's second characterisation is the use of appeal. In this regard, it is as important for Jude to demonstrate the evil nature of the Intruders as it is for him to display the desirability of the gospel. With respect to Mitchell's third criterion, proofs by example, there is an appeal to imitate the example described. In the case of deliberative rhetoric, the moral character of the author is critical to the effectiveness of the proof and the success of the argument.[104] In this regard, Jude shows his moral authority by referring to himself as a slave of Jesus Christ (v. 1). In 1 Corinthians, Paul employs proofs by example, using both positive (ch. 9) and negative (10:1–13) examples. Notwithstanding that he uses many examples from Hellenistic culture, it is interesting to note the extent to which Paul uses *himself* as an example of proper behaviour to his readers. Twice, Paul specifically instructs the Corinthians to imitate *him* (1 Cor. 4:16; 11:1). Jude cannot do this. He is using ancient examples of *bad* behaviour for deterrence, so he cannot use himself as exemplar! Jude considers that examples from the OT and Jewish writings are strong enough to be an effective warning for his readers.

Mitchell's fourth criterion for deliberative rhetoric is its appropriateness to issues of factionalism and concord (the restoration of unity). This is both Paul's and, to a lesser extent, Jude's thesis (vv. 3, 19, 20, 24), and, therefore, it is relevant to quote Mitchell's summary of this criterion's importance in this literary genre:

> This emphasis on the political questions taken up by deliberative rhetoric, particularly war and peace, which are in every list, is maintained in rhetorical theory down into the GrecoRoman period. Alongside deliberations on war and peace emerges the important and related political topic of ὁμόνοια [*homonoia*], 'concord', or unity within the political body. This is not surprising, as ὁμόνοια, the opposite of factionalism, is also discussed as a common subject of deliberative rhetoric in the rhetorical handbooks. Thus, according to theoretical

---

[104] . See Mitchell, *Paul and Rhetoric*, 39–46.

statements about the appropriate subjects of deliberative rhetoric, concord and factionalism are commonly treated in that species of rhetoric. Deliberative rhetoric, the rhetoric of the assembly, is often primarily concerned with such matters as political stability and unity.[105]

Paul's Jewishness neither compromises the form and content of 1 Corinthians nor calls into question the appropriateness of the letter or his ability to use such a literary style. It has been demonstrated that Jude's Jewish roots do not prevent him from using the same skills in his letter (but not to the height of Paul's competence). The contents and style of both *Jude* and 1 Corinthians require the writer to possess skills in deliberative rhetoric, but this does not have to imply a slavish copying of a particular style.

After spending 18 months in Corinth, Paul travelled to Ephesus, where he met Apollos, 'an Alexandrian by birth, a learned man (ἀνὴρ λόγιος—*aners logios*)...mighty in the Scriptures'.[106] Apollos eventually moved to Corinth (Acts 19:1), where he had such a powerful ministry that some Corinthians attached themselves more to Apollos than to Paul (1 Cor. 1:12, 3:6). It seems apparent that some Corinthians were attracted to Apollos' obvious intellectual ability and rhetorical skills. While Paul never criticised Apollos (or his techniques), he did condemn the Corinthians for being attracted to the 'Apollos' faction or the 'Paul' faction for the wrong reasons (1 Cor. 3:3–6). This issue concerned Paul enough for him to write 1 Corinthians, which obviously fell short of its purpose, since it was necessary for the apostle to reiterate his concerns in 2 Corinthians. This

---

[105] . Mitchell, *Paul and Rhetoric*, 60–61.

[106] . Acts 18:24. Most English translations (from KJV onwards) describe Apollos as 'an eloquent man' (ἀνὴρ λόγιος—*anēr logios*); however, as Bruce points out, 'the adjective means 'learned' in both classical and Modern Greek; the meaning 'eloquent' is secondary'. See F. F. Bruce, *The Book of the Acts*, New International Commentary on the New Testament (Grand Rapids: Wm. B. Eerdmans Publishing Co., 1988), 358 n. 64. Only the NIV uses 'learned man'; the NASB uses 'an eloquent man'. Both 'eloquent' and 'learned' are appropriate descriptions of Apollos' rhetorical ability (Acts 18:28).

occurrence of factionalism in Corinth demonstrates how easily some in Jude's congregation(s) in a large city like Antioch might have fallen under the influence of sophistic Intruders.

Corinthian Influences

At this point, it is relevant to note that several faults identified in *Jude* had already occurred in Corinth, e.g., Paul's letters to that assembly (see 1 Cor. 11:17–34 regarding the Lord's Supper). This is a point too readily overlooked by most commentators on *Jude*. There are several commonalities between the issues that arise from the behaviour of the Intruders in *Jude* and the problems that (by this time) *had already occurred* at Corinth.[107]

It seems at least possible that, having been rejected by the Corinthian congregation (or finding that Pauline Christianity was not to their taste), some of the disaffected members left that city to find more fertile ground for their deviant ways at the north-eastern end of the Mediterranean. It must be more than a coincidence that the underlying tensions in Corinth resurface in much the same way in another Christian community a few years later, with marked similarities.

The problems addressed by Paul concerning the Corinthian church begin in 1 Corinthians 1, when factionalism emerged between the few wealthy, wise (in worldly terms) and powerful members of the congregation and the majority remainder (1 Cor. 1:26). That division grows (e.g., 1 Cor. 4:18; 6:1; 11:19–20) and eventuates in gross misbehaviour in the *agapais* (the Lord's Supper). We find the same sequence of events in *Jude*. The Intruders wheedle their way into the congregation and trouble begins. The similarities between 1 and 2 Corinthians and *Jude* are illustrated below.

1 Corinthians	**Jude**

---

[107] . See 'Date and Place of the Letter' in the Introduction.

1:10	divisions; quarrels about	8	rejecting authority
11:17	which leader to follow not	11	Korah bad
1:26	many wise, powerful, or	16	behaviour
	noble people	19	creating divisions
2:14	natural man versus spiritual	8	reviling angels
	man	10	lack of understanding of spiritual matters
		19	devoid of the Spirit
3:18	wisdom in this age	19	worldly-minded
4:18	arrogance	8	rejecting authority
		16	speaking arrogantly, flattering
		18	scoffing
5:1	immorality worse than Gentiles	8	defiling the flesh
		10	bad behaviour
		13	shame
		16	sexual immorality
5:11	not associating with immoral	4	ungodly people
5:12	brothers judging those in the		
5:13	church removing wicked men		
6:9	condemnation of the	4	marked for condemnation
	unrighteous, especially for	15	ungodliness sexual
	sexual immorality	18	immorality
10:1	examples of Israel in the wilderness	5	Israel in the wilderness
11:2	holding firm to traditions	3, 20	contending for 'the faith'
11:20	the Lord's Supper	12	the Lord's Supper
11:33-34	food at the Lord's Supper	12	caring for themselves at the Lord's Supper
14:22-31, 40	prophecy	8	'dreaming'
15:33-34	stopping sinful behaviour and keeping bad company	12	blemishes at the Lord's Supper
		16	bad behaviour
16:13	standing firm in the faith	3, 20	contending for 'the faith'

2 Corinthians   **Jude**

10:13-18	boasting	16	boasting
11:12-15	false apostles and workers	4	ungodly persons
12:20	more bad deeds in Corinth	8	defiling the flesh
		16	bad behaviour
13:5	'in the faith'	3, 20	contending for 'the faith'

Some in the congregation at Corinth continued to perpetuate what was acceptable in secular society, despite Paul's emphasis on a community based on serving one another with a 'non-status' style of leadership. This worldly behaviour was reflected not only, primarily, in factionalism but also in strife through civil litigation, contempt of the poor, boasting about status, and applying the wisdom of the world instead of the wisdom of God to their life together. 'The behaviour Paul condemns appears to him to be all-too-human and worldly, involving rivalry, jealousy and strife.' This is reflected in factionalism (1 Cor. 1:10–13, 3:3–4), Paul's condemnation of 'worldly' wisdom (1 Cor. 1:19–25; 3:19–21) and God's rejection of the wise and powerful in human society (1 Cor. 1:18–29). Similarly, pride and boasting are rejected (1 Cor. 1:31; cf. 3:21). Much the same behaviour seems to have occurred in Jude's congregation(s). Clarke argues that the divisions in Corinth were the result of patronage (where it was personally advantageous to be associated with those of high rank), the influence of sophistic thinking (in which self-assertion, self-aggrandisement, and boasting were prominent characteristics), and political intrigue (whereby prominent individuals controlled factions and used rhetoric and litigation to influence their followers). These are the very issues that Jude addresses: factionalism (vv. 16, 19), deviation from taught behaviour (vv. 4, 8, 10, 12, 13, 16, 18, 19), seeking favour and gain (vv. 12, 16, 18), and elitist thoughts of superiority (v. 16).

The considerable similarity between the behaviour in Corinth reported to Paul (which compelled him to write 1 Corinthians) and the behaviour in Palestine reported to Jude are not distinctly separate and unrelated occurrences. This is particularly the case when the sophistic character of both the perpetrators in each place and the style of letter written to combat them is taken into account. Jude's Intruders were able to infiltrate the Palestinian Jesus movement because, initially at least, they would have spoken the *lingua franca* and shown familiarity with the practices (such as the *agapais*) of the early Jesus movement. It was only their subsequent attitudes and behaviour that betrayed their true nature to some mature believers, who reported the matter to Jude. It is certainly a speculative conclusion, but it is possible that some of Jude's Intruders may have been present in the Corinthian fellowship before rejecting Paul's standards of behaviour and moving on to shepherd themselves in more attractive pastures in Palestine where Paul was not present, although he had taught at Antioch for some years beforehand. It could well be the case that some of Paul's brothers in Christ in Antioch contacted Jude.

This conclusion is supported not only by the comparable behaviour noted above but also by the manner and style of Jude's letter. Is it possible that those in Palestine who fell under the influence of the Intruders were of similar standing to those described in 1 Cor 1:26 (i.e., wise, mighty, noble)? Antioch was a city large enough to have such residents. If so, it is likely that some members of the Palestinian fellowship were swayed by sophistic techniques; therefore, Jude writes in a style that these people would recognise and respect. By rejecting the behaviour of the Intruders through inter alia deliberative rhetoric, Jude undercuts the 'wisdom' (cf. 1 Cor. 1:26–29) of the Intruders' purported authority.

Jewish Influences

The Jewish influences that might have contributed to the denunciation of the Intruders should not be lightly dismissed. The Didache[108] describes itinerant prophets who followed the

---

[108] . A . Milavec, *The Didache: Text, Translation, Analysis, and Commentary* (Collegeville, MN: Liturgical Press, 2003), ch. 11–13. The Didache (meaning 'Teaching') was a writing of the early church used for instruction to train

practices of false teachers: initially welcomed but subsequently found to be fraudulent.

Notwithstanding its fluent style in Greek, *Jude* does not contain quotations from the LXX. When referring to the OT, Jude uses the Hebrew text. This is further evidence that the writer came from a background steeped in Jewish practices, such as living in Nazareth under the instruction of a rabbi using the Hebrew text. This lack of reliance on the LXX is consistent with an earlier date for the letter.

Jobes reinforces this:

> An important clue about a New Testament writer and his audience is given by whether he uses the Hebrew version of the OT Scripture or one of the standard Greek translations. Even though Jude does not fully quote an Old Testament verse, a couple clues [*sic*] point to his use of the Hebrew Scriptures. One of these clues is found in the likely allusion to Zechariah 3:3 in Jude 23. The Hebrew word for 'filth' in Zechariah 3:3 (Heb *so'îm*) more specifically defines the source and kind of filth than does the corresponding word in the **Old Greek** translation (Gk *rhupara*). It seems that Jude must have had the Hebrew text in mind, for in v. 23 he adds the prepositional phrase 'from the flesh' to make the allusion to the repulsive image of the Hebrew expression clearer (Gk *rhupara apo tēs sarkos*, 'filthy from the flesh').

> Perhaps more decisive is the allusion to Proverbs 25:14 in Jude 12, which is more fitting to Jude's context in its Hebrew version ('Like clouds and wind without rain is one who boasts of a gift never given') than in its Greek translation ('As winds and clouds and rains are exceedingly apparent, so are they who boast over a false gift').

> Similarly, the reference to shepherds who feed only themselves in Jude 12 stands closer to the Hebrew of Ezekiel 34:2 ('Ah, you shepherds of Israel who have been feeding yourselves!') than the Greek ('Oh, you shepherds of Israel, do

converts to Christianity in doctrine before baptism. It was compiled in the
first and second centuries.

> shepherds feed themselves?'). Finally, the allusion to
> Isaiah 57:20 in Jude 13 can be compared in its Hebrew
> and Greek versions:
>
> Hebrew: 'But the wicked are like the tossing sea
> that cannot keep still; its waters toss up mire and mud.'
>
> Greek: 'But thus shall the unrighteous be tossed
> like waves and shall not be able to rest.'
>
> Based on this evidence, it seems more likely that
> Jude was thinking of the Hebrew Scriptures even though
> he, or his amanuensis, was writing in Greek. In spite of
> this, Jude also uses expressions that are found in the
> Greek version of the Old Testament, probably because
> these expressions had become common idioms among
> Jewish people who used
> Greek, even if not as their first language.[109]

In addition to references to the OT, Jude includes examples from
extra-canonical Jewish sacred writings: 1 Enoch and the
Assumption of Moses.[110] There are several references (overt and
subtle) in *Jude* to 1 Enoch, which are commented upon in
individual verses. This book made a strong impression on Jude,
reflected in the examples he chose to use in condemning the
Intruders.

The influence of 1 Enoch on Jude can be briefly summarized:

1. Jude cites 1 Enoch 1:9 to demonstrate that it had been
   prophesied that 'the Lord' (here understood as Christ)
   would come to judge the ungodly. The quotation is
   introduced as a prophecy in precisely the language
   Matthew uses to cite Isaiah (Matt. 15:7). This is, in fact,
   the only formal citation in the Letter of Jude.
   Furthermore, Enoch is identified in no casual way, as

---

[109]. Jobes, *Letters to the Church*, 251–252.
[110]. See comments on verse 9. G. L. Green, *Jude and 2 Peter*, 26–33 provides an
excellent analysis of Jude's use of pseudepigraphic literature.

though Jude were merely citing a convenient passage; rather, Enoch is designated as 'the seventh from Adam', and thus given a special place as an antediluvian figure who spoke at a symbolic point in the created order, a man who lived before the flood, amidst the immoral generation that, for Jude, corresponds to his own.

2. Jude 6 makes reference to the fall of the angels as a paradigmatic sin. Such a reference need not depend directly on 1 Enoch, for Genesis 6:1–4 was itself widely interpreted as referring to the Fall of the Watchers (see below); but 1 Enoch 6–16 was the earliest and most influential version of this mythic event, and Jude's description evinces enough terminological similarities to 1 Enoch that we may safely presume that this was his source.

3. In Jude 12–13 the opponents are depicted as 'waterless clouds, fruitless trees, wild waves, wandering stars'—images apparently drawn from 1 Enoch 2:1–5:4 and 1 Enoch 80:2–88.11.

4. Other allusions to Enochic language and motifs have been detected in Jude 12 but the current examples are sufficient to demonstrate that "1 Enoch 1–5 and related passages in the Enoch literature lie at the foundation of Jude's exegetical work."

The use of 1 Enoch in Jude's letter indicates that Jewish believers in Palestine, even after their conversion to the Way, still thought in Jewish terms. Jude was an important figure in the Palestinian
Jesus movement, which had a strong apocalyptic flavour.[111]

> Certainly, Jude's indebtedness to Jewish apocalyptic tradition is irrefutable…Yet, at the same time, we are justified in maintaining that Jude is free to adopt apocalyptic themes and language without necessarily

---

[111]. This was not confined to Palestine. See this influence in 1 Thess. 4–5.

importing (and embracing) Jewish apocalyptic
theology. Indeed, while his mode is conspicuously
apocalyptic, his outlook, in theological terms, is
prophetic.[112]

It is evident that Palestinian Jews did not abandon their spiritual
heritage when they became members of the Jesus movement.
Indeed, *Jude* suggests that new meaning could be derived from
Jewish writings in view of Jesus' ministry, just as those Jewish
believers could (and we can now) view the OT through
Christological lenses.[113] This is not to say that what are now
regarded as extra-canonical (Hebrew) texts should hold the same
weight of authority as the Bible for Christians, but it is necessary
to realise that 'The Bible' had not yet been formulated at the time
Jude was written. Therefore, from Jude's perspective, any
Jewish religious text that might assist his argument was
helpful.[114] In the same way, Paul occasionally used texts from
pagan sources if they furthered his explanation (e.g., Acts 17:28;
Ti. 1:12), as well as Jewish non-canonical sources (2 Tim. 3:8).

Theology of Jude

Theological reflection must concern that which God
says about himself...Since the object of biblical
exegesis is a body of literature which purports to be
God's very word to mankind, it is evident that the
theological element is not one that follows upon
exegesis but, rather, is an integral element of exegesis.
It should be the biblical interpreter's aim to understand
the literature at hand, with the objective of

---

[112] . J. D. Charles, "Polemic and Persuasion: Typological and Rhetorical
Perspectives on the Letter of Jude," in *Reading Jude with New Eyes:
Methodological Reassessments of the Letter of Jude*, eds R. L. Webb and P.
H. Davids (London: T. & T. Clark, 2007), 89.

[113] . G. Goldsworthy, *According to Plan* (Leicester, UK: Inter-Varsity Press,
1991), 8: 'every part of the Bible is given its fullest meaning by the saving
work of Christ.'

[114] . S ee E. M. G. Green, *2 Peter and Jude*, 23, for a comparison with Paul's use
of contemporary literary sources.

> comprehending the mind of the Spirit who speaks in and through the Scriptures. In reading and interpreting, the biblical student seeks to acquire the knowledge of God which the literature imparts to the reader who is guided by the Spirit.[115]

Initially, I approached the word 'theology' with some hesitation. It has connotations of an area of religious analysis that is the preserve of highly-skilled, intellectual scholars who work in a world that is quite separate from the world in which 'ordinary' Christians exist. Without the background described above, one would hardly be bold enough to describe oneself as a 'theologian'. Many readers may sympathise with this idea but this view of 'theology' is wrong. All Christians should be, to a greater or lesser extent, theologians; i.e., they should attempt to understand what God is saying about himself in the Bible.

> Thus, much that surrounds us conspires to make us forget the importance of studying theology in the light of its Godintended practical purpose. But this is something that we must not allow ourselves to forget. For theology, the study of biblical truth in application and apprehension is the theory of religion in the same way that form, harmony, and instrumentation are the theory of music. As music theory is studied with a view to making music as composer or performer, so Christian theology should be studied with a view to furthering Christian life and ministry—faith and godliness, both individual and corporate; fruitful biblical interpretation in the pulpit and the class meeting; and overall competence in catechesis, apologetics, and the injecting of Christian contributions into the contemporary market-place of jostling ideas. Of no item in theology is

---

[115] . M. W. Woudstra, *The Book of Joshua, The New International Commentary on the Old Testament* (Grand Rapids, MI: Wm. B. Eerdmans Publishing Company, 1981), 27.

this more true [*sic*] than the doctrine of God Himself, which is my immediate concern.[116]

In seeking to discover Jude's theology, it is the process of assessing how he sees God, in terms of him fitting into Jude's life and understanding of the world in which he and his readers lived. In this letter, Jude explains how he makes sense of God's activity in history, his time when writing, and the future. Jude's understanding of God is not only monotheistic (v. 25) but also thoroughly Trinitarian (even if he did not realise it). He refers to God as Father, Lord, and Saviour (vv. 1, 5, 9, 25); he refers to Jesus as Christ, Master, and Lord (vv. 1, 4, 14, 17, 21, 25); and he refers to the Holy Spirit (vv. 19, 20). The extent to which this understanding (of what is now called the Trinity) emanated from contact with Jesus, divine revelation, or common beliefs of the early Jesus movement cannot be determined. Yet it is clear from *Jude* that first-century members of the early Jesus movement across the Roman Empire could speak to one another about Father, Son and Holy Spirit while yet believing in one God.

Notwithstanding his significant contribution to our understanding of *Jude*, I must express reservations about Davids' understanding of Jude's consciousness of Jesus' divinity.[117] Relevant passages from Davids' two books on the subject follow. They are necessarily lengthy to appreciate his position. Emphases (in italics) are added:

> If God is presented as the family head, as the framework, so to speak, of all the good his people have received, *Jesus is presented as his agent*, as the leader of the people of God, as *the sovereign of God's kingdom*.[118]

---

[116] . J . I. Packer, 'Theism for Our Time' in *God Who Is Rich in Mercy: Essays Presented to Dr D. B. Knox*, eds P. T. O'Brien and D. G. Peterson (Homebush West, NSW: Lancer Books, 1986), 3.

[117] . I stress that this is not a criticism of Davids' personal understanding of the Trinity, but, rather, his interpretation of what he thinks Jude understands about it.

[118] . Davids, *2 Peter, Jude*, 30.

Finally, *this Sovereign* is the one through whom honour is given to God (v 25), which means that he *is viewed as a subking under God as high king.*[119]

Quite possibly Jude is *not only viewing Jesus as the Sovereign within the contemporary period but also seeing him as God's agent in the Hebrew Scriptures* and other Jewish literature.[120]

Unlike 2 Peter, Jude does *not allow for the possibility* that the title 'God' is being applied to Jesus.[133]

Jesus, then, in Jude is the Sovereign who is coming at the end of the age to establish God's good order, but whose involvement with the world stretches back to the great events of Israel's history, as Jude, in common with other NT writers, retells Israel's history in terms of Jesus. *He is God's executive agent indeed, a Sovereign who is to be respected.*[121]

Unlike 2 Peter, Jude never uses language that explicitly identifies Jesus as anything more than God's agent in expressing his rule, God's Anointed One, but he does suggest this 'more' indirectly in his applying the title 'Lord' to Jesus.[122]

So *Jesus is read as God's agent, as world-ruler or Lord, but so identified with God that he can be seen as his agent throughout world history* (not forgetting the actions of vv. 6 and 7 are attributed to the subject of v. 5) and into the eschaton (v. 14).[123]

So we know that Jude views Jesus as *God's executive agent*, that he attributes to Jesus a number of the actions

---

[119]. Davids, *2 Peter, Jude*, 30.

[120]. Davids, *2 Peter, Jude*, 30–31.

133. Davids, *2 Peter, Jude*, 30.

[121]. Davids, *2 Peter, Jude*, 31. It appears that this Sovereign is worthy of 'respect' but not worship.

[122]. Davids, *Theology*, 283.

[123]. Davids, *Theology*, 284.

of God in the Hebrew Scriptures. We also know that Jude never says grammatically that Jesus is divine as 2 Peter 1:1 (or John 1:1 or Heb. 1:3) does. He is, perhaps, at an early, less self-conscious stage in the development of this doctrine. *But it is clear that Jesus is God's fully empowered agent and has been since at least early in the history of creation.*[124]

Thus in Jude we have the gracious, favourable Father and the Lord Jesus who has executed and will execute judgment, which certainly throws a monkey wrench in the works of the popular picture current in our culture of a judging Father and a caring Son (*Jude, of course, never uses Father-Son language for Jesus and God*, as John does, but rather Father/*empowered, authorised Agent*).[125]

There are references by Davids to Jesus as 'God's agent', 'sovereign of God's kingdom', 'a subking under God as high king', 'God's executive agent' and 'God's agent in the Hebrew Scriptures'. As a matter of law,[126] a principal can appoint and authorise an agent to do anything that the principal can or wishes to do. But the agent is not the principal. The principal can, for example, revoke the agent's power (partially or completely) at any time. The agent has no power of his own and, for the purposes of this point, it must be emphasised that *the principal and the agent must be two separate and distinct persons.*

Davids' description of the (Father) God/Jesus relationship in this agency form falls far short of the conventional Trinitarian doctrine of the godhead. A more promising alternative relationship might be that of a king and a crown prince, who acts on his father's behalf but also shares his father's nature and rights. Moreover, Jesus makes his dependence on the Father a central feature of his equality in John 5:18–23. Along with the description of Jesus as a 'subking', Davids clearly implies that

---

[124] . Davids, *Theology*, 284.

[125] . Davids, *Theology*, 284.

[126] . Whether English, American or Australian law. The author is an Australian

Jude did not understand that Jesus was God in human form, let alone the conventional Trinitarian position of three (equal) persons in one God, notwithstanding some subordination of functions within the Trinity (John 14–15). It was noted earlier that Paul influenced, and was influenced by, the early Palestinian Jesus movement and this is relevant to the discussion.

This suggests a dating of Jude that is around the same time as the Pauline correspondence (e.g., Colossians). In Colossians 1:19, Paul confirms that 'it was the Father's good pleasure for all the fullness [of deity] to dwell in Him [Jesus]' (NASB). Davids' analysis implies that neither Jude nor his readers can have had this understanding, even though they have received 'the faith once for all time entrusted to the saints' (v. 3). Could Jude and Paul have such varying concepts of Jesus' divinity around the middle of the first century? Was Jude unfamiliar with the expressions in John 14–15? Did all the other leaders of the movement in Jerusalem share Jude's opinion as described by Davids? This seems impossible to accept.

Davids' use of agency theory in Jude's theology must be rejected, both on the grounds of logic and conventional Trinitarian analysis. It must be replaced with an acknowledgement that Jude was well aware of Jesus' divinity. Just because Jude does not write

---

lawyer.

'Jesus is God' it cannot be argued that he did not believe that to be the case. *Jude* is as consistently Trinitarian as the Pauline Epistles and the Johannine Gospel.

This point is emphasised in verse 4, where Jude describes Jesus Christ as τὸν μόνον δεσπότην (*ton monon despotēn*): 'the only sovereign' (see also comments on v. 4). "During the first half of the third century, Julius Africanus, in his *Letter to Aristedes*, wrote of the *desposynoi* ['those who belong to the Master']—a term which, he explains, was used to designate the relatives of Jesus—that they preserved their family genealogy and interpreted it wherever they went on their travels throughout Palestine."[140] As Bauckham comments, "[t]he term δεσπότης for the relatives of the [sic] Jesus is only explicable if δεσπότης was commonly used to refer to Jesus in Palestinian Jewish Christianity. Jude's use of this term is, therefore an impressive, but neglected indication of his letter's origin in those Palestinian Christian circles in which the δεσπόσυνοι were leaders."[141]

Not only does *ton monos despotēn* denote the recognition of Jesus' status as Christ and Lord by his own relatives, but it is also an important pointer to Jesus' role in the Trinity. He is God. In verse 4, Jude combines the titles 'sovereign' (δεσπότης— *despotēs*) and 'lord' (κύριος—*kurios*) (as per the Granville Sharp rule)[142]

---

140. Bauckham, *Relatives of Jesus*, 60.

141. Bauckham, *Relatives of Jesus*, 283.

142. The terms 'Master' and 'Lord' both refer to the same person. The construction in Greek is known as the Granville Sharp rule, named after the English philanthropist-linguist who first clearly articulated the rule in 1798. Sharp pointed out that in the construction 'article–noun–καί–noun' (where καί [*kai*] = 'and'), when two nouns are singular, personal, and common (i.e., not proper names), they *always* had the same referent. Illustrations such as 'the friend and brother', 'the God and Father', etc. abound in the NT to prove Sharp's point; e.g. Ti. 2:13; 2 Pet. 1:1.

This has important implications for my criticism of Davids above in 'Theology of Jude' in the Introduction.

Strangely, Kelly, E*pistles of Peter and of Jude*, Bauckham, *Jude*, Davids, (three books) and G. L. Green, *Jude and 2 Peter*, do not refer to the Granville Sharp rule. Mayor, The Epistle of St Jude, 27, and Kistemaker, Epistle of Jude, 375, refer to the rule without naming it.

Granville Sharp (1735–1813) was an English political reformer, slavery abolitionist, and Greek language scholar known for his contributions regarding the translation of New Testament Greek as it relates to the divinity of

to denote the messianic ruler of the universe in whom all might and power resides. It is doing less than justice to describe this being, as Davids suggests that Jude does, as a 'subking' to God the Father. The use of *monon* not only reinforces the Judaic exclusivity for the divine name but also emphasises that this unique God is Jesus himself.

It should be noted that the theology of *Jude* does not include several fundamental themes, such as Christ's ministry on earth, or the cross. Three reasons can explain these absences. First, the urgent nature of the letter (v. 3): it was penned quickly to replace an intended letter about 'our common salvation'. (Perhaps that letter might have had time and space to consider such matters.) Secondly, the letter addressed the particular situation of the ungodly infiltration of false practices (and beliefs), which did not require mention of more fundamental aspects of Christian theology (already known to Jude's readers). Thirdly, and quite importantly, the readers themselves were quite mature in 'the faith'; it is quite clear from the letter that they had heard and believed the gospel. If, as suggested in verse 17, these believers heard and believed the words of the apostles, they would have understood the basic elements of the faith (i.e., the gospel). Their salvation was taken for granted by Jude.

There is also a strong apocalyptic theme running through *Jude*.

Christ. Sharp believed strongly in the deity of Christ and studied the New Testament in its original language to more ably prove Christ's deity. The Granville Sharp Rule was first noted in 1798 in his book, *Remarks on the Uses of the Definitive Article in the Greek Text of the New Testament: Containing Many New Proofs of the Divinity of Christ, from Passages Which Are Wrongly Translated in the Common English Version.*

The Granville Sharp Rule states, 'When the copulative *kai* connects two nouns of the same case, [viz. nouns (either substantive or adjective, or participles) of personal description, respecting office, dignity, affinity, or connexion, and attributes, properties, or qualities, good or ill], if the article ho, or any of its cases, precedes the first of the said nouns or participles, and is not repeated before the second noun or participle, the latter always relates to the same person that is expressed or described by the first noun or participle.' (*Remarks on the Uses of the Definitive Article*, 3).

See https://www.gotquestions.org/Granville-Sharp-Rule.html (Accessed 21 Jun 2021.)

In verse 1, the readers are those kept for Christ's return, although there is no indication as to when Jude might have expected it. Of course, a critical feature of Christ's return is to execute judgement on the ungodly. *Jude* makes constant reference to this regarding the Intruders in particular (vv. 4, 10, 13, 14, 15) and to others in the community (v. 23). There may be some sense of imminence in verse 23, where the readers are urged to snatch people from the flames (of judgement), although it could be interpreted as the need to rescue people before their physical death. Interwoven with this theme is the use of 1 Enoch to confirm the prophetic nature of the judgement that will befall the Intruders.

The theology of *Jude* is primarily concerned with the uniqueness of God and the people of God (vv. 3–4; 19–20), the need for their behaviour to conform to God's will and character, and the necessity for them to act whenever the body of believers is threatened by external dangers (vv. 3–5; 21). Key thoughts in *Jude* are encouragement and guidance for the leaders of God's people and the *mutual* action required to put the apostles' instructions into action. *Jude* is not like those letters of Paul that are instructions to new and immature communities of the early Jesus movement. Jude appears to assume that his readers possess a more robust, knowledgeable faith (v. 3). This would be the case for a city like Antioch, where Christianity took root at an early stage after the resurrection (Acts 11:19). It is much more like the Letter of James (the brother of Jude), with its practical instruction on how a congregation of the Jesus movement ought to treat its members and recognise Intruders.

In summary, the theology of *Jude* reflects God's sovereignty over the created order; his certain judgement against sin; his love, demonstrated in mercy for those who are saved by his grace, freely extended to his people through Christ. Jude also expresses his understanding of Jesus as God, Saviour and ongoing ruler of the universe, who will inevitably return to take his people home and who will ultimately destroy sin and death forever. There is an undoubted Trinitarian element to this understanding of (Father) God, Jesus, and the Holy Spirit.

Jude and Paul

It is unnecessary to assume that Jude relied on Paul for his theological terminology. There are several instances where *Jude* uses Pauline words or concepts, and these are explored in the comments on the text. This raises the question as to whether Jude met Paul and was familiar with any of the apostle's letters. It is conceivable that Paul might have met Jude when he visited Jerusalem (on the occasion of Acts 15:4–6 and Acts 21:15–19). Even if Jude had not read any of Paul's letters, it is not only quite possible that some 'Pauline' phrases had become widespread in the early 'global' movement, but also that Paul himself picked up and used language that was the *lingua franca* of the early Jesus movement in Palestine. Paul was in Antioch for some years after his conversion and undoubtedly adopted some early Christian sayings extant before he became a Christian.

The occurrence of 'Paulinisms' in Jude does not have to reflect a slavish following of the great apostle's words by the author just to be (using modern terminology) politically correct in Jesus movement terms. Indeed, it would be surprising if there was no overlap in the terminology of two men writing about the same broad subject for a (then) relatively small community. In this context, there is a need to remember the ready means of communication (oral and written) that undoubtedly would have been used by the early believers. There would also have been oral reports about what Paul and the other apostles had said. The Council of Jerusalem (Acts 15) was only possible because reports about Paul had reached the apostles in Jerusalem (and were undoubtedly heard by Jude). On the other hand, it is possible that Paul used terms from the Jerusalem (and Antioch?) believers, and the only reason we know of them is because they are contained in Paul's letters. It is widely assumed that all Pauline terms originated with Paul. Some undoubtedly did, but there is no need to be too insistent on this point.

Acts 21:17–19 describes Paul's arrival in Jerusalem, where he met James, the brother of Jude, 'and all the elders were present'. Had he been in Jerusalem, Jude would undoubtedly have been numbered among 'the elders'. Therefore, it seems most unlikely that Paul would not have also met with Jude. Given that Paul was in Jerusalem for more than a week, there might have been ample opportunity for the two to converse. On this basis, it is quite likely that Jude would have been familiar with Paul's expressions. It would be no surprise to find traces of them in this letter. But both probably used the same terminology in their letters, given their shared heritage as Jews familiar with the Greek language and the Jewish Scriptures. Nevertheless, it is interesting to note that Jude contains similarities to Paul's farewell speech to the Ephesian church (Acts 20:18–35) and to his letters to Timothy and Titus. Nevertheless, there is little evidence to suggest that the content of Jude is much indebted to Paul or Paulinisms.

Having provided a background to the Letter of Jude, we now consider what Jude wrote.

Commentary on Jude

The Author and His Blessing

Verse 1 Judas, a slave of Jesus Christ, but brother of Jacob, to the called: beloved in God the Father and kept for
> **Jesus Christ.**

Verse 2   May mercy and peace and love be multiplied to you.

Jude greets his readers in the normal style of a first-century letter, in which an author began with his self-identification and a description of his readers (often by name), followed by a greeting. Such introductions may be long (e.g., Rom. 1:1–7) or short (e.g., 3 John 1). The Letter of Jude is a little unusual in that it begins with a blessing on the readers rather than a salutation to them.

Verse 1 in Detail

Judas

Ἰούδας

The writer of this letter is variously called Judah (in Hebrew), Judas (in Greek), and Jude (in English). Judah was a common Hebrew name. For the reasons described in the Introduction, the writer is considered to be the half-brother of Jesus and brother of James, the (then) leader of the Jesus movement in Jerusalem. Unlike some letters in the NT, the writer simply describes himself in factual terms while making no attempt to justify his authority to write. In each of his letters, Paul offers some indication of his authority; the only exceptions being 1 and 2 Thessalonians. The absence of such a description indicates not only that his readers have no doubt about Jude's authority to write to them about an important matter but also that Jude is confident in his position in the early Jesus movement.

a slave of Jesus Christ

Ἰησοῦ Χριστοῦ δοῦλος

Jude is a slave of Jesus Christ (*Ἰησοῦ Χριστῷ—Iēsou Christō*). He mentions Jesus by name three times in his letter. On each occasion, it is 'Jesus Christ': i.e., Jesus the Messiah, the Anointed One. 'Christ' is the Greek equivalent of the Hebrew 'Messiah'. Throughout the NT, there are references to both 'Jesus Christ' and 'Christ Jesus', but Jude prefers the former style.[127] Just because Jude uses the Pauline description of a slave of Christ, he is not claiming apostleship.[128]

As with Paul,[129] Peter[130] and James,[131] Jude calls himself 'a slave (*δοῦλος—doulos*) of Christ.' This is one of the most common (early Jesus movement) descriptions of believers after the resurrection. It is also used of major figures in the LXX. 'Those called to special service in the OT were identified as the 'slave' (*doulos*) of the Lord: Abraham, Moses, Joshua, David, and the prophets (Josh. 14:7; 24:29; 2 Kings 17:23; Psalm 89:4, 20).' [132] However, many English translations of *doulos* in Scripture (especially those printed in the United States[133]) cannot

---

[127] . For example, Paul uses the order ἰησοῦς χριστός (*Iēsous Christos*—Jesus Christ) seventy-seven times and the order χριστὸς ἰησοῦς (*Christos Iēsous*—Christ Jesus) eighty-two times. It appears that this order is a matter of personal choice in a wide variety of references to the Lord.

[128] . See comments on v. 17 regarding the issue of whether Jude should be regarded as an apostle.

[129] . R om. 1:1; 1 Cor. 7:22; Gal. 1:10; Phil. 1:1; Col. 4:12; 2 Tim. 2:24; Ti. 1:1. Compare with Phil. 2:7.

[130] . 2 Pet. 1:1.

[131] . James 1:1.

[132] . Schreiner, *Jude*, 427–428. See also K. H. Rengstorf, '*δοῦλος*' in *Theological Dictionary of the New Testament*, vol. 2, ed. G. Kittel (Grand Rapids, MI: Wm. B. Eerdmans Publishing Company, 1964), 268, 276–277. (This dictionary is abbreviated *TDNT* throughout the rest of the notes.)

[133] . New International Version (NIV), English Standard Version (ESV), Good News, New English Bible (NEB), New Revised Standard Version (NRSV),

bring themselves to use 'slave'. This may reflect widespread modern revulsion (and, to many, embarrassment) at the practice of slavery in the United States and England for centuries.

The NASB is regarded as being one of the most literal translations of the Greek text, but it shows an inherent prejudice when translating *doulos*. It never uses 'slave' whenever *doulos* refers to someone (male or female) who is one of God's people, unless the notion of 'slave' is relevant to the particular text. Instead, it uses euphemisms like 'bond-servant' or 'bond-slave'. But the NASB always uses 'slave' whenever the word is used in a general context. The Book of Revelation is a clear example of this differentiation. The NIV deviates even further in its overwhelming use of 'servant' for *doulos* rather than 'slave'. But 'slave' is the only correct translation. The generally used alternative is 'servant' or 'bond-servant', as mentioned above. It must be emphasised that these are merely euphemisms. In the first century, there were slaves and servants—nothing else.

Rengstorf says about *doulos*:

> All the words in this group serve either to describe the status of a slave or an *attitude corresponding to that of a slave*... the meaning is so unequivocal and self-contained that it is superfluous to give examples of the individual terms or to trace the history of the group...Hence we have a service which is not a matter of choice for the one who renders it, which he has to perform whether he likes it or not, because he is subject as a slave to an alien will, *to the will of his owner*.[8]
>
> (Emphasis added.)

(NKJV) use 'bond-servant'. But The Message Bible (MSG), NetBible, and Recovery Version use 'slave'. Davids, 2 Peter and Jude, 33 uses the translation 'servant'; but agrees that it means 'slave' (34); however, P. H. Davids, 2 Peter and Jude: A Handbook on the Greek Text, Baylor Handbook

---

Revised Standard Version (RSV), and King James Version (KJV) use 'servant'; New American Standard Bible (NASB) and New King James Version

on the Greek New Testament (Waco, TX: Baylor University Press, 2011), 1 and Davids, Theology, 265–266 use 'slave'. Bauckham, Jude, 2 Peter, 19 uses 'servant' while acknowledging that doulos means 'slave' (23). Note Davids' change of emphasis in the importance of the 'slave' description between his two commentaries, where the latter is more sympathetic to my view.

8. Emphasis added. *TDNT*, vol. 2, 261, but see 261–278 for the full explanation. See also G. L. Green, *Jude and 2 Peter*, 45-46; J. MacArthur, *Slaves of Christ* https://www.gty.org/library/sermons-library/GTY112/slaves-of-christ. (Accessed 22 Jun 2021.)

It has been argued that 'servant' is an appropriate term because Jesus regarded himself as a servant (Matt. 20:28). However, the Greek in that verse uses the verb (διακονεω—*diakoneō*) for serving (i.e., being a servant), not for being a slave. In any event, it is not the role of Jesus that is under scrutiny but the relationship of the believer to the Lord. Similarly, 'bond-servant' is favoured by those who argue that 'it often indicates one who sells himself into slavery to another'.[134] This view gives far too much credit to the one who becomes the 'slave' and fails to recognise Paul's reminder to the Corinthians: '*you have been bought* with a price' (1 Cor. 6:20, emphasis added). It is God's grace and sacrifice, not human effort, that enables us to become Christ's slaves '*by the price He paid*' (Matt. 20:28, emphasis added).

There is no excuse for mistranslation of the original text just because the English meaning of the Greek word does not suit modern predispositions and sensitivities. This does no justice to the writer and thwarts the meaning he intended for his words. Nor does this reluctance to use 'slave' properly understand the role of a slave in the first century. Although the modern impression of slavery is that it is wholly repugnant (and appropriately so from the perspectives of creation (Gen. 1:27) and human rights), this is of little help in understanding the concept in the first century AD. Westermann's comprehensive analysis on the institution of slavery in ancient Greek and Roman times devoted a section to slavery in the context of the early Christians, which provides enlightenment on the use of *doulos*

---

[134] . *NetBible Commentary on Jude*, v. 1 n. 2, in https://bible.org/netbible ('NetBible'). (Accessed 21 Jun 2021.) This comment on 'bondservant' has adverse implications for the doctrine of predestination.

by Jude (and other NT writers). Some extracts follow to place our thoughts back in the first century:

> It would be self-deception if one failed to see that Jesus of Nazareth, the apostles and the Church, both in its formative period and in its later development, accepted the going system of labour of its time, including the slave structure, without hesitation or any expressed reluctance. It was there, and they took it.[135]

> To the apostle Paul slavery and freedom were facts of everyday life which were to be accepted and which could be expressed in simple terms and grasped readily by simple people.[11] ...What Paul had done for slavery as it applied to Christian believers was to accept it as a physical fact, but to spiritualise that acceptance so that it became almost, if not fully, meaningless for those who were imbued with his own fervent conviction that Jesus of Nazareth was the ordained Saviour of mankind.[12]

> [t]he accepted social distinction of legal status ceased to exist in their [Christian] communities along with the differences of racial origin and former religious belief. This may be ascribed, in part, to the conviction which they held that the Day of judgment, and with it the end of the existing world, was not far distant.[13]

A slave was the lowest position that a person could occupy in first-century society. There can be no doubt that most slaves in the Roman Empire were regarded as, and treated as little better than, animals; like animals, slaves were subject to the complete power of their masters. It could be argued that, having come from the glory of the Father to life as a Nazarene carpenter, Jesus himself displayed the elements of utter debasement. This would be demonstrated in the extreme (especially for the Jews) by his dying on a cross. Nevertheless, there were many slaves who occupied positions of responsibility and authority within

---

[135] . W. L. Westermann, 'The Slave Systems of Greek and Roman Antiquity,'

Memoirs of the American Philosophical Society 40 (New York: Noble Offset
Printers, 1955), 150. See also P. R. Coleman-Norton, *Studies in Roman
Economic and Social History* (Princeton, NJ: Princeton University Press,
1951), 158–159. See also M. J. Brown, 'Paul's Use of ΔΟΥΛΟΣ ΧΡΙΣΤΟΥ
ΙΗΣΟΥ in Romans 1:1,' *Journal of Biblical Literature* 120:4 (2001): 723-
737. Brown regards this title as 'an allusion to the *Familia Caesaris*, the
household of Caesar', but the article fails to recognise the term's primarily
spiritual significance.

11. Westermann, *Slave Systems*, 149. Westermann then uses this view to consider
Galatians 3:27–5:1.
12. Westermann, *Slave Systems*, 150.
13. Westermann, *Slave Systems*, 150–151. The expectation of Christ's imminent
return is an important element in *Jude*.

wealthy Roman households.[136] This latter understanding of the
role of a slave would certainly have been within the knowledge
of Paul, and perhaps Jude, even if not within their experience. In
any event, the particular role or physical circumstances of a slave
do not compromise the point at issue for Jude (or Paul) in this
self-description. Jude uses *doulos* simply to reflect the position
of the most subservient people in his society. That is his
understanding of his relationship to Jesus the Christ.[137]

The reason for Jude's self-description as a slave rests on two
premises: the first being the status of a slave. Slaves suffered
from institutional limitations on their freedom of action and
initiative. Slaves had no freedom at all, nor did they have any
entitlements.[138] A slave was his or her master's possession, with

---

[136] . See Garnsey and Saller, *Roman Empire*, 119, 132.
[137] . See M. J. Harris, *Slave of Christ: A New Testament Metaphor for Total
Devotion to Christ*, New Studies in Biblical Theology 8 (Downers Grove, IL:
Inter-Varsity Press, 1999).
[138] . Human rights *as they are understood today* were non-existent in the first
century; however, the concept of entitlements was recognised. The outcome
of the ancient Greek philosophical belief that ideals can be worth even more
than worthless (valueless) human beings meant that Plato considered that
every man had the right to a fair trial—even a slave! A slave only received a
fair trial because the importance of the argument for a fair trial had to be
upheld— even if it needed to be applied to a slave or criminal. None of these
concepts provide much comfort, in that ancient philosophers placed greater
value on ideals than human beings and that the entitlement to claim 'rights'

the same legal status as the master's other property, such as his house or horse. The slave's entire existence was determined by the master's will— for good or ill. As a slave of Christ, Jude is also subject to the will of his master, who will determine his role in life and control (own) his whole being.[139] In Jude's case, his master will control what happens to the slave in life *and death*. Unlike earthly equivalents, this slavery is not forced on Jude. It is a (low) status placed on him by God, to which he voluntarily and willingly submits because he wants to be wholly-owned and directed by the One who died for him. It should be noted that, in the OT, the slave/ master relationship is the 'commonest expression for the service of God in the sense of total allegiance and not just isolated acts of worship.'[140] This makes it less surprising that Jude uses this motif to describe his relationship to Jesus. The same, of course, could be said of Paul, the other apostles, and members of the early Jesus movement.

Jude's second premise for describing himself as a slave is the status of the master of the slave.[141] Slaves in a prestigious Roman household enjoyed the status of their master. Better to be a slave in Caesar's palace than one in rural Tuscany. But Jude is a slave of *Jesus Christ!* There could be no higher honour than to be a member of Christ's household (the King of Kings), no matter how menial the duties (cf. Psalm 84:10). Given the nature of Christ (2 Cor. 10:1), it is absurd to regard the slave nomenclature as a reflection of base existence and ill treatment in a Christian context. On the contrary, slaves of Christ will eventually reign with him (Rev. 20:6). This is a future for which no earthly slave could ever hope, let alone attain. In any event, Jude by now

---

was on a high pedestal. See J. M. Rist, *Human Value: A Study in Ancient Philosophical Ethics* (Leiden: E. J. Brill, 1982), 125–126.

[139] . Cf. Paul's determination to fulfil Christ's will in his path to Jerusalem when faced with godly advice to the contrary in Acts 21:10–14. A similar situation exists in the mistranslation of 1 Corinthians 16:12 where it is not Apollos' will but God's will that determines his decisions and actions.

[140] . C. E. B. Cranfield, *The Epistle to the Romans*, The International Critical Commentary (Edinburgh: T. and T. Clark, 1975), 1:51–52, 320–330.

[141] . See Harris, *Slave of Christ*, 135. Davids, *2 Peter, Jude*, 34–35 usefully notes that, when Jesus is referred to as 'servant of the Lord', in Acts 3:13; 4:27, 30, not *doulos* but παῖς (*pais*) is used for 'servant'.

recognises the divine nature of his brother, notwithstanding that he spent his early life with Jesus. Paul notes that Jesus was without sin (2 Cor. 5:21) and Jude makes no attempt to contradict this assertion. Again, the correct translation of *doulos* is 'slave', not euphemisms like 'servant' or 'bond-servant', which entirely misrepresent both the relationship described and the intention of the author. Note the frequent use of 'servant' (διάκονος—*diakonos*) in the NT to differentiate a servant from the lowlier designation of slave (cf. Matt. 25:14–30.) Mistranslations of *doulos* attempt to minimise the servitude of Jude (or Paul), whereas *they* wish to glory in their lowly position.[142]

but brother of Jacob

ἀδελφὸς δὲ Ἰακώβου

Jude did not just use his own name as author but also describes himself as the brother of Jacob (more commonly known as James). For his readers, there was only one James, the mention of whose very name would have engendered reverence in the readers. This was James, the leader of the early Jesus movement in Jerusalem and another brother of Jesus. So, by this association, Jude also describes himself as a brother of Jesus.[143] But why not say so directly? Bigg understands Jude's reluctance for self-aggrandisement in his comment that Jude is effectively saying, 'Jude, the slave, I dare not say the brother, of Jesus Christ, but certainly the brother of James.'[144] It is of note that James does not refer to his familial relationship to Jesus in the

---

[142] . Harris, *Slave of Christ*, makes the same point, at greater length, in Appendix 3.

[143] . Given Jesus' unique birth, James and Jude might be better called half-brothers of Jesus, with Joseph and Mary as their parents, as opposed to Jesus, who was born of the Holy Spirit and Mary. Jude's brotherhood with Jesus is disputed by T. W. Manson, *A Companion to the Bible* (Edinburgh: T and T Clark, 1949), 119, but endorsed by Guthrie, *New Testament Introduction*, 906–908; E. M. Blaiklock, *Commentary on the New Testament* (London: Hodder and Stoughton, 1977), 249. See also Bruce, *The Book of the Acts*, 42; L. L. Morris, *The Gospel According to John*. The New International Commentary on the New Testament (Grand Rapids, MI: Wm. B. Eerdmans Publishing Company, 1995), 187–188.

[144] . Bigg, *Jude*, 323.

first verse of his letter. Perhaps the brothers had a joint understanding that this was not to be referred to, lest they appear to be boosting their status.

Bauckham makes an important point when he mentions 'the fact that to identify oneself by reference to one's brother, rather than one's father, was extremely unusual and requires explanation.'[145] This particularly points to James being that well-known leader of the Jesus movement. 'The author's designation of himself as 'brother of James' is unique. No other New Testament writer introduces himself by identifying his family connections.' [146]   Schreiner correctly notes that ἀδελφός (*adelphos*) means 'brother' in the context of familial relationships (or the family of God) and dismisses Ellis' contention that the word means a 'co-worker in the gospel'.[147] Such a designation would be συνεργὸς (*sunergos*— fellow-worker), as in Romans 1:9 and Philemon. 1.

The use of δὲ (*de*) should be mentioned. This little word is used nearly 2,800 times in the NT (thirteen times in Jude) and has a variety of meanings, depending on the context. It is one of Jude's favourite connecting words. In this context, *de* is translated 'but'.[148] There is similar usage in verses 17 and 20, where Jude writes, 'But you'. The sense of Jude's description may be: I am a slave of Jesus (many members of the early Jesus movement could have used this self-description, following the usage of James, Peter, Jude and Paul), *but* (as a point of distinctiveness) I am also James' brother—no one else could make that claim.

Therefore, Jude has incredibly special personal credentials: a brother of the ascended Christ and a brother of the earthly

---

[145] . Bauckham, *Jude, 2 Peter*, 23.

[146] . D . E. Hiebert, *Second Peter and Jude: An Expositional Commentary* (Greenville, SC: Unusual Publications, 1989), 192; Kelly, *Epistles of Peter and of Jude*, 242.

[147] . Schreiner, *Jude*, 483; Ellis, *Prophecy and Hermeneutic*, 226–230.

[148] . The only other similar usage is found in Titus 1:1; see P. H. Towner, *The Letters to Timothy and Titus*, The New International Commentary on the New Testament (Grand Rapids, MI: Wm. B. Eerdmans Publishing Company, 2006), 666 n. 12.

leader of his movement. This alone would give him sufficient authority to write in his own name.

When attesting one's qualifications and the people one knows, it is normal to list them in order of impressiveness. First impressions count, so the saying goes. But Jude begins his letter by appearing to identify his relationship to two people in the opposite manner: the first, a lowly relationship (a slave); and the second, a high one (in worldly terms), as brother of the leader of the movement. Jude is a slave and a brother. This is a differentiation between his two brothers. Considering the matter from a human point of view (cf. 2 Cor. 5:16), to one (Jesus), he is a slave; to the other (James), he is a brother. However, the reality for Jude is reversed. Being a slave of Christ was far more valuable and prestigious to him than any earthly relationship, no matter how close and significant that person might be. Do we value our relationship with Jesus as more valuable (and more impressive) than, say, our relationship (if it existed!) with the President of the United States or the Queen of England? A similar question might also be asked of our relationships with family and friends, particularly those we wish to impress (consider Luke 14:26).

to the called

τοῖς...κλητοῖς

The intervening words describe the status of the called and are better understood in an English translation if they follow this description of Jude's readers.

By NT comparison, it is unusual that Jude does not name the recipients of his letter. They are just 'the called'. This has led a few commentators to consider that *Jude* is one of the 'catholic' epistles. [149] This interpretation is rejected by most modern

---

[149]. This is using 'catholic' in its proper meaning of 'universal'; i.e. the letter was supposed to be addressed by Jude to members of the Jesus movement in general, like a sermon. The term has nothing to do with Catholicism, nor is the letter associated with the Roman Catholic Church. See further comments on v. 3.

scholars. Nevertheless, the way the readers are addressed is of significance. The doctrine of election (regarding God's calling of people to himself) is not some construction of modern theologians. It was at the centre of Jesus' message. Jesus was clear that he would have followers who had been called by God (John 15:16; 17:24). Jude is writing to a group of people who were chosen (predestined) by God to become believers in Jesus. These believers are not just called. They are *τοῖ* κλητοῖ (*to klētoi—the* called): a specific group that God has chosen (Rom. 1:6; 1 Cor. 1:24). Cranfield notes that to be called 'denotes God's effectual calling: the *klētoi* are those who have been called effectually, who have been summoned by God *and have also responded to His summons.*'[150] Jude's readers are members of this group. To be 'called' by God is not a matter of human effort or achievement: it is solely effected by God's amazing grace.

'Called' is a particularly Pauline phrase (Rom. 1:1, 6, 7; 8:28; 1 Cor. 1:1, 2, 24; but see also 2 Pet. 1:10). Paul used it of himself and others. However, the term does not have to be a Paulinism that was adopted by Jude. 'The word κλητός here expresses the thought of divine calling in opposition to human self-appointment—it is not based on presumptuous human ambition but based on God's call that Paul is an apostle.'[151] As well as referring to God's intervention in human activity, the word is also used in Revelation 17:14 to describe those who dwell with Christ in heaven. This is the final destination of the called. To be called by Christ is to be set apart on earth for an ongoing relationship after death. It is an eternal concept.

This description links the readers and Jude to OT concepts with which both would have been well versed: Isaiah 41:9; 42:6; 48:12, 15; 49:1; 54:6; Hosea 11:1. In Deuteronomy 4:37, God's choice is solely dependent on his own love of Israel.

'Called' is preferred to the alternative translation of 'chosen', not only because of its long association with biblical precedent

---

[150] . Cranfield, *Romans*, 1:69 (emphasis added); see also C. E. B. Cranfield, *The Epistle to the Romans*, The International Critical Commentary (Edinburgh: T. and T. Clark, 1979), 2:581–582 regarding its irrevocability.

[151] . Cranfield, *Romans*, 1:51.

and reformed theology[152] but also because that is the primary meaning of *klētoi*.[153] This term may be a hint to Jude's readers that the Intruders are not called. One verse in which the two concepts of 'called' and 'chosen' are compared is Matthew 22:14. However, in that verse, κλητοὶ is used for 'called', and ἐκλεκτοὶ (*eklektoi*) is used for 'chosen'. Interestingly, it is the only instance where the NIV translates κλητός as 'invited' and not 'called' (out of nine instances, including *Jude*). The NASB uses 'called'.

beloved in God the Father

ἐν Θεῷ πατρὶ ἠγαπημένοις

Some Bibles[154] have translated the phrase ἐν Θεῷ πατρὶ (*en Theō patri*) as 'by God the Father'. A more literal translation is 'in God the Father',[155] which suggests a closer relationship (see John 17:21; 1 John 2:24). 'In Christ' is one of Paul's frequently used descriptions of the believer's relationship with God. Paul claims that he and all believers are 'in Christ'.[156] It is assumed that Jude was familiar with Paul's terminology *and vice versa*, perhaps even from discussions with the apostle himself. Therefore, it would not be surprising to find Jude using something like Pauline terminology here to refer to the relationship between the believer and the Father, instead of Christ. This is a relationship that Jesus himself used to describe his and his followers' relationship with the Father and with him

---

[152]. See R. W. A. Letham, 'Calling' in *New Dictionary of Theology*, eds S. B. Ferguson and D. F. Wright (Leicester, UK: Inter-Varsity Press, 1988), 119–120.

[153]. J . R. Kohlenberger III, E. W. Goodrick and J. A. Swanson, *The Greek English Concordance to the New Testament with the New International Version* (Grand Rapids, MI: Zondervan Publishing House, 1997), 431.

[154]. NIV, MSG, Bible in Basic English, NKJV, KJV.

[155]. NASB, ESV, NRSV.

[156]. Rom. 8:1; 16:3, 7, 9; 1 Cor. 1:2, 30; 3:1; 4:10, 15, 17; 15:18, 22, 31; 16:24; 2 Cor. 1:21; 2:17; 5:17; 12:2; Gal. 1:22; 2:4; 3:27, 28; Eph. 1:1, 3, 12; 2:6, 10, 13; Phil. 1:1; 4:21; Col. 1:2, 28; 1 Thess. 1:1; 2:14; 4:16; 2 Tim. 1:9; 3:12; Phlm. 23. Note the opposite ('Christ in…') in 2 Cor. 11:10; 13:5; Eph. 1:10; Col. 1:27. See J. S. Stewart, *A Man in Christ* (London: Hodder and Stoughton, 1935) for an excellent discussion of this phrase.

(John 17:21–23).[157] While it is true that Jude's readers are loved *by* the Father (as in some translations), there is a far deeper significance in their being loved *in* the Father—the relationship that Jesus desired. 'The preposition ἐν (*en*) is constantly used to express the relation in which believers stand to Christ: they are incorporated in Him as the branches in the vine, as the living stones in the spiritual temple, as the members in the body of which He is the head.'[158] So it is with the believer and the Father. 'In' seems a more suitable translation for *en*.[159] (See also comments on v. 21.)

For a Jew like Jude, being in the love of God could come as a natural name for his readers because it was a readily accepted description of Israel (Deut. 10:15; Hos. 11:1). This may indicate an early realisation by the Jesus movement that it was destined to be the real Israel (Isa. 41–49; Rom. 9:6) and fulfil in spiritual terms the earlier national and political destinies of OT Israel.[160]

The phrase *en Theō patri* only occurs two other times in the NT. When writing the first of his letters to the believers in Thessalonica, Paul greets them as being both 'in God the Father *and* the Lord Jesus Christ' (1 Thess. 1:1). But in his second letter to them, Paul greets them as being 'in God *our* Father and the Lord Jesus Christ' (2 Thess. 1:1).

The readers are 'beloved' (ἀγαπάω—*agapaō*) in God the Father, reflecting the participle's derivation from ἀγάπη (*agapē*), the word widely used by the early members of the Jesus movement to denote that self-effacing love that puts others first. But it was not a specifically Christian description, as many tend to regard it.[161] This word is a present perfect participle, as is the

---

[157] . See also John 17:21; 1 John 2:24; 3:24; 4:13, 15, 16.

[158] . Mayor, *Jude*, 17.

[159] . But see Schreiner, *Jude*, 430; G. L. Green, *Jude and 2 Peter*, 47, for compelling interpretations where *en* is translated 'by'.

[160] . See W. Dumbrell, *Covenant and Creation: An Old Testament Covenantal Theology* (Homebush West, NSW: Lancer Books, 1984), ch. 5.

[161] . Mark 12:30–31; 1 Cor. 13:1–13. Nobbs points out that 'the adjective ἀγαπητός is used from the very beginnings of Greek literature'. A. Nobbs, "'Beloved Brothers" in the New Testament and Early Christian World,' in *The New Testament in its First Century Setting: Essays on Context and*

participle in the following phrase. The perfect tense is used to indicate that both participles are 'envisaging the lasting result of past action',[162] but it can also describe the present, as in 1 Corinthians 1:2. God has loved them from the outset and will always do so. This theme is developed more fully in the comments on verse 3.

and kept for Jesus Christ καὶ

Ἰησοῦ Χριστῷ τετηρημένοις

The perfect participle τετηρημένοις (*tetērēmenois*) means 'kept'. (For the context of 'kept', see John 15:10; 17:11; 1 Thess. 5:23; 1 Pet. 1:4.) Sometimes 'kept' is used in the context of guarding or protecting someone (vv. 21, 24; Matt. 27:36), obeying an instruction (v. 6; John 17:6–15) or being kept in custody (vv. 6, 13). 'Kept' is a key word in this letter, given that it is used six times (vv. 1, 6 [twice], 13, 21, 24).[163] Here, the sense is that the readers are being preserved for the day of Christ's return.[164]

An important aspect of 'the faith' of the early Jesus movement was certainty about the return of Jesus from heaven. Its timing was obviously unknown (John 14:28–29), but texts like 1 Thessalonians 5:23 and 1 Peter 1:5 give the impression that Jesus' return was expected to occur well before the now two thousand years since his ascension. *Jude* 24 also reflects that expectation. The sense in that verse of being kept safe for Christ's return will give Jude's readers proportionally more reassurance as their expectations come closer to the present time.

Background in Honour of B. W. Winter on His 65th Birthday, ed. P. J. Williams (Grand Rapids, MI: Wm. B. Eerdmans Publishing Company, 2004), 143. This adjective was also used in the LXX: Gen. 22:2, 12; Amos 8:10; Zech. 12:10.

[162] . M. Zerwick and M. Grosvenor, *A Grammatical Analysis of the Greek New Testament* (Rome: Biblical Institute Press, 1979), 2:738.

[163] . The Greek in v. 24 uses a different word, but it has a slightly stronger meaning.

[164] . See Kelly, *Epistles of Peter and of Jude*, 243; Schreiner, *Jude*, 430–431.

Translators vary in their understanding of Ἰησοῦ Χριστῷ (*Iēsou Christou*) in this phrase. The variants are *for*,[165] *by*,[166] or *in*[167] Jesus Christ. Each alternative has its own truth and relevance. There is no doubt that believers are kept safe *by* their Saviour (John 10:28). It could also be said that believers are kept safe *in* Jesus Christ, using the Pauline phrase discussed above. However, earlier in the verse, Jude has discussed being *in* the Father, which makes the translation 'in Jesus Christ' somewhat redundant. Jude's readers are called by God to live for Him and to inherit the kingdom. Therefore, *for* is preferred because of its forward-looking implications and the eschatological illusions in the letter (v. 21).[168] These believers are kept safe until Christ's return.

Verse 2 in Detail

may mercy and peace and love be multiplied to you

ἔλεος ὑμῖν καὶ εἰρήνη καὶ ἀγάπη πληθυνθείη ἔλεος

This phrase is more a blessing on the readers than a greeting to them. It follows closer to a Jewish form of greeting than do other NT letters. Jude is fond of triplets. The previous verse had 'called', 'loved' and 'kept'. Here, there is 'mercy', 'peace' and 'love'. Other examples will be seen in due course. Mercy (ἔλεος—*eleos*), peace (εἰρήνη—*eirēnē*) and love (ἀγάπη—*agapē*) are the three great gifts of grace. 'They are not self-acquired Christian virtues, but the gifts of God, which, the author prays, may be abundantly bestowed upon his readers. Nevertheless, by a divine alchemy, the gifts of God are transformed into human characteristics.'[169] Jude's ordering of the divine blessings has its own logic and significance. He does

---

[165] . NET, NASB, ESV, BBE, NRSV.

[166] . NIV, MSG.

[167] . NKJV, KJV.

[168] . See Davids, *2 Peter, Jude*, 39; Davids, Handbook, 2; G. L. Lawlor, *Translation and exposition of the Epistle of Jude* (Nutley, NJ: Presbyterian and Reformed Publishing, 1972), 25–28.

[169] . Wand, *St Peter and St Jude*, 196.

not mention the source of the blessings, but they obviously flow from God, because of verse 1.

God is rich in *mercy* (Eph. 2:4). Without God's mercy, it would be impossible for humanity to survive his wrath. The first mention of mercy (Hebrew: *hesed*) in the Bible is God's mercy, which occurs in Genesis 19:19, with the story of Lot and his family being saved from the destruction of Sodom. Mercy is not a human construct. Mercy is a divine prerogative and, by grace, God has imbued it in the human conscience. It is appropriate that God is the first-mentioned giver of mercy in the story of redemption. It is from his mercy towards helpless sinners that God set in plan the redemption of humanity through Christ before the foundation of the world (Eph. 1:4).[170] Mercy is closely linked to rescue (Gen. 19:19) and salvation. When Mary learns of her pregnancy, she exclaims that 'He [God] has given *help* to Israel his servant, in remembrance of his *mercy*' (Luke 1:54, emphasis added). When John the Baptist is born, his father, Zecharias, pronounces that his son will be a prophet who will give Israel 'the *knowledge of salvation* by the forgiveness of their sins, *because of the tender mercy of our God*' (Luke 1:77–78, emphasis added).

Jude would have been quite familiar with *hesed* from his reading of the OT Scriptures in Hebrew. It is a concept of deep significance in Judaism, for it is probably the closest OT term for the NT term 'grace' (Χάρις—*charis*).[171] *Hesed* is closely associated with the Abrahamic covenant (Gen. 12)[172] and Dumbrell notes importantly that *hesed* 'does not arise from a sense of obligation, i.e. merely from a legally binding commitment, but from a sense of personal loyalty which the

---

[170] . See L. Berkhof, *Systematic Theology* (Edinburgh: Banner of Truth, 1976), 72.

[171] . The parallel meaning of hesed and charis is not universally accepted by commentators.

[172] . See Dumbrell, *Covenant and Creation* for a comprehensive analysis of the continuity of God's covenant with humanity (and the created order) from creation to eternity. See also F. I. Andersen, 'Yahweh, the Kind and Sensitive God,' in *God Who Is Rich in Mercy: Essays Presented to Dr D. B. Knox*, eds P. T. O'Brien and D. G. Peterson (Homebush West, NSW: Lancer Books, 1986), 41–44.

relationship involves. The point has been made that the word *hesed* is not applicable to the establishment of a relationship, but *reflects rather fidelity and loyalty to an existing relationship*. The aim of the hesed exhibited is to preserve the tenor of the relationship which already exists.'[173]

Jude begins his greeting with 'mercy', because that is the foundation on which the readers' relationship with God is based: the divine initiative to extend mercy and blessing to Abraham, even before he recognised its existence.

From mercy emanates *peace*. This can be peace in a general sense, but it is much more likely to be the peace of God the Father and the Lord Jesus Christ (Phil. 1:2; 1 Thess. 1:1; 1 Tim. 1:2). The primary Jewish greeting is *shalom* (peace) and it seems obvious that Jude would wish this for these particular readers. Note that all these references are greetings at the start of a letter. For Jews like Jude, this automatically recalls the concept of peace (favour, safety, welfare) conveyed by *shalom* (Gen. 15:15). Having accepted God's gift of mercy through the atoning sacrifice (propitiation) of Christ, Jude's readers can then enjoy peace with God. The divine/human relationship has been restored through Christ. This also means that the individual's peace with God can then flow outwards to fellow believers and others. In this way, the peace of God is multiplied towards these believers as the church grows.

From mercy and peace flow *love*. Initially, this is the love of God himself seen most directly in Jesus Christ (John 17:23, 25; Gal. 2:20). Jude wants that love to be multiplied to his readers. Only those called by God's mercy and enjoying peace with him can then display God's love to others (Eph. 5:2) and especially fellow believers (Gal. 6:10; Rom. 12:10; Heb. 13:1). This is the only NT letter in which love is used in a greeting. Cranfield observes that '"Love" is not used anywhere else in the New Testament in the opening greeting of a letter, though 'grace', which is very close to it in meaning, often is.'[174] Perhaps Jude is

---

[173] . Dumbrell, *Covenant and Creation*, 106 (emphasis added); see also 19, 194.

[174] . Cranfield, *Jude*, 153.

simply reaffirming his statement in verse 1, as pointed out by Kelly:

> According to some, the prayer draws out ideas latent in
> 1, **mercy** being the effective action of God's call, **peace**
> the serenity of soul which springs from the assurance of
> being **kept safe**, and love the charity appropriate to
> people who are themselves **beloved**. But since **mercy** is
> clearly God's objective gift, it seems arbitrary to give
> the other two terms a subjective interpretation; all three
> surely denote coordinate aspects of God's grace.[175]

As noted earlier, it was a normal custom for the members of the early Jesus movement to include a greeting at the commencement of their letters, usually in terms of bestowing some spiritual blessing upon their readers. In this case, Jude wishes mercy, peace and love on his readers. This must have become an accepted Christian greeting because a virtually exact repetition of it occurs a century later in the *Martyrdom of Polycarp*,[176] which has no similarity in subject matter with *Jude* at all. Polycarp was the bishop of Smyrna (modern Turkey) in the second century and it seems likely that *Jude* had been transmitted this far from its place of origin. Verses 1 and 2 enable Jude to tell his readers that he and they are on the same side against opponents who are shortly to be revealed.

Paul usually greeted his readers with 'grace and peace'[177] in that order, but he included 'mercy' in his letters to Timothy (1 Tim. 1:2; 2 Tim. 1:2), using the order of grace, mercy and peace. This order is also used by John in his second letter (2 John 3). As noted above, peace is the natural consequence of God's grace and mercy.[178] Jude's use of mercy to address a primarily Jewish audience closely matches Paul's use of grace to the primarily

---

[175] . Kelly, *Epistles of Peter and of Jude*, 244 (original emphasis).

[176] . See Davids, *2 Peter, Jude*, 40.

[177] . Rom. 1:6; 1 Cor. 1:3; 2 Cor. 1:2; Gal. 1:3; Eph. 1:2; Phil. 1:2; Col. 1:2; 1 Thess. 1:1; 2 Thess. 1:2; Tit 1:4; Phlm. 3. Similarly, 1 Pet. 1:2; 2 Pet. 1:2.

[178] . See I. H. Marshall, *The Epistles of John*, The New International Commentary on the New Testament (Grand Rapids, MI: Wm. B. Eerdmans Publishing Company, 1981), 63 n. 24.

Gentile readers of his letters. In verse 21, Jude reintroduces the linking of *eleos* and *agapē*.

From a spiritual perspective, it is more appropriate to translate πληθυνθείη (*plēthunthein*) as 'multiplied' rather than 'increased'.

The word's general usage in the NT is to describe considerable expansion (Acts 6:7; 7:17) or abundance (1 Pet. 1:2).[179] Jude wishes God's gifts to be showered down upon his readers. The tense of the verb is the aorist optative passive, where the use of the optative denotes a wish.[180] Hence, the translation: 'may (these things) be multiplied to you.'

As Schreiner comments:

> It is also notable that the source of mercy, peace and love is not specified, though God is surely in view (cf. also 1 Pet. 1:2; 2 Pet. 1:2). This is no indication of a low Christology in Jude, for he had already noted in v. 1 that he was a slave of Jesus Christ. We saw in the Old Testament that Moses, David and others were servants of Yahweh. Furthermore, v. 1 constructs a parallel between the love of God and being kept by Jesus Christ, suggesting that Jesus Christ deserves the same honour as the Father. *Jude did not present an explicit doctrine of the Trinity, and yet he provided the data from which such a doctrine was constructed. Interestingly, a Trinitarian formula is found in vv. 20–21.*[181]

Having identified himself, Jude identifies his readers as those who are secure in God's safekeeping, both in the present and until that time when Christ returns. This will provide them with the certainty they need to oppose the incorrect behaviour (and implied doctrinal errors) of the Intruders and the confidence that God's hand is on the matter.

---

179. See also Daniel 4:1; 6:25 (LXX); 2 Pet. 1:2.
180. Zerwick and Grosvenor, *Grammatical Analysis*, 2:738.
181. Schreiner, *Jude*, 432. Emphasis added considering the discussion in 'Theology of *Jude*' in the Introduction.

The Urgency of the Letter, and Jude's Thematic Statement

Verse 3 Beloved, I was eagerly making every effort to write to you concerning our common salvation (but) I felt compelled to write to you imploring that you contend earnestly for the faith once for all time entrusted to the saints.

Verse 3 in Detail

Beloved

Ἀγαπητοί

This term introduces a new section, as it does in verses 17, 20. It has a linguistic connection with ἠγαπημένοις (*ēgapēmenois*) in verse 1 and ἀγάπη (*agapē*) in verse 21. The word Ἀγαπητοί (*Agapētoi*) 'is most frequently used in the NT with reference to the love of Christians for their fellow Christians'.[182] There is a seriously disturbing tendency in the twenty-first century church (carried on from the second half of the twentieth century) to water down the strong language of the Bible to a weak and wimpy version that lacks the force and intention of the Greek terms used by the writers of the NT. Jude's greeting to these believers is 'Beloved!' It now suffers the same fate in the NIV as it does in the Australian version of the Anglican Book of Common Prayer. Compare these two greetings: 'Dearly beloved brethren'[183] and 'Dear friends'.[184] The first (in *Jude*) is a Christian greeting full of meaning to the hearers: brothers and sisters in Christ who are dearly loved by God (and Jude). The

---

[182]. Cranfield, *Romans*, 1:69.

[183]. The Order for Morning Prayer, in *The Book of Common Prayer*; NASB, NKJV, NRSV, KJV.

[184]. Morning and Evening Prayer, in *A Prayer Book for Australia, The Anglican Church of Australia* (Mulgrave, Victoria: Broughton Books, 1999), 4. Initially, in *2 Peter, Jude*, 41, Davids translates Ἀγαπητοί as 'dear friends', but, in his (later) Handbook, 3, he translates the word as 'loved ones', which more closely reflects its Christian context. Schreiner, *Jude*, 433, regards 'dear friends' as 'a remarkably weak translation'.

second greeting would not be out of place at a meeting of the Country Women's Association or any social gathering.

Jude's deeply meaningful and heartfelt 'beloved' has been reduced to a greeting that has no Christian context whatever and is as much at home in the secular world as it is in church on Sunday. These weak forms of Christian greeting reflect an attempt (probably well meant) to make Christianity more acceptable to a broader audience and to remove from its liturgy terms that outsiders might find 'threatening'—although it is difficult to see how calling people 'beloved' would put them ill at ease. We are who we are. Let us not be ashamed of it (Rom. 1:16) or weaken the theology of our status before God. Let Christians then greet one another in a manner and form befitting the One who caused them to be loved in the first place.

Jude and Paul use 'beloved' in different ways. Whereas Paul uses the term to conclude an argument, Jude uses it to introduce a new section of the letter.

I was eagerly making every effort to write to you

πᾶσαν σπουδὴν ποιούμενος γράφειν ὑμῖν

It appears that Jude intended to write a letter to some believers about 'our common salvation', but something intervened. Instead, he wrote what is now before us. Was the other letter ever written? We do not know. Jude stresses the strength of his desire to write to his readers by using πᾶσαν (*pasan*—all), which has a sense of completeness (Matt. 3:15, 4:23; John 5:22). The verb σπουδή (*spoudē*) means 'earnestness' or 'diligence'. The tense 'here, as often, denotes an action in progress when something intervened'.[185] Jude was in the process of writing one letter when he was distracted by this more pressing matter. Richard offers the obviously false (and uncomplimentary) opinion that Jude was just making this up as an excuse for 'a self-serving defence made by the author to blunt the negative polemic character of the letter that is being composed.'[186]

---

[185] . Zerwick and Grosvenor, *Grammatical Analysis*, 2:738.

[186] . E. J. Richard, *Reading 1 Peter, Jude and 2 Peter* (Macon, GA: Smyth and

If Jude initially intended to write in such inclusive terms about beliefs that he and his readers shared, it seems most likely that he would have composed a letter of encouragement. On that basis and, given his affection towards these beloved in the Father, it justifies the inclusion of 'eagerness' to his desire to write the first letter. This raises the unanswerable question of how much correspondence occurred between the early congregations of the Jesus movement and how much we have lost over two millennia.

concerning our common salvation

περὶ τῆς κοινῆς ἡμῶν σωτηρίας

The NT was written in κοινῇ (*koinē*—common) Greek because that was the language spoken by everyone who lived in the eastern Mediterranean world controlled by the Romans. Here, the same word is used to describe κοινῆς ἡμῶν σωτηρίας (*koinēs hēmōn sōtērias*—'our common salvation'); the salvation possessed by all those who have put their faith in Jesus. Jude and his readers share that salvation derived from faith in the atoning sacrifice of Christ and his resurrection (Rom. 10:9). For Jude to write in such inclusive terms, he must have had some knowledge of his readers as stable believers with faith the same as his own. If this were not the case, he would not have made the request in the second half of this verse. This use of 'salvation' is not a reference to Christ's death on the cross, but to the mutual comfort enjoyed by the writer and his readers in being part of the salvation community. This differentiates them from the Intruders who face condemnation and punishment, not salvation.

G. L. Green makes a strong case for translating *sōtērias* here as 'security':

> In the wider sphere of Greek usage, 'salvation' could mean simply 'bodily health', 'well-being', or 'safety' (cf. Acts 27:34; Phil. 1:19; Heb. 11:7; MM 622), but within biblical literature the word repeatedly points to God's great redemptive acts or deliverances that he effects on behalf of his people, all the way from the Exodus from Egypt (Exod. 14:13; 15:2; Acts 7:25) to

Helwys, 2000), 251.

the messianic salvation through Jesus Christ, both as a present reality (Luke 1:69, 77; 19:9; Acts 4:12; Rom. 10:10) and a future hope (Rom. 13:11; 1 Thess. 5:9; 1 Pet. 1:5). It is God's victory over his enemies.

But as tempting as it is to read Jude's summary of his intended correspondence completely within this frame, the description of the letter's contents as 'our common salvation' or 'our common security' (τῆς κοινῆς ἡμῶν σωτηρίας) adopts another well-known concept from their wider world. Amidst the struggles against national enemies, concerns for the 'common safety' or 'security' of a people were paramount (similar to the contemporary idea of a 'national security'). Those worthy of leadership sought to secure it, and the human cost to obtain it could be high.[187]

The description of *our common salvation* 'brings out the corporate nature of salvation as understood by Judaism, with its consciousness of being the people of God, and even more vividly by Christianity, with its conviction of fellowship in Christ.'[188]

(but) I felt compelled to write to you imploring that you contend earnestly

ἀνάγκην ἔσχον γράψαι ὑμῖν παρακαλῶν ἐπαγωνίζεσθαι

The matter that has come to Jude's attention is so serious that he is not letting this opportunity pass. His use of ἔσχον (*eschon*—I had) reflects that he is taking charge of the matter.[189] His need to do so verges on distress, as reflected in ἀνάγκη (*anagkē*— distress/ crisis), but in this context, it has the force of

---

[187] . G. L. Green, *Jude and 2 Peter*, 54. In this context, the extent of Christ's commitment to give his people security (salvation) is amazing.

[188] . Kelly, *Epistles of Peter and of Jude*, 246.

[189] . See Matthew 7:29 for the use of the same verb where Jesus had authority that no one else possessed.

compulsion: 'I felt compelled to write to you.'[190] In Luke 21:23 and 1 Corinthians 7:26, this word is used for the distress accompanying tribulation and the persecution of Christians, respectively. Jude is deeply moved by what he has heard. His proposed earlier letter needs to be abandoned because he considers it necessary to implore (παρακαλέω—*parakaleō*) his readers to act (cf. Mark 1:40). 'This is one of the principal verbs that NT authors employ in moral instruction (Rom. 12:1; 1 Cor. 1:10; Eph. 4:1; Phil. 4:2; 1 Thess. 3:2; 4:1; 5:11; 2 Thess. 3:12; 1 Pet. 2:11; 5:1), and its presence signals Jude's hortatory aim.'[10]

He wants them to 'contend earnestly'. Jude uses ἐπαγωνίζεσθαι (*epagōnizesthai*), an emphatic form of the verb ἀγωνίζομαι (*agōnizomai*), from which is derived the English word 'agony'. This is its only occurrence in the NT; however, milder forms of the verb are found in 1 Corinthians 9:25, Colossians 1:29; 4:12, 1 Timothy 4:10; 6:12; and 2 Timothy 4:7:

> To 'contend earnestly for' (*epagonizesthai*) is an expressive compound infinitive which appears only here in the New Testament. The simple form of the verb (*agonizomai*), which appears as 'agonise' in its English form, was commonly used in connection with the Greek stadium to denote a strenuous struggle to overcome an opponent, as in a wrestling match. It was also used more generally of any conflict, contest, debate, or lawsuit. Involved is the thought of the expenditure of all one's energy in order to prevail.[11]

Bigg comments that 'it is as strong a word as could be found'.[12] It appears that the situation advised to Jude is quite alarming, requiring him to plead to his readers to take the matter seriously and do everything within their power to turn the situation around. 'The present tense of the infinitive, ἐπαγωνίζεσθαι, denotes that the contending has no end. It goes on and on, during our whole

---

[190]. Mayor, *The Epistle of St Jude*, 22: 'The aorist γράψαι, contrasted with the preceding present γράφειν, implies that the new epistle had to be written at once and could not be prepared for at leisure, like the one he had previously

contemplated. It was no welcome task: 'necessity was laid upon him.' The
watchman was bound to give warning, however much the people might
resent it (Ezek. 3:17–19; 33:6–9).'

10. G. L. Green, *Jude and 2 Peter*, 55.
11. Hiebert, *Second Peter and Jude*, 142–66, esp. 144. See also Pfitzner, *Paul
and the Agon Motif*.
12. Bigg, *Jude*, 325.

lifetime.'[191] They will have a real struggle on their hands. Mayor
provides a thoughtful analysis of how Christians should contend
for the faith, depending upon the circumstances in which they
find themselves. He gives persuasive arguments, using the
examples of Jesus and Paul to support both carrot and stick
methodologies in different situations.[192]

The task that Jude sets before his readers is neither unusual
nor historic. From the first century onwards, it has been the *duty*
of every Christian to contend earnestly *for* 'the faith'. Jude's plea
resonates with Paul's and other NT writers' ongoing
exhortations for believers to stand up for what they believe as
the truth of the gospel (Rom. 15:30; Eph. 6:18; Phil. 1:27; 1 Tim.
6:11; Heb. 10:32–34; 1 Pet. 5:9). Philippians 1:27–30 contains
the same sentiments as this verse, where Paul contrasts the
salvation of the faithful and the destruction of opponents. Jude
will repeat these exhortations in verses 20–23, where he urges
his readers to build themselves up in their faith, keep themselves
in the love of God, and attempt to save those who are falling
away from the faith. The purpose of *Jude* is to spur the readers
to action.

We 'contend earnestly for the faith' best by remaining
faithful to it personally, and by demonstrating an example of
faithfulness to others. This is Jude's method. He did not have in
mind apologetics and Christian evidences, though there is a place
for those endeavours. Second, what is the 'contending' that
defends the faith? It is essentially volitional submission to God's
authority. It is also behaviour that is morally in harmony with His

[191] . Lawlor, *Epistle of Jude*, 43.
[192] . The arguments in Mayor, *The Epistle of St Jude*, 70–71 should be considered
in full.

will. It is also conviction that is intellectually consistent with His revelation. This is the calling of each Christian.[193]**for the faith once for all time entrusted to the saints τῇ ἅπαξ παραδοθείσῃ τοῖς ἁγίοις πίστει**

The readers of Jude's letter must contend earnestly in a struggle to maintain the fundamental beliefs of the early Jesus movement. Faith (πίστις—*pistis*) has a few different meanings in the NT. It often refers to belief and trust in Christ for salvation (Luke 7:50; Rom. 4:5; 1 Thess. 1:8). In this verse, it refers to a body of doctrine that had already been taught by Jesus' apostles and Paul (2 John 7–11). These were accepted as the basic tenets of belief of the early Jesus movement—*the* faith—even though no 'official' codification had occurred. Jude was confident that his readers knew and understood 'the faith' because he depended upon them to defend it. These Christians had a common salvation because they had a common faith.

There is much debate as to the meaning and content of his simple term 'the faith'. Two types of faith should be considered here. The first is *fides quae creditur,* which is an objective, established body of doctrine or belief that can be documented and assented to.[194] The second is *fides qua creditur,* which is a believer's own acknowledgement of faith in God. To which does Jude refer? It is the first in this instance. In the NT, Paul uses several terms when discussing what Christians should believe, particularly in circumstances where they are subject to challenge or where contrary beliefs are asserted.

These beliefs were delivered from God the Father through the Holy Spirit (John 15:26–27), just as the Mosaic law had its divine origin at Mount Sinai (Exod. 34:27). These beliefs were entrusted to the apostles in the first century for all time. The verb παραδίδωμι (*paradidōmi*), meaning 'deliver or hand on to', is an aorist passive participle, which gives an air of finality. In this context, the verb gives the sense of handing something over by

---

[193] . Constable, *Notes on Jude*, 5. See F. F. Bruce, *The Defence of the Gospel in the New Testament* (Grand Rapids, MI: Wm. B. Eerdmans Publishing Company, 1959), 80.

[194] . Examples are the Apostles' Creed and the Nicene Creed.

passing on a tradition. A better translation is 'entrust'. 'The faith' is therefore entrusted from one generation to another *without alteration.* Jude's use of ἅπαξ (*hapax*—once for all) should be understood in the light of Hebrews 9:26–28 and 1 Peter 3:18. The meaning here is 'something done uniquely only once, once for all'.[195] It is not just that God has provided insight into his purposes on one occasion and this might change over time. On the contrary, these basic tenets of the faith were intended to stand forever. It is this firm foundation that Jude encouraged his readers to defend (Matt. 16:18). The later-dated books of the NT stress this need to adhere to tradition more strongly than earlier ones.

The extent to which 'the faith' (the gospel) might be subject to alteration is well explained by Marshall. His comments are particularly relevant to *Jude:*

> Two points, however, must be noted. On the one hand, the writer is not saying anything handed down from the past is true and reliable simply because of its antiquity. He regards the teaching given at the beginning as issuing from the Lord through the apostles and hence bearing the stamp of divine revelation; it is 'the word of Christ' which is to 'dwell in you richly' (Col. 3:16). On the other hand, while the writer is clearly opposed to new fashions and innovations in doctrine which are false, he would no doubt allow that what has been handed down as 'truth unchanged, unchanging' may need to be re-expressed in fresh ways if it is to make the same impact on modern readers as it made on its first readers. The art of translation is to reproduce by means of the receptor language the same impression on the readers in its original language. What is true of different languages is also true of presenting the gospel to people in different ages and cultures.[18]

There has been a good deal of debate as to the nature and, particularly, the content of this faith that had to be protected. Some commentators regard this 'faith' as a term comparable to the beliefs that Paul espoused when he used the term 'gospel'

---

[195] . T. Friberg, B. Friberg and N. F. Miller, *Analytical Lexicon of the Greek New Testament* (Grand Rapids, MI: Baker Books, 2000), 61. See G. L. Green,

(cf. Phil. 1:27). Others have enlarged its meaning to encompass a set body of doctrine that might have even been reduced to written form. While this latter suggestion is going too far at the time *Jude* was written, it is the case that Paul's letters do contain what we might call doctrinal propositions (e.g., 1 Cor. 15:1–8, 11.)

Jude and 2 Peter, 56–57 concerning the importance in the first century of the handing down of tradition.

18. Marshall, *The Epistles of John*, 160.

Even when Paul wrote his letters, it is difficult to assert that, apart from some fundamental statements, he would have regarded 'the faith' as a rigid statement of belief. Paul refers to the same concept in the same context as *Jude*, using the same word (*pistis*) in Colossians 2:7: 'now being built up in Him and established in your faith, *just as you were instructed*' (my emphasis). It was not until ad 325 that the Nicene Creed was adopted as a definitive statement of Christian belief. Nevertheless, Jude insists that 'the faith' (however defined) is an unchanging truth. With this, Paul would be in complete agreement (1 Cor. 16:13; Gal. 3:23, 25; 6:10; Phil. 1:25; Col. 1:23), as would the author of Hebrews (3:6, 14; 4:14; 10:23). Because there is no indication in *Jude* of formal church structure or organisation, it is reasonable to assume that Jude's 'faith' is more equivalent to Paul's 'gospel' than to the later formulations of a more established church. But this conclusion should not rule out the possibility that Jude's 'faith' contained elements of both *fides qua creditur* and *fides quae creditur,* even if more of the latter: 'only earnest believers contend for what they believe.'[196] This interpretation is consistent with an earlier date for *Jude*.[197]

It needs to be said that Jude's use of 'the faith' does not imply that his letter contains so-called early 'catholicism'; i.e., that either an established (written) body of belief existed or an institutional organisation was being developed. The Jesus

---

[196]. Lenski, *Interpretation*, 610.

[197]. See P. B. Harner, *What Are They Saying About the Catholic Epistles?* (Mahwah, NJ: Paulist Press, 2004), 105.

movement was still in its formative stage when *Jude* was composed and such developments occurred later than the middle of the first century.

The characterisation by many scholars that *Jude* is an early catholic epistle has considerably muddied the waters of understanding its context and meaning. It has also forced a later date than ad 70 for its composition. This 'early catholic' label must now be removed from *Jude*.

This body of truth was entrusted to 'the saints'—perhaps one of the most misunderstood terms in the Christian lexis. To the man in the street, the broad meaning of 'saint' is the connotation of a special, holy person who has done great deeds or shown great compassion. Names like Mother Teresa and Francis of Assisi come readily to most people's minds when they hear the word 'saint'. But this understanding (primarily derived from Roman Catholicism) is completely at odds with its meaning throughout the NT. The saints (ἁγίοι—*hagioi*) in the NT[198] were certainly special people—*but not because of anything that they had done*. In *koinē* Greek, *hagioi* means set apart from ordinary use. It is used of Christians to describe *God's act* in setting them apart from the world for his own use. This setting apart of Christians has nothing to do with any outstanding attributes or actions of those set apart but, rather, reflects God's free grace in election. Therefore, *every Christian is a saint in a biblical context*. Nevertheless, the colloquial meaning of the word ought to spur Christians on to greater and better deeds so that they might demonstrate their right to be (and to be called) 'saints'.

---

[198] . And up to the present day!

The Reason for the Letter

Verse 4 For certain men have crept in unnoticed; ungodly men: those long ago marked out for this condemnation, transforming the grace of our God into licentiousness and denying our only Sovereign and Lord, Jesus
Christ.

Verse 4 in Detail

For certain men have crept in unnoticed
παρεισέδυσαν γάρ τινες ἄνθρωποι

This is the reason for Jude's anxiety in writing immediately. Some men had infiltrated the fellowship(s) of Jude's readers. They were clearly not from within the congregation. Through charm and persuasion (described as boasting and flattery in v. 16), they seduced their audience and gained influence over some believers. This is quite consistent with sophistic techniques (as described in the Introduction). It is possible that their dress supported their boasting about superior spirituality and opinions. They appeared to be believers in Jesus (and, no doubt, regarded themselves as such) and thus were initially welcomed, but they were wolves in sheep's clothing (Matt. 7:15; Acts 20:28–30). Jude does not know who they are, but the need for this letter makes it clear that at least some of his readers were unaware of what was happening in their midst.

Jude's use of the prefix παρ–εισ in παρεισέδυσαν (*pareisedusan*—crept in unnoticed) gives this sense of unawareness. [199] A similar lack of discernment is found in Galatians 2:4 and 2 Peter 2, although different words describe the situation. With the current deviation of many 'evangelical' churches (both congregations and denominations) towards liberal theology, *Jude's* message is particularly relevant to the twenty-first century. Christians eager to maintain 'the faith' for which Jude was contending must be constantly vigilant against

---

[199] . Zerwick and Grosvenor, *Grammatical Analysis*, 2:738.

men and women whose views deviate from the fundamentals of Christian belief (i.e., biblical truth). For this reason, it is sound practice for congregations to repeat confessional statements, such as the Nicene Creed or the Apostles' Creed, regularly. Those who murmur against the need for, let alone the validity of, these statements ought to be noted. Their repetition is not just for the benefit of believers. It informs visitors of what '*we believe*'. But there are far more subtle ways to undermine biblical doctrines, as explained by Francis Schaeffer.[200]

> The word παρεισέδυσαν, which he uses, denotes an indirect and stealthy insinuation, by which the ministers of Satan deceive the unwary; for Satan sows his tares in the night, and while husbandmen are asleep, in order that he may corrupt the seed of God. And at the same time he teaches us that it is an intestine evil; for Satan in this respect also is crafty, as he raises up those who are of the flock to do mischief, in order that they may more easily creep in.[201]

The use of τινες (*tines*—certain) to describe these men is common in the NT and often implies denigration of an opponent. 'The verb "crept in" [παρεισδυω—*pareisduō*]...indicates a secret, stealthy, and subtle insinuation of something evil into a society or a situation.' [202] Jesus himself warned of such infiltration (Matt. 7:15). Jude's use of the adjective τινες may, again, point to the origin of the Intruders as Corinth (cf. 2 Cor. 10:12; Gal. 1:7).

ungodly men
ἀσεβεῖς

The word ἀσέλγεια (*aselgeia*) broadly means 'immorality' but, in the Greek of the first century ad, it had the particular

---

[200] . See Preface.
[201] . J. Calvin, *Commentaries on the Catholic Epistles*, ed. and trans. J. Owen (Edinburgh: Calvin Translation Society), 391. See www.ccel.org. (Accessed 1 June 2021.)
[202] . W. Barclay, *The Letters of John and Jude*, Daily Study Bible Series, 2nd ed. (Edinburgh: Saint Andrew Press, 1960), 211.

connotation of sensual (and especially sexual) immorality. In verse 15 Jude will use it four times to allege 'ungodliness' on the part of these Intruders. This was not a new phenomenon in the early church (Rom. 3:8; 1 Cor. 5:1; Gal. 5:13); indeed, it was one of the more common problems to be overcome (Rom. 6:1–2). This is hardly surprising given the pagan environment from which new Gentile converts emerged. In this regard, we should not only search the NT for its occurrence but also look for its absence by means of praise to believers (e.g., Philippi and Thessalonica). Leaders had to work hard to dispel these practices (Ti. 1:10–14).

The Corinthian church was particularly prone to this type of behaviour (1 Cor. 5:1–6; 6:12–20; 10:21–33), which went well beyond sexual issues to include misbehaviour at the Lord's Supper (cf. *Jude* 12) and the eating of food sacrificed to pagan idols. There was a severe problem with antinomianism (disregard for God's law) in Corinth. We find a repetition of much of it in the behaviour of *Jude's* Intruders. This may be further evidence of a Corinthian connection with the Intruders.

This Greek word occurs seventeen times in the NT, six of which are in Jude's short letter. The word is self-explanatory, emphasising that these people are entirely opposed to God. In the first century ad, this term was used to describe moral outrage against a deity, or unrighteous, sinful behaviour. It is likely that Paul's behaviour in Ephesus (Acts 19:23–41) came within this description, as far as the people of that city were concerned. The use of ἀσεβεῖς (*asebeis*) also has strong links to the LXX, where the Wisdom literature compares ungodly and godly (righteous) people. It was also carried forward to the writings of some of the early church fathers.

For Christians, the concept of godlessness should raise the spectre of *behaviour* that is derived from an irreverent attitude towards God's holiness and his laws. It is a concept that should go together with the expectation of divine condemnation and punishment of the offenders. The crime is not disbelief; it is moral rebellion against a deity. Its use in the NT accompanies descriptions of people far from God and in need of salvation. Although the ungodliness of the Intruders is the rationale for

Jude's letter, it is not the main point, which is described in the previous verse: the need to contend for the faith. The strength of Jude's accusation conveyed in this word opens up the question as to the strength of the opposition displayed by churches (individual congregations as well as denominations) in modern times towards those who seek to deviate Christians from the gospel (the faith) once delivered to the saints. 'An "ungodly" person is one who has within himself refused to submit to God's authority over him. He may be a non-Christian or a Christian. He does not have the appropriate reverence for God. This involves a volitional choice.'[203]

In Australia, tolerance is regarded as one of the great virtues, epitomised by the expression 'No worries; she'll be right, mate.' In other words, do not get too excited; everything will work out OK. Well, as far as Jude is concerned, everything will not be OK! The errors witnessed among Jude's readers must be stopped immediately because of the inherent nature of the Intruders. It is not being 'loving' (a singularly misused term for tolerance among many modern Christians) to tolerate error. Contending for the faith is a battle for truth. Teachers in the classroom would not tolerate children whispering to their fellow students that two plus two really equals five. In the same way, Christians must be equally anxious to oppose those who distort the truth of 'the faith'.

those long ago marked out for this condemnation οἱ πάλαι προγεγραμμένοι εἰς τοῦτο τὸ κρίμα

Jude pauses to describe these interlopers. The preferred translation of πάλαι (*palai*) is 'long ago' in the present context.[204] The next word, προγεγραμμένοι (*progegrammenoi*), means 'written out beforehand'. This is its only occurrence in the NT. It is the word from which we derive the English 'programme'. Just as a programme tells us beforehand what we are about to

---

[203] . Constable, *Notes on Jude*, 3.

[204] . It can have the meaning of 'former times', but Jude is emphasising the historicity of the determination of their fate, as in Matthew 11:21.

witness in a play or musical event, so were these men's fates programmed long ago (written about in ancient Hebrew texts). The use of this word has the sense of the public announcement of their fates. The origin of the ancient denunciation of these ungodly men is unknown, but there may be an allusion to Exodus 32:32 and (or) Isaiah 4:3. Mayor regards *palai* as derived from the passage of 1 Enoch quoted in verses 14, 15 and suggests the reading of 'designated beforehand';[205] 1 Enoch 108:7 is also relevant. The material to follow in the letter will make it clearer why their fate is already sealed. The end point occurs in verses 14 and 15.

Another possibility might be that Jude has the long-term focus of the OT in mind. From the outset of biblical history, God has punished evil and, particularly, licentious behaviour (Genesis 19). From that perspective, it would be readily apparent to Jude that the punishment of the past would not be withheld in the present. He surely does not need extra-Scriptural prophecy to confirm this most basic principle of divine justice. Their fate is certain, just as an event follows its programme. Indeed, there is a special announcement if the programme is not to be followed. In our current technological age, programmes are associated primarily with computing. They are the fundamental tools that make computers do what they do. Again, in this context, the programme sets the computer on a predetermined course that cannot be altered. So it is with divine judgement on the last day.

These men are designated for 'this condemnation' (τοῦτο τὸ κρίμα—*touto to krima*). The use of 'this' is puzzling because judgement has not previously been discussed in *Jude*. But, for the moment, he does not describe the specific judgement to which these men will be subjected; instead, he proceeds to describe the condemnation that comparable characters in the OT suffered. Jude will describe the judgement to be exercised against the Intruders as a future event, with 'this' only emphasising its future certainty. Although not yet indicated, 'this' condemnation will be described in detail in verses 5–19.

---

[205] . Mayor, *The Epistle of St Jude*, 24–26, provides a lengthy explanation of the way in which *palai* can be understood in the context of v. 4.

'Since the Bible is primarily a revelation of redemption, it naturally does not have as much to say about reprobation as it does about election. But what it says is quite sufficient.'[206] Jude is referring to ancient texts that see part of their fulfilment in the future judgement to be exercised against such Intruders. Let the reader (ancient and modern) be warned! **transforming the grace of our God into licentiousness** τὴν τοῦ θεοῦ ἡμῶν χάριτα μετατιθέντες εἰς ἀσέλγειαν

The root (μετατίθημι—*metatithēmi*) of the participle μετατιθέντες (*metatithentes*—transforming) occurs only six times in the NT. The word implies a certain finality to what it describes. On one occasion, it has a negative connotation when Paul admonishes the Galatians (Gal. 1:6) for 'deserting' the grace of God: they had changed from a true doctrine to a false one. In Hebrews 7:12, the writer refers to a positive transformation that has occurred with the Jewish priestly office. It is in this context that 'transforming' is preferred to 'changing'. The Intruders have transformed a good thing (grace) into an evil thing (sensuality). Jude uses an unusual variant for 'grace' (χάριτα—*charita*)—which is also found in Acts 24:27—rather than the more common χάρις (*charis*) that occurs 42 times in the NT. 'The verb is a present tense: these men keep right on with their perversion of grace. There is no cessation.'[207] Jude's use of 'our God' is an attempt to differentiate himself and his readers (and their God) from the Intruders and their errors.

This allegation is a critical insight into the beliefs of the Intruders. Their words are never described, but the thoughts underlying their actions are clear and revealed by Jude. If their theology did indeed emanate from Corinth, they have misapplied Paul's teaching about free grace (Rom. 3:1–8). They considered that, having been justified by grace, there was no longer any obligation on them to pursue good works and serve others in obedience to Christ's commands. They had been freed from such obligations and were now allowed to do as they pleased in sensual and self-indulgent behaviour (e.g., feasting and sex). They reached the wrong conclusion about the nature and

---

[206] . Berkhof, *Systematic Theology*, 118.
[207] . Lawlor, *Translation and Exposition*, 52.

implications of grace: their behaviour overtly demonstrated this lack of understanding (cf. Rom. 3:8).

and denying our only Sovereign and Lord, Jesus Christ καὶ τὸν μόνον δεσπότην καὶ κύριον ἡμῶν Ἰησοῦν Χριστὸν ἀρνούμενοι

The root word for deny is ἀρνεομαι (*arneomai*). It is used throughout the NT for disowning or rejecting someone, including Peter's denial of Jesus (Matt. 26:34, 35, 70, 72, 74). Other references are Matthew 10:33; 1 John 2:22; Titus 1:16; and there is a relevant verse in 1 Enoch 38:2. By perverting grace into sensual behaviour, these men have denied the Lord Jesus. They are not denying Christ's existence but, rather, his lordship over their lives and behaviour.

> All antinomianism is a radical denial of Christ and of God. And antinomianism is by no means merely a thing of the past. It is present wherever zeal for the Christian religion, of worship, theology, and all manner of other Church activities is unaccompanied by moral earnestness, wherever Christians can complacently and without any sense of incongruity combine piety with indifference to their neighbours' need and a comfortable acquiescence in social and political injustice.[208]

It may appear from the Greek τὸν μόνον δεσπότην καὶ κύριον ἡμῶν Ἰησοῦν Χριστὸν that Jude is referring separately to both the Father (Sovereign) in τὸν μόνον δεσπότην (*ton monon despotēn*)—'the only Sovereign'—*and* the Son in καὶ κύριον ἡμῶν Ἰησοῦν Χριστὸν (*kai kurion hēmōn Iēsoun Christon*—'and our Lord Jesus Christ'). However, this is an incorrect understanding of the Greek. According to the Granville Sharp rule,[209] the correct translation is 'and our only Sovereign and Lord, Jesus Christ'. In the paragraph above, the Intruders reversed the grace of 'our God'; now they have denied the One who dispenses this grace to humanity.

---

[208]. Cranfield, *Jude*, 158.
[209]. The terms 'Master' and 'Lord' both refer to the same person. See p. 163.

Three Proofs from the Old Testament and Jewish Tradition

Verse 5   Therefore I resolved to remind you, although you know all about these things, that the Lord, having saved a people from the land of Egypt once for all time, later destroyed those who did not believe.

Verse 6   Moreover, the angels, having not kept their position of authority but having abandoned their own dwelling
place, he keeps (them) in eternal chains under deep darkness for (the) judgment of (the) great day.

Verse 7   Likewise Sodom and Gomorrah, and the towns around them in like manner with them, having indulged in sexual immorality and having gone after strange flesh, are set forth as an example undergoing
the penalty of eternal fire.

Verse 8   Nevertheless in the same way these men, in their dreaming, not only defile flesh but also reject authority
and defame things and persons in whom shines the divine majesty.

Verse 9   But Michael the archangel, when disputing with the Devil, argued about the body of Moses, did not dare to bring a judgment against him for slander, but said,
'The Lord rebuke you.'

Verse 10   But these men speak evil of whatever things they do not understand; whatever things they do understand
naturally—like irrational animals—in these things they corrupt themselves.

The outworking of ungodliness is illustrated by three groups: two from the Old Testament and one from Jewish sacred writings. They are ancient predecessors of the Intruders and Jude intends that we should learn from their behaviour and what happened to them. 'Each of these stories is told, not with direct reference to the OT, but in the form in which it was told in various Jewish circles during the Second Temple period.'[213] Verses 5–7 begin this part of the letter with warnings of judgement, just as similar warnings in verses 14–16 end it.

The Exodus from Egypt

Verse 5 in Detail

Therefore I resolved to remind you

Ὑπομνῆσαι δὲ ὑμᾶς βούλομαι

The Greek in this verse presents some difficulty when translating it into English. There are also disputes about the content of the original text.[214] In this verse, δὲ (*de*) is translated 'therefore'. It is the link between the announcement of 'this condemnation' in verse 4 and the commencement of its description in the fifteen verses that follow. Since condemnation was prophesied long ago (v. 4), it is appropriate that Jude will use examples from long ago to prove his point.

Ὑπομνῆσαι (*hupomnēsai*), which means 'to bring to remembrance', is in the aorist infinitive active tense of the verb. The aorist infinitive does not express a progressive aspect. It presents the action expressed by the verb as a completed unit with a beginning and an end. Similarly, the use of βούλομαι (*boulomai*) for 'I resolved' indicates the strength of Jude's desire to bring the matter to the forefront of his readers' minds. The point for Jude is that something valuable is at stake and he is prepared to go to extreme lengths to make this apparent. Jude's intention is clear. His resolution to write (and its accomplishment in the written document) is firm. Its purpose is to 'remind'. This

---

[213] . Davids, *2 Peter, Jude*, 47.
[214] . See Mayor, *The Epistle of St Jude*, 28–30 for a discussion of these technicalities.

reminder relates to verses 5–16: the prophetic material in the OT and 1 Enoch.

Some translations give the impression that the readers knew these truths once upon a time and, having forgotten them, now need reminding.[215] It is not that the readers have forgotten but that Jude wants to emphasise and reinforce that his subject matter lies at the centre of their life in Christ. This passage is reminiscent of 2 Peter 2. As noted in the Introduction, there are many similarities between *Jude* and 2 Peter. This is one of them. Peter reminded his readers that 'there *will be* false teachers among you (my emphasis)'. In his letter, Jude is writing to warn his readers that these Intruders (not necessarily false teachers) *have already arrived.* This situation is, therefore, much more urgent than the later case in 2 Peter 2:1. In Romans 15:15 and 1 Corinthians 15:1, Paul uses a similar rhetorical style to encourage his readers.

although you know all about these things

εἰδότας ὑμᾶς πάντα

Jude interrupts his train of thought with this aside. He reminds his readers that he knows that they are aware of what he is writing about. This is to encourage their adherence to what they already know of Christian discipleship and their practice of it.

that the Lord, having saved a people from the land of Egypt once for all time

ὅτι [ὁ] κύριος ἅπαξ λαὸν ἐκ γῆς Αἰγύπτου σώσας

There is considerable debate about the placement of ἅπαξ (*hapax*) and I defer to G. L. Green's analysis:

> The second textual issue, not discussed in the commentary, has to do with the position of ἅπαξ (*hapax*). Should it be read with πάντα (ἅπαξ πάντα, *once and for all*), as in A, B, 33, 81, 2344 (Osburn 1981: 108–10; Metzger 1994: 657–58), or does it stand near the

---

[215] . NKJV, KJV, ESV, NASB, RSV, NIV incorrectly link ἅπαξ (*hapax*) (see below)

head of the following ὅτι (*hoti, because*) clause as in 322, 323, 1241, 1739, 1881, 2298 (Wikgren 1976: 147–48)? Whether κύριος (*kyrios*) or Ἰησοῦς (*Iēsous*) is read as original, the MS evidence is diverse regarding the position of ἅπαξ, as is scholarly opinion. With the evidence being less than clear at this point, internal evidence would favour reading it within the ὅτι clause and so setting up the contrast with

---

with this reminder.

the following τὸ δεύτερον (*to deuteron*) later.[216]

This is the first of three examples given by Jude concerning the destruction of those who do not believe the gospel, who defy God's will and engage in immorality.

Notwithstanding the text, God did not save Israel from a land[217] but from an enemy (a people): *people* who wanted to kill the Israelites (Numbers 14). Jude is making the point that, just as some people in the past (the Egyptians) wanted to harm God's people physically, so there are men in the present time who wish to harm God's people spiritually. In one sense, nothing had changed over the course of 1,500 years, from the time of Moses to Jude's day. It was just that the men to whom Jude refers are set on a subtler course of destruction that might not be as easily recognised. The subsequent 2,000 years from Jude's era to the present time only serve to confirm that the one thing that changes is the skill and subtlety with which Satan continues to try to deceive God's people. His destructive intention is relentless and just as ruthless as that of the Egyptians, even more so, now that Jesus' saving power is vindicated by his resurrection.

The usual translation of ὁ Κύριος (*ho Kurios*) is 'the Lord'. However, Hamann discusses the possibility that 'Jesus' is the best translation for this saver of God's people. He notes that this

---

[216] . G. L. Green, *Jude and 2 Peter*, 78. See also Bauckham, *Jude, 2 Peter*, 43, Note a regarding the placement of ἅπαξ.

[217] . Indeed, Israel had prospered greatly in and from the land of Egypt (Exod. 1:7). But see Exodus 20:2 for this terminology.

possibility (i.e., an event before Christ's birth) is 'not completely unparalleled (see 1 Cor. 10:4)'.[218] Jude's reference point is the Hebrew Scriptures, where 'the Lord' in the case of Exodus is plainly stated to be Yahweh; this seems clear, given what follows in the rest of the sentence. Paul's reference to the same matter in 1 Corinthians 10 seems to refer to Yahweh in the OT contexts. However, the issue at hand is not what the OT or Paul says, but what Jude wrote. **Hamann's view finds strong support from Bruce in his commentary on Hebrews 3:7–11.**[219] Therefore, *ho Kurios* in *Jude* should be translated as 'the Lord' but seen as a reference to Christ.

later τὸ δεύτερον

These words are translated 'later', although τὸ δεύτερον (*to deuteron*) literally means 'the second time'. Jude is making a contrast. On one occasion God acted decisively in history to save his people but that did not imply that they were immune from later judgement. Accordingly, God did *later* execute judgement on Israel for their sins of unbelief in the desert (Num. 14:11–12; 26–35; 26:64–65; Psalm 78:21–22; 95:8–11; Heb. 3:18–19).

destroyed those who did not believe τοὺς μὴ πιστεύσαντας ἀπώλεσεν

The verb for believing is derived from πιστεύω (*pisteuō*), a common word in the NT, meaning 'to believe in something or someone'. It does not refer simply to acceptance of a fact like 'I believe that two plus two equals four.' It is closely aligned with faith (trust) in something that will result from our acting on that faith/trust. For example, if someone reads the railway timetable and believes that the train will depart the station at 4:40 p.m., they will be on the platform at 4:35 p.m. to ensure that they catch the train. This is having faith in the timetable because they have

---

[218] . H. P. Hamann, *Chi Rho Commentary on James–Jude* (Adelaide, SA: Lutheran Publishing House, 1980), 92.

[219] . F. F. Bruce, *The Epistle to the Hebrews*, The New International Commentary

put belief (trust) into action. This is the sense of belief described here and throughout the NT. To complete the analogy, when the train arrives at 4:40 p.m., their faith is vindicated. Over time, experience will deepen their faith in the timetable. So it is with Christian faith.

The ongoing experience of God's goodness and faithfulness leads believers to ever-deepening faith. But there must be a starting point—using the timetable for the first time. Those who will be destroyed are those who have read the timetable and completely ignored it. In verse 3 Jude uses the noun πίστις (*pistis*—belief) to

---

on the New Testament (Grand Rapids, MI: Wm. B. Eerdmans Publishing Company, 1964), 63 n. 46; see also 77, 351.

describe the *faith* of his readers. It is belief in action.

The Introduction noted that Jude likes to use strong language against his opponents. This is typified in his used of ἀπώλεσεν (*apōlesen*), meaning 'He destroyed'. Both *apōlesen* and the earlier σώσας (*sōsas*—having saved) are in the aorist indicative tense, indicating the complete finality of these events. The only other occurrences of this particular word in the NT are comments by Jesus in Matthew 22:7 (the parable about those who refused to come to the king's wedding feast for his son—destroyed by an army); Luke 17:27 (the destruction of the flood in Noah's time); Luke 17:29 (the destruction of Sodom). In each case, God levied horrific destruction against those who refused his ways. Jude uses the same verb and tense (aorist indicative active) as in the gospel events to emphasise the utter and complete destruction of these godless men. In the twenty-first century, most people (including many Christians) seem to discount the likelihood, let alone the severity, of the wrath of God against unbelievers who have refused his grace or undermined his church. To them, this God seems unacceptably nasty, dealing out retribution to those who do not really deserve it. *Jude* will have none of this; nor will the remainder of Scripture (Isa. 29:6; 30:27, 30; 34:8–10). God will utterly destroy those who do not—or will not—believe.

Schreiner discusses the implications for the church of Jesus Christ of Jude's summary that those who were saved from Egypt were subsequently destroyed. Does the fact that the eventual destruction of those who were saved from Egypt imply that true believers can succumb to apostasy? His conclusion that 'true believers can lose their salvation is mistaken, even though it appears on first glance to be convincing'[220] is correct.

Evil Angels

Verse 6 in

Detail

moreover the angels having not kept their position of authority ἀγγέλους τε τοὺς μὴ τηρήσαντας τὴν ἑαυτῶν ἀρχὴν

Jude's second example uses angels. The insertion of τε (*te*—moreover) is a means of continuing the sentence beginning in verse 5. These angels rebelled against God and did not remain in the domain 'over which lordship was accorded them'.[221] Their proper 'domain'[222] (ἀρχή—*archē*—position of authority[223]) was that to which they were *first* appointed. The word is used of office and dignity, as in Genesis 40:21 (LXX). Whether the angels' domain is physical or spiritual (or both) is a matter of debate, but irrelevant. Their sin was to move away from God's will for them. The word ἀρχή is used in Ephesians 6:12 to describe demonic 'rulers' that are spiritual forces, quite likely similar to such beings as the evil angels.

Jude's likely reference in the OT is to be found in the Genesis 6:1–4 description of the angels leaving their heavenly realm,

---

220 . Schreiner, *Jude*, 447.

221 . Zerwick and Grosvenor, *Grammatical Analysis*, 2:739.

222 . Most translations use some form of 'dwelling' to translate ἀρχή: 'domain' (NetBible), 'home' (NIV), 'abode' (NASB, NKJV), 'dwelling' (ESV, NRSV), 'habitation' (KJV).

223 . Kohlenberger, *Greek English Concordance*, 90.

coming to earth and having sexual relations with women. This sin fits much more neatly with the example that follows. Jude's main reference point, however, is 1 Enoch, especially regarding the angels' punishment:

v. 4 'Enoch, thou scribe of righteousness, go, declare to the Watchers of the heaven who have left the high heaven, the holy eternal place, and have defiled themselves with women, and have done as the children of earth do, and have taken unto themselves wives: "Ye have wrought great destruction on the earth:

v. 5 And ye shall have no peace nor forgiveness of sin: and inasmuch as they delight themselves in their children,

v. 6 The murder of their beloved ones shall they see, and over the destruction of their children shall they lament, and shall make supplication unto eternity, but mercy and peace shall ye not

attain."

v. 1 And Enoch went and said: "Azazel, thou shalt have no peace: a severe sentence has gone forth against thee

v. 2 to put thee in bonds"'

1 Enoch 12:4–13:2 [224]

The angels' behaviour was both a violation of their proper place in their heavenly 'dwelling' and, also, as Jude describes it in his next example, 'going after strange flesh.' These angels were behaving in a manner that was not only immoral but also contrary to their very nature. Angels do not have sexual relations with humans.

Jude uses the word 'kept' with opposite meanings. In verse 1, the believers are 'kept (safe) for Jesus Christ'; in verse 21, the believers are 'kept in the love of God'; also, God can 'keep them from stumbling'. However, in this verse, the evil angels *have not*

---

[224]. R. H. Charles (ed.), *The Apocrypha and Pseudepigrapha of the Old Testament* (Oxford: Clarendon Press, 1913). See *https://www.ccel.org/c/charles/otpseudepig/enoch/ENOCH_1.HTM.* (Accessed 21 Jun 2021.)

kept their proper position and, so, a place of doom and darkness is 'kept' for them by God.

but having abandoned their own dwelling place
ἀλλὰ ἀπολιπόντας τὸ ἴδιον οἰκητήριον

The sense is not that the angels just left, but that they *chose to leave*. They swapped one position for another. But this also involved leaving (in some metaphysical sense) their own dwelling. The use of an aorist active participle ἀπολιπόντας (*apolipontas*—having abandoned) indicates that the angels deserted their place forever. There was no going back. Jude is claiming that, by first renouncing their God-given status, it was inevitable that they would also have to abandon their actual presence before God. Jude chose an interesting word to describe the angels' place of residence (οἰκητήριον—*oikētērion*). This word's only other NT occurrence is in 2 Corinthians 5:2, where Paul refers to 'our dwelling *in heaven*' (emphasis added)—the same place from which the angels came. Perhaps Jude had heard this term from Paul's letter as it spread throughout the Christian community to describe their final resting place in heaven.

The place that the angels abandoned is described as τὸ ἴδιον (*to idion*), 'their own' dwelling place. These angels not only had a God-given status but also had a God-appointed place to live appropriate to their special nature. The latter cannot be maintained if the former is renounced.

In this and the earlier part of verse 6, Jude seems to be differentiating between the angels' position of authority (ἀρχή) and their dwelling place (οἰκητήριον). The sense seems to be that the angels left their rightful relationship (status) with God and that this inevitably led them to abandon their actual place (dwelling) with God.

he keeps (them) in eternal chains under deep darkness for (the) judgment of (the) great day εἰς κρίσιν μεγάλης ἡμέρας δεσμοῖς ἀϊδίοις ὑπὸ ζόφον τετήρηκεν Here again Jude's reference point is the Book of Enoch:

v. 4 And again the Lord said to Raphael: 'Bind Azâzêl hand and foot, and cast him into the darkness: and make an opening in the desert, which is in Dûdâêl, and cast him therein.

v. 5 'And place upon him rough and jagged rocks, and cover him with darkness, and let him abide there for ever, and cover his face that he may not see light.

v. 6   'And on the day of the great judgment he shall be cast into the fire.'

1 Enoch 10:4–6

[225]There is a positive and negative wordplay in Jude's use of 'keep' (τηρέω—*tēreō*), as discussed earlier. In verse 1, the readers are 'kept safe for Jesus Christ'. However, in this verse, while the angels *did not keep* (cf. verses 1, 13, 21, 24) their first state, God subsequently *does keep* them in chains. While Jude's use of this picture of punishment for the evil angels is probably influenced by 1 Enoch 6–10, it may also be a reference to Isaiah 24:21–22, where the host of heaven and the kings of the earth rebel against God and are consigned to prison.[226] The perfect tense of τετήρηκεν (*tetērēken*) indicates that the angels' imprisonment in chains is an ongoing occurrence. The faithlessness of the angels is contrasted with the steadfast nature of God, who is faithful to his character and his word. Although the text says that these angels are bound forever in deep darkness,[15] it is only for so long as the Day of Judgement is delayed. The word ἀΐδιοις (*aidiois*—eternal) has the same meaning as αἰωνίος (*aiōnios*) in the following verse. It appears only here and in Romans 1:20. They await a crisis. The *Oxford English Reference Dictionary* defines a crisis as 'a decisive moment; a time of great danger or difficulty; the turning point.'[16] It is that time when events come to a head and a decision must be made. That reflects its origin in Greek, where κρίσις (*krisis*) means 'decision'; or, more commonly, 'judgement' in the NT.

The Great Day (μέγας ἡμέρα—*megas hēmera*) will be that time when Christ returns in glory to judge the living and the

---

[225] . Charles, *Apocrypha*.

[226] . See J. N. Oswalt, *The Book of Isaiah*, Chapters 1–39, The New International Commentary on the Old Testament (Grand Rapids, MI: Wm. B. Eerdmans

dead.[17] The Great Day (sometimes abbreviated to just 'the Day') is an expression common to both the OT (Isa. 2:12; 13:6; Joel 2:11, 31; Mal. 4:5) and the NT (Matt. 24:36; John 6:39; Acts 2:20 [quoting Joel]; Phil. 1:6 [the day of Christ]; Rev. 6:17; 16:14). Sometimes 'the Day' is described as 'great' or 'awesome'. But, in every case, it is *the* day when God's final vindication of Jesus, and his vanquishing of sin and Satan, will be demonstrated overwhelmingly.

In the twenty-first century, Christians are no longer consumed by discussions about angels and other heavenly beings but these were matters of considerable interest in Jude's day. The intervening period between the last book of the OT, Malachi (which was written around 400 bc), and the time of Christ was filled with a range of Jewish scriptural interpretations and prophetic utterances. Calvin's comment on whether we need to know about such matters is relevant in the light of 1 Timothy 4:7 and 2 Timothy 2:23:

Publishing Company, 1986), 455.

15. The word ζόφος (*zofos*—deep darkness) is used only five times in the NT: twice in 2 Peter, twice in Jude, and once in Hebrews 12:18. Jude 6 parallels 2 Peter 2:4; Jude 13 parallels 2 Peter 2:17.

16. *The Oxford English Reference Dictionary* (Oxford: Oxford University Press, 1996), 338.

17. Revelation 21, Nicene Creed.

> Some persons grumble that Scripture does not in numerous passages set forth systematically and clearly that fall of the devils, its cause, manner, time, and character. But because this has nothing to do with us, it was better not to say anything, or at least to touch upon it lightly, because it did not befit the Holy Spirit to feed our curiosity with empty histories to no effect.[227]

---

[227]. J. Calvin, *Institutes of the Christian Religion*, ed. J. T. McNeill and trans. F. L.
Battles (Philadelphia: Westminster Press, 1960), 1:14:15.

Sodom and Gomorrah

Verse 7 in Detail

Likewise Sodom and Gomorrah, and the towns around them in like manner with them, having indulged in sexual immorality and having gone after strange flesh, are set forth as an example undergoing the penalty of eternal fire.

ὡς Σόδομα καὶ Γόμορρα καὶ αἱ περὶ αὐτὰς πόλεις τὸν ὅμοιον τρόπον τούτοις ἐκπορνεύσασαι καὶ ἀπελθοῦσαι ὀπίσω σαρκὸς ἑτέρας, πρόκεινται δεῖγμα πυρὸς αἰωνίου δίκην ὑπέχουσαι.

Like ὅτι (*hoti*) in verse 5 and τε (*te*) in verse 6, ὡς (*hōs*—likewise) introduces the third group which fell afoul of God's judgement.

This is the third of Jude's examples. The use of *hōs* also links the fate of the evil angels with the fate of Sodom and Gomorrah. It differs from the first two in that it speaks only of divine judgement and does not mention a falling away from God. The story of Sodom and Gomorrah (Genesis 18–19) is one of the bestknown catastrophes in the Bible. But what is Jude's specific point here? Take note of the linkage provided by τὸν ὅμοιον τούτοις τρόπον (*ton homoion toutois tropon*), meaning 'in like manner with them'. The Greek word for *them* is masculine and, therefore, refers to the fallen angels, not Sodom and Gomorrah (feminine in Greek). The others referred to are the disobedient angels of verse 6. Jude wants to associate both parties with the same type of evil. When reading of Lot's experience in Sodom, it is easy to find evil abounding among its inhabitants but Jude is referring to one particular sin. Note that the offenders included καὶ αἱ περὶ αὐτὰς πόλεις (*kai hai peri autas poleis*—and the towns around them). The generally accepted reason for the cities' fate is that their men indulged in homosexuality and there is no doubt that this would have incurred severe divine anger.

However, given Jude's prior reference to the angels and their desire for 'strange flesh', it appears that Jude is referring to a quite specific sexual sin. The link appears to be an instance of humans wishing to have sexual intercourse with angels, and vice versa; i.e., both are seeking after 'strange flesh'. Although we may know that this is the case, the men of Sodom did not. They thought that these visitors were mere men, so, clearly, their own wish was to have homosexual relations with 'men'. The fact that the visitors happened to be angels only made their crime more egregious.

If it seems that homosexual sin is being downplayed as a reason for the destruction of the cities, nothing could be further from the truth.

> It is only fair to remember that Greece and Rome had no monopoly in homosexuality: it was common also in the Semitic world. To the Jews it was an abomination (see Gen. 19:1–28; Lev. 18:22; 20:13; Deut. 23:17f.; 1 Kings 14:24; 2 Kings 23:7; Isa. 1:9; 3:9; Lam. 4:6; *Wisdom* 14:26; *Test Levi* 17:11; *Or Sib* 2:73; 3:596f; Philo, *Spec Leg* 3:39, etc.), and Paul clearly shared his fellow-countrymen's abhorrence of it. In the NT compare 1 Corinthians 6:9; 1 Timothy 1:10; 2 Peter 2:6f.; Jude 7; and also—for dominical words which must not be overlooked in this connexion—Matthew 10:14f; 11:23f.[228]

There is a need to return to a first-century ad understanding of the account in Genesis 6:1–4. When Jude composed this letter, the standard interpretation of the passage was that the angels referred to in verse 6 were known as the Watchers, a direct link from 1 Enoch 6–19.[229] It is these angels that were sentenced to be bound in chains until the Great Day.

The sin of the Watchers and that of Sodom and Gomorrah was particularly egregious because, through the sexual union of humans and heavenly beings, it violated the natural order. This is not to diminish in any way God's abhorrence of homosexuality (Rom. 1:26–27): note Jude's inclusion of *kai* (and). Jude does not provide sufficient information to allow us

---

[228] . Cranfield, *Romans*, 1:127.

[229] . Bauckham, *Jude, 2 Peter*, 51; 50–53 provides extensive background material about these angels and Jude's linkage of them to Sodom and Gomorrah.

to conclude that the Intruders indulged in homosexuality, although Kelly suggests that it is 'probably legitimate to infer that he is snidely accusing the innovators of homosexual practises'.[230] More important for Jude is that the Intruders' licentiousness contravened God's laws for human behaviour and should be regarded as being as shocking as the ancient examples of sexual sin.

This verse concludes with Jude's assessment that Sodom and Gomorrah serve as an example of those who deserve the penalty of *eternal* fire. Sodom and Gomorrah are used in Scripture to refer to divine punishment, especially in the NT, with reference to the end of time (Isa. 1:9–10; 3:9; Luke 17:28–29; Rom. 9:29; 2 Peter 2:6–10; Rev. 11:8). Throughout the NT, the word αἰώνιος (*aiōnios*—eternal) usually means not only 'everlasting' but also a 'superior quality' (e.g., John 3:16). In this case, the implication is that this punishment is both complete and of a most severe kind. These cities were destroyed by fire and, unlike many other cities around Palestine, never rebuilt. This punishment evokes the same picture as Revelation 20:14–15. In Matthew 18:8; 25:41, eternal fire also stands for divine judgement (see also Isa. 66:14–16).

The words 'gone after' are reminiscent of frequent OT passages where God condemns Israel for having 'gone after' other gods. Jude's condemnation equates Sodom and Gomorrah's evil desires and practices with a rejection of God and with the worship of other deities (Deut. 6:14; Josh. 23:16; Jdg. 2:12; Jer. 2:23).

Jude has provided three examples of those who deserve God's condemnation: those who do not believe; those who rebel against God's will; and those who commit gross immorality. It will be evident that Jude does not present these examples in chronological order. As will be seen in verse 11, Jude's progression is from one level of sin to an even more egregious level. Sodom and Gomorrah depict all the sins of Israel in the desert, all the sins of the evil angels, plus more. Sodom and

---

[230] . Kelly, *Epistles of Peter and of Jude*, 259.

Gomorrah come last not only because of the grossness of their sin but also because they best represent the sins of the Intruders.

As Lawlor comments:

> In a disintegrating civilisation, where lust, greed and hatred are predominant, where love is largely interpreted in terms of physical attraction and sexual allure, it is indeed blessed and assuring to know that in God our Father we are beloved, and that such a state never changes. While the apostate religious leaders of our time talk much of the love of God and the God of love, and engage in lengthy, high-sounding discourses to show how such a God and such a love assures all men everywhere of divine favour and entrance into heaven, the called ones, beloved in God the Father, know this to be completely false, a gigantic religious hoax, a diabolical deception, which actually blinds the minds of men to the reality and wonder of the immeasurable love of God.[231]

These comments were published in 1972. In the subsequent fifty years, unbelief, rebellion against God and his revealed truth, immorality and anarchy in our Western society have flourished. All this, despite the fact that these societies were established on Christian principles. Where Christian values once held sway over the majority (even if they were not believers), they are now accepted by an increasingly less-vocal minority. Swearing that would have been banned on television in 1970 is now heard from schoolchildren on public transport, without any rebuke from adults. Over the same period, sexual behaviour that was generally kept hidden is now flaunted as the new normal. The list goes on into the public sphere, with the degenerating moral and civil standards of many politicians, public figures and 'celebrities'.

---

[231] . Lawlor, *Translation and Exposition*, 24–25.

First Description of the Intruders

Verse 8 in Detail

Nevertheless in the same way, these men, in their dreaming

Ὁμοίως μέντοι καὶ οὗτοι ἐνυπνιαζόμενοι

Jude's use of 'these men' (οὗτοι—*houtoi*) is 'a reiterated literary device, repeated five times in the verses we are using to gain a profile.' [232] As noted in the Introduction, it is as if Jude remembers some ancient wrongdoings and then says, 'See! "these men" (*houtoi*) are just like that!' The four other instances of this reference are verses 10, 12, 16, 19.

Jude confirms that, 'nevertheless' (μέντοι—*mentoi*), the Intruders commit the same types of sins as those of old. 'Nevertheless' is often not translated in English Bibles but this omission limits our understanding of Jude's thoughts on the matter. There is a sense of his frustration that, even though all the past incidents that he has (and will) describe warn against incurring the wrath of a holy God, these people *nevertheless* ignore the lessons of (spiritual) history and persist in their wickedness. Jude also notes that the sin he confronts is of the same nature ('in the same way' [ὁμοίως—*homoiōs*]) as that committed by the three groups described above. This phrase is Jude's link between the past and the present. History is simply repeating itself.

The Intruders are accused of sinning 'in their dreaming'.[233] Hamann describes this as 'deceitful dreams from the father of lies'. [234] The only other occurrence of ἐνυπνιαζόμεναι (*enupniazomenai*) in the NT is Acts 2:17, in Peter's sermon at Pentecost, where he cites Joel 2:28. We might initially suppose that Jude is accusing the Intruders of what we would call 'daydreaming' or imagination: indulging in non-productive, futile thinking. But this interpretation seriously underestimates the danger that Jude has detected. The type of 'dreaming'

---

[232] . Martin, *Theology of Jude*, 71. Bauckham, *Jude, 2 Peter*, 45 provides a detailed comment on the use of this word.

[233] . Zerwick and Grosvenor, *Grammatical Analysis*, 2:739.

[234] . Hamann, *Chi Rho Commentary*, 94.

described by Jude is condemned in Deuteronomy 13:1–5. It comprises leading people away from God by signs or wonders. The Intruders boasted of their spiritual superiority (v. 16) and impressed some by their worldliness (v. 19). The OT remedy for such behaviour was death because the dreamers 'counselled rebellion against the Lord your God who brought you from the land of Egypt and redeemed you from the house of slavery to seduce you from the way in which the Lord your God commanded you to walk. So you shall purge the evil from among you.' (Deut. 13:5; cf. Jude 4, 5, 8, 11, 16, 19.)

This is why Jude's attitude towards the Intruders is so hostile. 'Dreaming' is an important code word in both the OT and the NT for spiritual discernment or revelation.

In Genesis 20:3, God shows mercy via a dream (revelation) to Abimelech, who was deceived by Abraham about the identity of Sarah as his sister, not his wife. [235] From then on, God sometimes used dreams and their interpretation to confirm his will (Gen. 31:10; 37:5–11; 40:8; Daniel 2; Joel 2:28). This type of dreaming extended into the NT (Matt. 1:20; 2:12–23—God's will for Joseph and Mary). On the other hand, dreams could be misused by those who did not acknowledge God to lead his people astray. These were false prophets (Jer. 23:23–40; Zech. 10:2). Dreams could also be used to refer to God's judgement (Isa. 7:8–14; Daniel 4). Visions and trances can also come within the ambit of 'dreams' (Acts 10:3, 10; 16:9; 2 Cor. 12:2). Paul's warning in Colossians 2:18 is particularly pertinent to the matter addressed in *Jude*.

With this OT background, Jude's accusation best fits within the condemnation of Jeremiah against false prophets and (relevantly for this letter) the certain punishment awaiting them (Jer. 23:34; 39–40). The Intruders claimed revelations and knowledge derived from their 'dreams' that were false and deceptive. By their actions, the Intruders claimed to be the

---

[235] . Sarah was actually Abraham's half-sister (Gen. 20:12) but Abraham was economical with the truth. He was more concerned about his own safety than the honour and safety of his wife.

recipients of divine revelation. All such messages from God must be tested against Scripture to verify their legitimacy.

There is a tendency among some Christians (particularly charismatics) in modern times to offer comments like 'The Lord told me (such and such)' or 'God spoke to me about (such and such).' While one cannot discount the possibility that God could audibly speak to someone today, it is difficult to take these sorts of statements at face value. Often, after some delving by another Christian, the first person will concede that God did not actually speak to him or her. The insight was generally derived from reading Scripture or speaking with other Christians or contemplating some issue in the light of Christian principles. This manner of speaking (unless genuine) is, in general, only used by those who seek to boost their own status among other believers, as if they are the special recipients of divine revelation. It is just a form of boasting. In the same way, Jude does not accept the 'revelations' of the Intruders as readily as some of the early believers apparently did: it is relevant that the Intruders are also accused of boasting (v. 16). Jude regards the Intruders as 'dreamers' in the Jeremiah 23:23–40 context. They are to be discerned and rejected: their fate is inevitable.

By enacting their 'revelations', the Intruders' behaviour will lead believers to copy their evil example, thereby defiling their own bodies through sexual immorality. The behaviour of the Intruders is not a matter for theorising or debate. It has dire practical (as well as spiritual) consequences. Three of them are now explored.

not only defile flesh

σάρκα μὲν μιαίνουσιν

This is a reference to the sexual immorality of the Intruders, particularly after the references to the practices of the evil angels (v. 6) and Sodom and Gomorrah (v. 7). The verb μιαίνω (*miainō*— defile) only occurs four other times in the NT. It refers to ceremonial uncleanness (John 18:28) or defilement (Ti. 1:15 [twice]; Heb. 12:15). Its usage suggests that this defilement may spread to others who encounter it.

As far as the issue of 'purity' is relevant to Jude's readers, Lockett considers Jude's contrast of purity and pollution:

> A nuanced use of these categories [purity and pollution] reveals that Jude's polemical language not only functions negatively to draw stricter boundaries between Jude's audience and his opponents, but it also functions positively to reinforce a theological world in which purity is important—not only in terms of the readers' present state but also their eschatological future.[236]

The conjunction μὲν (*men*) is translated 'not only' here and is another of Jude's triplets. It links with the following two occurrences of δὲ (*de*) 'but also' in this verse.

but also reject authority

κυριότητα δὲ ἀθετοῦσιν

What type of authority is being rejected? Calvin, following Luther, considered that it is a reference to certain types of *human authority*.

> Though, indeed, their chief object is to be free from every yoke, it yet appears from the words of Jude that they were wont to speak insolently and reproachfully of magistrates, like the fanatics of the present day, who not only grumble because they are restrained by the authority of magistrates, but furiously declaim against all government, and say that the power of the sword is profane and opposed to godliness;[237]

This interpretation must be rejected. The whole focus of Jude's discussion concerns violations of *divine law*, not human rules. The text makes it clear that the Intruders have rejected the

---

[236]. Lockett, *Purity and Polemic*, 3.

[237]. J. Calvin, *Commentaries on the Catholic Epistles*, ed. and trans. J. Owen (Edinburgh: Calvin Translation Society), 397. See www.ccel.org. (Accessed 21 Jun 2021.)

authority of 'the faith' (v. 3), the apostles (v. 17) and Christ himself (v. 4). The word κυριότητα (*kurioteta*) is derived from *kurios* (lord). This rejection of authority is juxtaposed against the angels of verse 5 who flouted divine authority. Like them, the Intruders are rejecting the authority of God. This phrase is really a reiteration of verse 4, but its repetition demonstrates how seriously the early Jesus movement insisted on adherence to the established teachings of Jesus and the apostles. It could be said that rejecting the authority of God is common to each of the three groups mentioned in verses 5–7, but it occurs in different ways: from physical sin to rejection of the spiritual order of things. The same can be said of the Intruders. They do so initially by 'dreaming' and then by putting their evil ideas into practice.

and defame things and persons in whom shines the divine majesty δόξας δὲ βλασφημοῦσιν

It takes quite a few words in English to describe what Jude is referring to. This translation attempts to capture the sense of δόξας (*doxas*—glories). The word δόξα (*doxa*) means glory but here Jude refers to 'glories'. What are they? The accepted interpretation is that it is a reference to God's angels, who reflect God's glory and majesty. The Intruders' sin is described by the verb βλασφημέω (*blasphemeo*), to defame (or malign)[238] the angels of God, whereas the godly would be in awe of beings so strongly associated with God. It is the derivative of the English word 'blaspheme'. Rather than respect the position of God's angels, the Intruders malign them and, in so doing, defame God's holy name. They are unable to distinguish between holy and profane things.

In summary, Jude has demonstrated that the current behaviour of the Intruders is no different from that of sinful people in ancient times. Why should their fate be any different? The same conclusion applies today.

---

238 . Zerwick and Grosvenor, *Grammatical Analysis*, 2:739.

Example of Judgement: Satan and the Body of Moses

Verse 9 in Detail

But Michael the archangel, when disputing with the Devil, argued about the body of Moses, did not dare to bring a judgement against him for slander, but said, 'The Lord rebuke you.'

Ὁ δὲ Μιχαὴλ ὁ ἀρχάγγελος, ὅτε τῷ διαβόλῳ διακρινόμενος διελέγετο περὶ τοῦ Μωϋσέως σώματος, οὐκ ἐτόλμησεν κρίσιν ἐπενεγκεῖν βλασφημίας ἀλλ᾽ εἶπεν, Ἐπιτιμήσαι σοι κύριος. This verse has a clearer meaning when we consider it in the light of two passages from Jewish writings: the Book of Zechariah in the OT, and the *Assumption of Moses*, which was likely written in the early part of the first century ad.[239] Zechariah 3:1–2, written around 500 bc, says:

v. 1 Then he showed me Joshua the high priest standing before the angel of the Lord, and Satan standing at his right hand to   accuse him.

v. 2 And the Lord said to Satan, 'The Lord rebuke you, Satan! Indeed, the Lord who has chosen Jerusalem rebuke you! Is this not a brand plucked from the fire?'

This situation in Zechariah was subsequently replicated in the *Assumption of Moses*, in an event concerning the body of Moses after he died. The events surrounding the death of Moses are sketched briefly in Deuteronomy 34:5–6. His burial place was unknown. In brief, the *Assumption of Moses* relates a (fictional) story that, after Moses was buried, Satan challenged God for Moses' body. Satan said that Moses' body belonged to him because Moses was a murderer (Exod. 2:11–14). The continuation of the dispute is related in *Jude 9*:

---

[239] . 'In its present form the Testament of Moses must be dated around the turn of the era, since there is a clear allusion to the partial destruction of the temple in the campaign of Varus in 4 BC (TMos 6:8–9). The document shows no awareness of the final destruction of AD 70' in J. J. Collins, 'The Assumption of Moses' in *Outside the Old Testament*, ed. M. de Jonge (Cambridge: Cambridge University Press, 1986), 148.

131

Jude 9 refers to a story in which the archangel Michael disputes with the devil about the body of Moses. Although the story cited by Jude has not been preserved, the literature of early Judaism contains several traditions that can inform one's understanding of Jude's source. This article explores these traditions, especially early Jewish interpretations of Zechariah 3, in an effort to throw light on this story and its use in the epistle of Jude. These traditions suggest that the disagreement between Michael and the devil over Moses' body pertained not to the burial of Moses' corpse, as previous scholarship has assumed, but to Moses' bodily ascent into God's presence. In this ascent account, the devil would have opposed Michael on the grounds that Moses' fleshly, human body was inadequate for God's presence. Further, it is probable that *Jude* 22-24 alludes to the same ascent story.[240]

Jude uses κρίσιν (*krisin*) to describe the dispute. Remember that, in Greek, *krisis* means a time of decision; the English 'crisis' derives from the Greek, meaning 'a time when a decision needs to be made'. In a theological context, 'crisis' is often used to refer to divine judgement (see v. 15). The author of the *Assumption of Moses* brings the archangel Michael (ὁ Μιχαὴλ ὁ ἀρχάγγελος— *ho Michaēl ho archaggelos*) into the dispute. Michael then uses the same words as occur in Zechariah 3:2. Note the use of ἐπιτίμησεν (*epitimēsen*) in Matthew 17:18, when Jesus rebukes a demon, which is derived from the same verb as in 'The Lord rebuke (ἐπιτιμήσαι—*epitimēsai*) you' (v. 9).

Note the 'but' (δὲ—*de*) at the beginning of the verse. There is clearly a comparison to be made. Jude contrasts the arrogance of the Intruders' crimes in verse 8 with the restraint shown by Michael. There is also a comparison between the behaviour of the (good) archangel and the (bad) angels of verse 6. For other

---

[240] . R. E. Stokes, 'Not Over Moses' Dead Body: Jude 9, 22–24 and the Assumption of Moses in Their Early Jewish Context,' *Journal for the Study of the New Testament* 40:2 (2017): 192–213, 192.

biblical references to Michael, see Daniel 10:13, 21; 12:1; and Revelation 12:7. 'He is thought of as pre–eminently the protecting angel of the Jewish people and the opponent of Satan.'[241] The word archangel occurs in the Bible only here and in 1 Thessalonians 4:16. The critical part of the text is that Michael 'did not dare to bring a judgement against him [Satan] for slander.'

In response to Satan's slandering of Moses (for murder), Michael has two responses. First, he recognised his subordination to God and did not bring a charge of slander against Satan because that was not his prerogative (cf. 2 Peter 2:10–11). Only God could bring such a charge against Satan. Michael's self-restraint here is contrasted with the actions of the evil angels in verse 6. Secondly, Michael went to the highest authority, appealing to God himself by calling out, 'The Lord rebuke you.' Only God is the final judge, so it is appropriate that Michael need not slander or rebuke Satan; God is willing and able to do that.

Satan was put in his place by a word from God. There was no need for God to even abuse Satan.

Second Description of the Intruders

Verse 10 in Detail

But these men speak evil of whatever things they do not understand οὗτοι δὲ ὅσα μὲν οὐκ οἴδασι βλασφημοῦσιν

For the second time, Jude points to the Intruders as 'these men' (οὗτοι—*houtoi*). Again, he uses *de* to contrast them with Michael. The contrast is evident between good and bad, right and wrong. Jude now considers why the consistently bad behaviour of the Intruders occurs. The reasons are a lack of understanding and a lack of perception.

The initial criticism is that the Intruders speak evil of whatever things they do not understand. The verb οἴδασιν

---

[241] . Cranfield, *Jude*, 161.

(*oidasin*) has the meaning of 'understand', as per its use in Mark 4:13, where Jesus questions his disciples' capacity for *spiritual* discernment. The Intruders have clearly not understood angels. Their knowledge about heavenly beings is astray. Accordingly, rather than accepting the sovereignty of God to order creation (in heaven and on earth) as he sees fit, they 'defame things and persons in whom shines the divine majesty' (v. 8). The use of βλασφημοῦσιν (*blasphēmousin*) here has the same sense as it does in verses 8, 9: defaming or speaking evil of someone (cf. 2 Pet. 2:10–12). It is no coincidence that this word describes the behaviour of both the devil and the Intruders. But Salmond goes further and is more to the point:

> The idea is that high and holy things are beyond their knowledge and their understanding is limited to the senses, the physical wants and appetites which they have in common with the brutes. In the case of the former, they are rash and profane of speech where they should be silent and restrained; in the case of the latter they use them only to their own undoing. The turn of the phrase, "in these they are destroyed" (or, "destroy themselves"), indicates, perhaps, how absolutely they are lost in the service of the physical appetites.[242]

In their 'dreaming', the Intruders are claiming to possess knowledge of heavenly realities, but Jude counters this by saying that they do not really understand the role of angels; otherwise, they would not be defaming them. They are not only claiming to have revelations but also suggesting that their perception of heavenly realities is superior to God's. Understandably, Jude should want to clearly identify 'these men' who have such preposterous self-aggrandisement. What better way to expose their evil notions and warped behaviour (v. 8) than by contrasting them with the behaviour of the archangel Michael himself!

---

[242] . S. D. F. Salmond, *The General Epistle of Jude*, The Pulpit Commentary (New York: Funk and Wagnalls, 1944), 10.

**whatever things they do understand naturally—like
irrational animals—in these things they corrupt
themselves** ὅσα δὲ φυσικῶς ὡς τὰ ἄλογα ζῷα
ἐπίστανται, ἐν τούτοις φθείρονται

Michael's response to Satan showed that he *understood* that God
is sovereign and knew the proper way to act in the light of that
knowledge. On the other hand, the Intruders *did not understand*
this fundamental principle and replaced godly understanding
(with all that this word implies—see Prov. 1:7; 1:30–2:2) with
instinct (φυσικῶς—*phusikōs*). Whatever 'natural' understanding
the Intruders possessed was from instinct. Jude describes them
as 'irrational animals': they do not even have the understanding
of a primitive human being. For this reason, they have no
understanding of God and his requirements for living. Paul said
the same thing in Ephesians 4:22 and Philippians 3:19. Their
dreams may provide insights (v. 8), but they are of the basest
kind. They corrupt themselves and, even worse, are corrupting
believers of the Jesus movement (cf. 1 Cor. 2:7–16, especially v.
10; vv. 15–16).[243]

For Christians, there must be a clear differentiation between
using God-given intellect and reasoning (in a biblically-oriented
manner) and resorting to 'gut feeling' or a surrender to natural
impulses. Again, this sort of *instinct* is like that of 'unreasoning
animals' (v. 10); it is instinct without any reasoned analysis of its
validity. This type of 'gut feel' ministry is seen in some churches
where preachers regularly pronounce what God has told them—
not by reference to Scripture, but by what they feel or perceive.
This is foolishly arrogant behaviour and should be avoided—
both by preachers and their hearers. MacArthur correctly
observes that many contemporary Christians lack spiritual
discernment, to their own and the church's cost. He gives six
reasons 'for the disturbing lack of discernment that characterises
much of contemporary Christianity'.[244]

---

[243] . See Kistemaker, *Epistles of Peter and the Epistle of Jude*, 387.
[244] . MacArthur, *Commentary*, 195 (emphasis added); see 195–197 for a complete
discussion of these six reasons.

A summary of the six reasons suffices for our purposes here:

1.   the trend among many evangelicals to minimise the importance of doctrine;

2.   the church's trend towards a less objective outlook, substituting unconditional truth for moral relativism and postmodern subjectivity;

3.   the church's abandonment of the power of Scripture, substituted with its preoccupation with its own image;

4.   pastoral laziness, exegetical sloppiness and a general attitude of indifference to God's Word, all of which have plunged God's people into error;

5.   God's people's failure to confront sin and heresy, leading to unchecked wickedness within the church body and the congregation's inevitable accumulation

of more and more unregenerate members—unbelievers who feel comfortable that their sin issues are never addressed—grievous immorality and major ethical lapses may sometimes even be overlooked or ignored, under a false pretence of love;

6.   a rampant void of spiritual maturity within the ranks of the church—including individuals with a superficial understanding of Scripture (cf. Mark 12:24), a weak grasp of sound doctrine and a deficient view of God, which means that they cannot be discerning.

Three Further Proofs from the Old Testament and Jewish Tradition

Verse 11   Woe to them! Because they walked in the way of Cain and plunged into the error of Balaam for reward and perished in the rebellion of Korah.

Verse 12   These men are reefs in your love feasts, feasting together (with you), fearlessly shepherding themselves; clouds without water being carried about by winds; autumnal trees without fruit, having died twice, having been uprooted;

Verse 13   wild waves of the sea, tossing up (the) foam of their own shame; wandering stars for whom the gloom of darkness for the age has been reserved.

Jude had previously used *three groups* (vv. 5–9) to illustrate the outworking of ungodliness. Their relevance to Jude's argument is that they typify general examples of sin that were exemplified by the Intruders. Lest his readers think that this type of behaviour occurs only in groups, he now particularises his message by considering the lives and outcomes of *three individuals*. The same can be said for the verbs: *walked, plunged, perished*. Jude's message in v. 11 is more particularised because he concentrates on the bad example that the Intruders display to his readers.

His warning is clear: be aware of the teaching that is implied by the Intruders' behaviour. It is imperative that every Christian congregation is similarly aware of the behaviour of its leader(s). Godly examples are to be admired and replicated by church members, but ungodly leaders are to be shunned. Furthermore, it is of equal importance that Christians should constantly test the teaching of their leaders against the word of Scripture so that 'the faith' is maintained and practised.

It needs to be recognised that Jude is not just using three examples from the OT and allowing his readers to draw their own conclusions from Scripture alone. His method incorporates the Jewish traditions about these characters from the targums. The Hebrew word *targum* (plural *targumim*) refers to an Aramaic translation of the Hebrew OT. By the first century ad, these

translations were sometimes literal translations of the Hebrew
and sometimes paraphrased, like a commentary on the OT.
Occasionally, NT quotations from the OT are closer to the
targumim than to the Hebrew OT.

Cain, Balaam, and Korah

Verse 11 in Detail

Woe to them!

οὐαὶ αὐτοῖς

'Woe' is a word of warning.[245] It never connotes good news.[246]
Jude may have been influenced to use οὐαὶ (*ouai*—woe) because
of its repeated use in 1 Enoch (especially ch. 94–100). This cry
immediately takes us to Matthew 23:13–36. In that passage,
Jesus uses this word of warning eight times.[247] Its occurrence
always denotes the expectation of a major calamity. In both the
OT and NT this word's usage is increasingly associated with the
condemnation of sin as well as predicting dire events. Paul uses
it only once: of himself in 1 Corinthians 9:16. It is frequently
used by the OT prophets to warn of God's severe judgement
against Israel and heathen nations alike.[248]

> The Hebrew word 'woe' (*hôy*) is used fifty-one times,
> always by the prophets. Over forty of these instances are
> in passages where warnings are being given, such as
> here [Isa. 5:8]…The oracles provide a picture of society
> in Isaiah's day, to which he gives expression in the
> following chapter when he confesses

---

[245] . Generally, this word is intended for the ungodly, but see Lamentations 5:16, for 'woe' to believers.

[246] . In the same way, the phrase 'the writing's on the wall' always announces bad news at the least and, generally, worse than that (see Daniel 5).

[247] . Jesus also utters this warning in Matthew 11:21 (twice); 18:7 (twice); 24:19; 26:24. Its other major occurrences are in Revelation 8; 9; 11; 12; 18.

[248] . Numbers 21:29; Isaiah 3:9, 11; 45:9–10; Jeremiah 4:13, 31; 10:19.

that he lives among a people of unclean lips (6:5).[249]

> Six sermonic warnings are grouped together, each one beginning with the word 'Woe!' (cf. the six woes in chapter 5, and see the comments on 5:8 for the usage of the Hebrew word.) One important feature is that there is alteration between threat and promise in this section. Each woe is accompanied by a corresponding promise.[250]

Jude follows this dire warning with brief references to three OT characters. Their choice is not random. The listing of Cain, Balaam and Korah is not in the chronological order of the OT: Cain came first, but Korah came before Balaam. So, there must be some rationale for this order, which becomes evident as we examine each person and his deeds. There is a progression in sin from one to the other. This reflects the errors committed by the Intruders. In the same way that God punished these earlier transgressors with an increasing degree of severity, Jude is confident that he will deal with their modern equivalents (then and now). Jude's words have a sense of increased tempo and seriousness as he moves from one character to another. The intensity of sin goes from 'way' to 'error' to 'rebellion'. The verbs move from 'go' to 'rush' to 'perish'. The punishment increases in severity from 'banishment' to 'death in battle' to 'divine destruction'.

The lessons that *Jude* taught in the first century are still relevant in the twenty-first.

because they walked in the way of Cain ὅτι τῇ ὁδῷ τοῦ Κάϊν ἐπορεύθησαν

The reason for the declaration of woe is explained by ὅτι (*hoti*): 'because'. 'To walk in the way of' someone was a standard term

---

[249]. A. M. Harman, *Isaiah: A Covenant to be Kept for the Sake of the Church*, Focus on the Bible (Fearn: Christian Focus, 2005), 65.

[250]. Harman, *Isaiah*, 189.

in the OT for following the moral example of someone (1 Kings 15:26, 34; 2 Kings 8:18; 2 Chron. 11:17). The term itself is neutral. One can walk in God's way or Satan's way.

Cain was the first son of Adam and the first murderer, slaying his younger brother, Abel. But that is not the issue in focus here; it is what went before. Jude writes that the Intruders 'walked in the way of Cain'. The story of Cain in Genesis 4 is relatively short. His error was that his offering to God was not as acceptable as that of his younger brother, Abel.[251] Jealousy took hold and Cain killed Abel. Cain's punishment was exile from the land. We also need to take account of Jewish traditions prior to the first century ad, understanding that Jude would have been familiar with them. In summary, Cain stood accused of a variety of sins, including lust, jealousy, murder and (perhaps, most importantly, for Jude's context) self-love. Even Josephus, the first-century Jewish historian, mentions that Cain was guilty of leading others into sin.[252]

For Jude, Cain is an example of the evil practices and attitudes displayed by the Intruders. Their sin can be traced back to the beginning of history. It begins with asserting oneself against the righteous judgement of God.

and plunged into the error of Balaam for reward καὶ τῇ πλάνῃ τοῦ Βαλαὰμ μισθοῦ ἐξεχύθησαν

It should be noted that there are two different Jewish traditions about Balaam. The main story is told in Numbers 22–24, but there are also references to him in Deuteronomy 23:4–5 and Nehemiah 13:2, both of which describe Balaam as cursing Israel. Numbers 31:16 has Moses ascribing responsibility to Balaam for the sins committed at Peor (Num. 25:1–3), which resulted in the

---

251 . See D. Atkinson, *The Message of Genesis 1–11*, The Bible Speaks Today (Leicester, UK: Inter-Varsity Press, 1990), 102–106.

252 . Flavius Josephus, *Antiquities of the Jews*, Book 1, 2.2.

death of 24,000 Israelites. None of the Balaam traditions views him in a favourable light.

For Jude's purposes, the story of Balaam is one of duplicity and greed. To use an analogy from American western films, Balaam was a 'prophet for hire'. Balaam was a well-known seer in the Jordan region when the people of Israel were camped in Moab, on the eastern side of the River Jordan. By this time, Israel had wandered in the wilderness for nearly forty years and was close to entering the promised land on the other side of the river.

Israel had already defeated Sihon, king of the Amorites, and Og, king of Bashan, so Balak, king of Moab, was appropriately concerned that he would also suffer defeat at the hands of these new people in the land. Accordingly, Balak sent messengers to Balaam (a non-Israelite), who lived in Ammon, requesting that he use his spiritual powers to curse Israel. Rather strangely, Balaam replies that he can only do what Yahweh, the God of Israel, commands him to do, and that this Yahweh had told him in a dream not to go to Bashan.

Not to be deterred, Balak sends more impressive messengers, who offer Balaam considerable wealth. Overcome by greed, Balaam argues with God that he should be permitted to go to Bashan. God eventually allows him to go, on condition that Balaam only speaks the words given to him by God. Balaam sets out on a donkey but God repents of his earlier decision and sends the angel of the Lord to prevent Balaam's onward journey. The angel blocks the donkey's path. We are told that only the beast can see the angel. Unaware of the reason for the donkey's refusal to move forward, Balaam begins to beat it but the donkey is miraculously enabled to speak and asks why it is being beaten. At this point, Balaam sees the angel, who reveals that Balaam's life has been spared only for the sake of the donkey.

When they meet, Balak orders Balaam to curse Israel but, instead, Balaam blesses Israel, explaining that he can only say what God tells him to say. This occurs on another two occasions, infuriating Balak. Eventually, Balaam goes home after failing to do what he had been paid to do. But that was not the end of the story. Perhaps Balaam felt some unfulfilled obligation to Balak; or perhaps he was concerned that his reputation as a prophet for hire and resultant ability to gain large fees from his spiritual power would be damaged by his failure to meet Balak's demands. In any event, Balaam hatched a plan for Balak whereby Israel would curse itself by sinning against God. In due course, Balak offered the Israelites prostitutes and unclean food (i.e., food sacrificed to idols—see Acts 15:20; 1 Cor. 8:1, 4, 7; 10:20; Rev. 2:14), which were accepted by them (Numbers 25). In response, God sent a deadly plague upon the Israelites. This is interpreted in Numbers 31:16 as a direct result of Balaam's evil.

The language becomes more forceful in this second example. Whereas the Intruders *walked* in the *way* of Cain, they now *plunge into* the *error* (τῇ πλάνῃ—*tē planē*) of Balaam. It is relevant to note that the word for Balaam's error (*planē*) means 'wandering', as in wandering off the right path. Cranfield notes that 'Error (AV and RV) is an adequate rendering of πλάνη here only if it is understood in the strongest sense it can have, as denoting a thoroughly serious going astray from the truth in thought and/or conduct.'[253] Jude's choice of offender here links with 'walking in the way' of Cain. In both cases, there is the sense of a journey gone wrong. Like Cain, Balaam's error also has the effect of leading Israel into error. There is a progression from the sin of an individual to the leading of a broader community into sin. In the same manner, the sin of the Intruders has led others to abandon 'the faith'.

The basic meaning of ἐγκέω (*echkeō*) is 'to pour out', and, thereby, 'to plunge into'.[254] The Intruders have not slipped into an error. They are wholeheartedly committed to this course of action. The verb is in the aorist tense, signifying their complete absorption to derive material benefit from their intrusion into this group of believers. The NASB 'rushed headlong' has a better strength than the NIV 'rushed'. As indicated above,

---

[253] . Cranfield, *Romans*, 1:127.
[254] . See Lawlor, *Translation and Exposition*, 87.

Balaam's error was not just his lust for gain but also his persistent efforts to obtain it.

Jude refers to 'the error of Balaam for reward'. His emphasis is on Balaam's greed and his willingness to do whatever is necessary to obtain (and maintain) his ill-gotten gains. Notwithstanding the incident with his donkey and God's obvious power, Balaam was prepared to deceive Israel to keep his lucrative spiritual business alive. So it is, says Jude, with the Intruders. Jude's emphasis here is their willingness to do whatever is required for material gain. Paul condemned the same behaviour in 1 Timothy 6:5 and Titus 1:11. The expected consequence is that their example will encourage others to leave the straight and narrow path (Matt. 7:13–14) and follow the way of Balaam. It is no coincidence that Jude chose an OT character who stood condemned of *both* greed and leading God's people into error through sexual immorality.

The three main dangers causing Christians (and Christian leaders, in particular) to desert the faith are sex, money and power. As in the case of Balaam, all three were at work in the Intruders as they undermined the congregations to whom Jude was writing.

In the latter part of the twentieth century, there were several publicly prominent Christians (particularly evangelists on US television) who were seduced by money, sex or publicity—a form of power—and who subsequently faced disgrace, humiliation and even imprisonment for their egregious crimes. At the same time they were also false teachers leading their followers to a path of destruction. This continues today, but most Christians seem to remain silent about this type of disgraceful behaviour. The more liberal the doctrine of a church or denomination, the more likely it is that their leaders will go astray. Consequently, believers are dragged down with them.

In Australia, a Royal Commission into Child Sexual Abuse that began in 2014 (and ended in 2017) found that some of the most serious offenders were within Christian denominations and organisations. By far, the most disgusting behaviour occurred in the Roman Catholic Church, but men from all denominations, who were once renowned for their 'gospel ministry' or senior church-leadership positions, were revealed as those who were aware of and deliberately covered up incidents of serious sexual abuse of children. Other such individuals engaged in disgusting criminal acts which were discovered many years later. Both the Christian church and the broader community in Australia are now reeling from these shameful episodes that occurred and were hidden deliberately for decades. Similar incidents have been uncovered in the United Kingdom and the United States. Thousands of adults now suffer permanent disablement (particularly mentally, psychologically, and emotionally) from the abuse they received as children. The credibility of the Christian message has been seriously destabilised among many non-believers, as senior church figures across Australia were shown to have demonstrated utter disregard for Jesus' stern warning in Matthew 18:6, Christian behavioural norms *and criminal law*. The offenders have shown little or no remorse.

Jude serves as a major wake-up call to Christians in terms of understanding how insidious is sexual misbehaviour, especially against children, in its congregations and institutions. The sins that *Jude* addresses in the Intruders' behaviour have multiplied exponentially in recent decades, with the moral relativism of modern society and the easy access to pornography via the internet. The Christian church contributes to this problem by means of the lax attitudes and behaviour of many of its adherents (including highly-placed clergy), who tolerate standards of sexual behaviour among their own people that would have been anathema less than a century ago.

and perished in the rebellion of Korah

καὶ τῇ ἀντιλογίᾳ τοῦ Κόρε ἀπώλοντο

The rebellion of Korah was the most serious challenge to Moses' leadership of Israel in the desert after the people's departure from Egypt. It was serious, both in the level of discontent that was engendered and the degree of planning that went into the uprising. The story is related in Numbers 16. Korah was a senior member of the priestly tribe of Levi as well as a great-grandson of Levi himself (Num. 16:1). Korah had an important role in the administration of the tabernacle but was not a priest, a position he clearly desired.

Korah devised a plan to usurp Moses' role as leader. The conspiracy began with Dathan and Abiram, two influential members of the tribe of Reuben. Eventually, these three were joined by an additional 250 rebels. Together, they gathered the people of Israel to challenge directly the authority of Moses and Aaron, under the guise of what we might now call the democratic right of all the people to be regarded as equal. But, as Moses pointed out, the God of Israel did not run a democracy (this is as true now as it was then). The kingdom of God is a theocracy. God is King. *He* set his chosen leaders over Israel. Korah's challenge to Aaron (Num. 16:10–11) and the Reubenite leaders' challenge to Moses (Num. 16:13–14) was, in effect, a challenge to God's sovereignty to choose the leaders he desired: Moses and Aaron.

For Jude's purposes, Korah represents those who stand in defiance of God's law and God himself, rather than opposing earthly leaders. Korah's challenge is described as τῇ ἀντιλογίᾳ (*tē antilogia*), the 'rebellion'. The transliteration of the Greek makes it clear that the underlying meaning of the word is 'speaking against'.

Moses' primary response was not to challenge Korah but to appeal to God directly. We saw similar behaviour in the case of Michael the archangel in *Jude* 9 above. As Moses said, 'The Lord will show who belongs to him and who is holy, and he will have that person come to him' (Num. 16:5). Being confident of God's favour, Moses knew that God would vindicate him and Aaron. The divine proof emanated in actions, not words. The earth opened up and swallowed Korah, Dathan and Abiram, along with their families and possessions. The 250 rebels were destroyed by fire. Their crime was to worship God in an unacceptable manner; i.e., they ignored God's specific commands (Numbers 16).[255] Unfortunately, Korah's personal jealousy and self-seeking had broad consequences. Persuasive leaders can turn their own ambitions into national demands that bring division and ruin. In the same way that Hitler's persuasive oratory transformed Germany into the Nazi warmonger, Korah was able to persuade the Israelites to rise up in *his* cause. Both examples of self-promotion ended disastrously for far more people than just those who began these revolts. Nations came to grief.

Jude's language goes further than that of his account of Cain and Balaam in this third example. He writes that, like Korah, the Intruders *have* rebelled and perished (ἀπώλοντο—*apōlonto*). The verb is in the aorist middle voice. It is as if the punishment of the Intruders has already occurred. Examples of Korah-like behaviour are found in the NT in 3 John 9, 10, Titus 1:10, 11; 2 Timothy 4:14, 15, and, particularly, 2 Timothy 3:1–9.

Notwithstanding Korah's ignominious end through the overt display of God's wrath and judgement (and vindication of Moses!), the Israelites continued to rebel openly against God's chosen leader. Despite this open rebellion, Moses begged God not to destroy his own people. However, a plague began to consume Israel, killing 14,700 people before Aaron rushed to make atonement. Therefore, nearly 15,000 people died because of one man's overweening ambition, incitement of factionalism and deliberate refusal to accept God's will. It is clear why Korah provides such an obvious example for Jude's purposes.

Constable summarises these three offenders—Cain, Balaam, and Korah—in the following manner:

> Individual #1: Jude used 'Cain' to illustrate apostasy because Cain did not submit to God's will for him volitionally (v. 11). He was a self-righteous person.

> Individual #2: Jude used 'Balaam' to illustrate apostasy because Balaam advocated to Balak that the Moabites

---

[255] . The same sin was responsible for the earlier death of Aaron's sons (Num. 3:4). These people should have known the likely outcome of their misdeeds.

> seduce the Israelites to participate in their immoral feast
> (v. 11). He was a greedy person who lusted after money.
>
> Individual #3: Jude used 'Korah' to illustrate apostasy because
> Korah tried to make wrong 'right', and right
> 'wrong' (v. 11). He was a presumptuous person.[256]

Cain's sin was punished by exile; Balaam died in a battle (Num. 31:8; Josh. 13:22); Korah's demise was overtly public. There is a progression in the severity of punishment meted out to each person. More significantly for Jude, there is a progression in the seriousness of sin, even if it is of the same type. Cain disputed God's right to find his offering unacceptable; his self-righteousness eventually led him to commit murder. Balaam challenged God's authority to protect Israel (despite an unequivocal manifestation of his power). He added greed and immorality to his errors. Korah's presumption eventually resulted in open rebellion against God's appointed leaders, with 250 rebels rallying behind him. The biblical record shows God's relentless punishment against such sin (cf. Acts 5 for a NT example). Jude's conclusion is clear: the Intruders will suffer the same fate.

Third Description of the Intruders

Verse 12 in Detail

These men are reefs in your love feasts, feasting together (with you) οὗτοί εἰσιν οἱ ἐν ταῖς ἀγάπαις ὑμῶν σπιλάδες συνευωχούμενοι Verse 11 contains a woe oracle. This theme continues in verse 12, where Jude alludes to OT texts that are themselves woe oracles. Even though they may be destined for eternal punishment, Jude has not finished with the Intruders. Note his third particularisation of '*these* men' (*houtoi*) at the beginning of the verse. Jude denounces their ideas and behaviour in verse 8. In verse 11, he considers the damage that their behaviour had on the believers *as a congregation*. Now he focusses on their impact on the lives of the believers *personally*.

---

[256]. Constable, *Notes on Jude*, 4–5.

Condemnation of sin is not a theoretical issue. It is about what goes on in day-to-day life for every Christian.

This and the next verse use a range of rural and seasonal images to describe the Intruders, which would have been familiar to Palestinian readers.

Jude's first condemnation is directed at the behaviour of the Intruders at the communal ἀγάπαις (*agapais*), the so-called love feast of the early Jesus movement that we now call the Lord's Supper. The term for this gathering of believers was derived from the Greek ἀγάπη (*agapē*) for 'love'—that Christian form of love that always seeks the betterment of another (Rom. 13:10). This is the earliest recorded use of *agapais*,[257] again giving credence to an early date for *Jude*. It is the same gathering as that referred to in 1 Corinthians 11:20–22. The love feast involved the community of believers coming together to share a common meal in the evening (Acts 20:7, 11) and remember Christ's last meal with his disciples. Christians should contemplate the following comments seriously in relation to social interaction and behaviour at their churches.

> That is, it was a common potluck meal with bread broken at the beginning and a cup of wine shared at the end (cf. Ignatius, *Smyrn.* 8:2; Hippolytus, *Apostolic Tradition 26*; *Epistle of the Apostles* 15). We see this custom reflected in 1 Corinthians 11:20-22, where an abuse of the meal allowed social distinctions in the church to be underlined as the upper-class Christians ate and drank their rich food, leaving either only poorer food or scraps for the slaves and the other low-class folk in the church; this practice followed the normal social customs for a *collegia* (club). However accepted the social custom might be in the Greco-Roman world around them, Paul is upset that rather than celebrating the unity of Christians (i.e. that they were one family), it reinforced social distinctions that belonged to the surrounding pre-Jesus humanity.

---

[257] . See Davids, *Handbook*, 19.

Here in Jude the problem at the meals is different: these teachers whom Jude opposes are a danger to the community...And since the meal was at least in part a re-enactment of the Last Supper, where the participants were to be ritually pure and the animal 'without blemish', it would be quite improper that such 'blemishes' be present.[258]

In his comments on verse 12 Davids speaks of the Intruders as 'teachers' and 'leaders' but the text of *Jude* cannot support that interpretation of their position.[259]

Jude's use of σπιλάδες (*spilades*) to describe the Intruders has caused much discussion regarding its meaning. It is a stark example of the wordplay that Jude sometimes employs to underline the point he is making. There are two words derived from the stem *spil:* σπίλάς (*spilas*—rock) and σπίλος (*spilos*—blemish). Accordingly, there has been considerable debate about which word (and, therefore, which meaning) Jude intended. Although the differentiation is important to understand Jude's meaning, the outcome of the following discussion reveals a surprisingly satisfactory conclusion of the matter for those holding opposing views. When he wrote this, Jude may have been smiling in anticipation of the future debate.

Many commentators [260] (and some translations of the Bible[261]) regard Jude's use of σπιλάδες (*spilades*) as simply the plural of *spilas*. This particular word is used to describe rocks in the sea: 'a ledge or reef of rocks in the sea', as Strong puts it.[262] In *Jude*, this meaning has generally been translated along the lines of 'hidden rocks' or 'hidden reefs'. Whether or not they are

---

[258] . Davids, *2 Peter, Jude*, 70. See Lockett, *Purity and Polemic* for his discussion of the importance of purity in this context.

[259] . Davids, *2 Peter, Jude*, 68-70.

[260] . For example, Mayor, *Epistle of St Jude*, 40; Kelly, *Epistles of Peter and of Jude*, 270; Bauckham, *Jude, 2 Peter*, 85; Lawlor, *Epistle of Jude*, 89; Davids, *2 Peter, Jude*, 69-70; Davids, *Theology*, 276.

[261] . NASB, ASV, ESV, HCSB, Recovery Version.

[262] . Strong, *Greek Dictionary*, 66, 4694. Strong notes that this word should not be confused with *spilos*, 66, 4696.

hidden is another matter of debate, and, in this context, irrelevant.[263] Using *spilades*, the meaning would be that the Intruders are like reefs in the sea that snag unwary vessels and destroy them. By the time you are aware of their presence, it is too late, because the damage has already begun. It is not only the destructiveness of the reef but some also argue that it is the reef's hiddenness that is emphasised. Kelly makes the useful point that the word 'reefs' fits more easily into these descriptions because the entire phrase alludes to nature.[264]

The Intruders were part of the fellowship and had some influence in it. However, at the same time, there was a certain 'hiddenness' about their behaviour. Although some people informed Jude about their activities and behaviour, it is evident that the sinful ways of the Intruders were hidden from the perception of some believers. So, it can legitimately be argued that the Intruders were both visible and hidden, depending upon whose perception is considered. The analogy of the reef (hidden or visible) is particularly valid. Even though the presence of reefs may be known from nautical charts, it only takes a moment of carelessness on the helmsman's part for a ship to founder. The sinking of the *Costa Concordia* in 2012 provides ample evidence of this possibility. So it was with some members of the congregation who did not keep to 'the faith' (v. 3) but, instead, were distracted and fell foul of the reef of the Intruders' evil ways.

We now consider the case for 'blemish'. Some commentators[265] (and most Bibles[266]) consider that the correct text is *spilos*, 'a blemish'. The translation of 'blemish' has merit because it refers to another aspect of Jude's message and has linkages elsewhere in the letter (v. 23), where Jude uses the verb σπιλόω (*spiloō*) to describe the stain on a garment. The

---

[263] . Lenski, *Interpretation*, 645 objects to 'hidden', because the Intruders were in the midst of believers.

[264] . Kelly, *Epistles of Peter and of Jude*, 270.

[265] . Bigg, *Jude*, 333; Cranfield, *Jude*, 163 assesses that 'blemishes' is the more appropriate word, in light of 2 Peter 2:13, but this must be rejected. See also G. L. Green, *Jude and 2 Peter*, 94–95.

[266] . RSV, NEB, KJV, NKJV, NIV, Barclay NT, Good News Bible.

ceremony in point is the Lord's Supper, the remembrance of Christ's death for the atonement of sin. This was the culmination of all the OT animal sacrifices, where only the death and shedding of blood of the perfect Son of God was a full, complete sacrifice for the sins of the whole world (Heb. 9:22). Jude would have recalled the sacrifices that continued in his day at the Temple in Jerusalem at Passover. The only acceptable animal was a sheep or goat *without blemish*. So, it is understandable that Jude would have regarded the Intruders' behaviour at the *agapais* as a blemish on the inherent purity of the ceremony.

Here we come to Jude's play on words. Although the Intruders may be regarded as 'reefs' to be avoided by believers lest their faith be wrecked, they can also be regarded as 'blemishes' that spoil the purity of the *agapais*. Of course, each interpretation has its own validity. This is the best example of Jude's use of wordplay to make two points with the one word. The translation 'reefs' is preferred, both for the arguments provided above and the fact that Jude ought to be allowed to write what he wants to write. It is unacceptable to put words in his mouth (or, more precisely, on his pen) that are not his just to fit some theological perspective or assumption. The text is plain, and the meaning is clear: the word is 'reefs'.

fearlessly   shepherding   themselves

ἀφόβως ἑαυτοὺς ποιμαίνοντες

The characterisation of God as the shepherd of his people has a strong tradition in the OT and the NT. It reflects the intimate care of the Good Shepherd for the creatures that depend on him for their sustenance and well-being. The most famous is 'The Lord is my shepherd' (Psalm 23). Other references follow (emphases added):

> Like a shepherd He will tend His flock, in His arm He will gather the lambs, and carry them in His bosom; He will gently lead the nursing ewes.
>
> Isaiah 40:11

I am the good shepherd; the good shepherd lays down
His life for the sheep.

John 10:11

the great Shepherd of the sheep ... *even* Jesus our Lord.

Hebrews
13:20 And when the Chief Shepherd appears, you will
receive the unfading crown of glory.

1 Peter 5:4

for the Lamb in the centre of the throne shall be their
shepherd.

Revelation 7:17

But Scripture does not always have this favourable view of
shepherds. There can also be bad shepherds. This is a theme in
Zechariah and Ezekiel. The earlier mentioned reference to woe
resounds in the passages below, relating to shepherds:

v. 2 Therefore, the people wander like sheep, they are afflicted, because
there is no shepherd.

v. 3   My anger is kindled against the shepherds

Zechariah 10:2–3

v. 16 For behold, I am going to raise up a shepherd in the land who will
not care for the perishing, seek the scattered, heal the broken, or sustain
the one standing, but will devour the   flesh of the fat sheep and
tear off their hooves. v. 17 'Woe to the worthless shepherd   Who
leaves the flock! A sword will be on his arm   And on his right
eye!

His arm will be totally withered,
And his right eye will be blind.'

Zechariah 11:16–17

Jude's reference to shepherds feeding themselves has its closest
connection to Ezekiel 34:1–8. Chapter 34 should be read in its
entirety. It dwells on this theme at length and compares bad

(human) shepherds with the loving care provided by God, the Good Shepherd, who is personified in Jesus (cf. Psalm 23:1):

v. 1   Then the word of the Lord came to me saying,

v. 2 'son of man, prophesy against the shepherds of Israel. Prophesy and say to those shepherds, "Thus says the Lord God, 'Woe, *shepherds of Israel who have been feeding themselves!* Should not the shepherds feed the flock?

v. 3 You eat the fat and clothe yourselves with the wool, *you slaughter the fat sheep* without feeding the flock.'"'

v. 8 'As I live,' declares the Lord God, 'surely because My flock has become a prey, My flock has even become food for all the beasts of the field for lack of a shepherd, and my shepherds did not search for My flock, but *the shepherds fed themselves and did not feed My flock.*'

Ezekiel 34:1–3, 8

'Fear' (φόβος—*phobos*) is an oft-used word in the NT. Most often, it describes fear or terror. (e.g., John 20:19; Acts 5:5), but is also used for reverence towards God (e.g., Acts 9:31; Eph. 5:21). However, the adjective 'fearlessly' (ἀφόβως—*aphobōs*) occurs infrequently in the NT (Luke 1:74; 1 Cor. 16:10; Phil. 1:14). The fearlessness of the Intruders could refer to two possibilities. The first is fear of a holy God himself. It would certainly be appropriate for sinners to fear (have reverence for) a God who is pure and holy (Lev. 20:7, 26; 1 Sam. 2:2–10; 1 Chron. 16:28–31; Prov. 15:16). Secondly, there is the fear of the righteous judgement to be exercised by Christ (God) in punishing sin, in contrast with his mercy in verses 2, 22. It is appropriate to fear the righteous judgement of God (Psalm 1:5; Heb. 10:26–27; Rev. 19:2). These two possibilities are closely connected. A proper fear (reverence) of the holy God ought necessarily to include fear (terror) of his power to punish sin. Thirdly, there could be fear of self-contamination from associating with these wicked Intruders. There is, perhaps, less fear associated with continuing association with sinners (1 Cor. 5:11; 2 Thess. 3:14–15; Ti. 3:10) than the first two possibilities.

The use of *aphobōs* in the NT suggests that the second possibility, above, is the preferred meaning. The Intruders have no fear that God's wrath will fall on them, and so they 'shepherd themselves' without any qualms. The same issues arise in understanding verse 23.

The *agapais* was a special occasion in which unity and care for the brethren was to be especially evident, but the Intruders did not exhibit this. Instead, they were more interested in looking after themselves than others. Given Jude's reference to 'feasting', it may be the case that the Intruders were so overt in 'feeding themselves' that they went so far as to eat more than their fair share of what had been prepared for the meal. However, Jude's particular point is their role as teachers in this community of believers. The *agapais* was a time not only of fellowship and worship but also of teaching. The boastful and self-seeking behaviour of these interlopers would have been influential because they were presumably role models. Jude is anxious to denounce the lessons that their *behaviour* has revealed.

Given previous intimations about the background of the Intruders, it is pertinent to draw parallels between Jude's description of them and Paul's condemnation of the same type of inappropriate behaviour in Corinth (1 Cor. 11:18–22). Note the factions that developed at Corinth and Jude's assertion that the Intruders were keeping to themselves (possibly also with their followers). In Corinth, there is the same behaviour of overindulgence by the wealthy group at the expense of poorer brothers and sisters. It may be the case that the Intruders did not learn their lesson in Corinth and perpetuated their sin in a new environment where disapproval was less likely.

Because of the centrality of the *agapais* to the believers' fellowship, the improper behaviour of the Intruders had an opportunity to be evident to all and, therefore, to taint (blemish) the whole community.

Relevant examples in modern times are the pastors (shepherds) of megachurches in the United States, Australia and elsewhere—especially those on television—who enjoy expensive lifestyles and parade themselves in lavish surroundings, while delivering messages that are primarily about self-motivation, material prosperity, their own spiritual superiority and (sometimes) distortions of the plain meaning of Scripture. In short, their messages are *not* about the heart of the gospel. These people constantly seek donations for their 'ministries', preying upon the easily manipulated, but are really 'feeding themselves'. They are fulfilling Ezekiel's prophecy. They should be denounced by mature Christians.

clouds without water being carried about by winds

νεφέλαι ἄνυδροι ὑπὸ ἀνέμων παραφερόμεναι

The following references to natural phenomena (air, earth, sea, heaven) have some resemblance to 1 Enoch 2–5, which may have been in Jude's mind; the implications of 1 Enoch contrast the apparent order in the natural world to the disorder evident in the behaviour of the Intruders. Jude's examples will be self-evident to readers who lived in the dry Palestinian environment near the Mediterranean Sea. There is a clear allusion here to Proverbs 25:14: 'Like clouds and wind without rain is a man who boasts of his gifts falsely' (Hebrew text). This is further evidence of Jude's familiarity with the Hebrew Scriptures since the LXX has a somewhat different text. This is the type of man who talks big but does not deliver. However, the stronger reference is to 1 Enoch 80:2–6, particularly because it refers to sinners (the Intruders), and Jude immediately quotes 1 Enoch after this section of his letter. Davids' translation appears below:

v. 2 In respect to their days, *the sinners* and the winter [rainy season] are cut short. The seed(s) shall lag behind in their lands and in their fertile fields, and in all their activities upon the earth. He will turn and appear in their time, and *withhold rain*, and the sky shall stand still at that time.

v. 3 *The vegetation shall slacken and not grow in its season, and the fruit shall not be born in its (proper) season.*

v. 4   The moon shall alter its order, and will not be seen according to its (normal) cycles...

v. 6 Many of *the chiefs of the stars shall make errors with respect to the orders given them*; they shall change their courses and functions and not appear during the seasons which have been prescribed for them.

1 Enoch 80:2–4, 6 (emphases added)

The Intruders boasted about their spiritual superiority, but without good cause. They were deceivers. Farmers keep a constant eye on the weather. When clouds and winds appear they hope that rain will follow. These clouds (the Intruders) never deliver the expected benefits, thus leaving expectations disappointed. The verb παραφερόμεναι (*parapheromenai*—carried about) has an association with περιφερόμενοι (*peripheromenoi*) in Ephesians 4:14, where Paul rebukes his readers for being 'carried about by every wind of doctrine'. In the same verse, Paul refers to trickery and craftiness of men—the very deeds of the Intruders. Perhaps Jude had heard this Paulinism.

autumnal trees without fruit, having died twice, having been uprooted δένδρα φθινοπωρινὰ ἄκαρπα, δὶς ἀποθανόντα, ἐκριζωθέντα Jude uses ἄκαρπα (*akarpa*) to describe the works and worth of the Intruders. There are two possible translations of *akarpa*. In Titus 3:14 and 2 Peter 1:8, Zerwick and Grosvenor use 'unfruitful'; an alternative is 'unproductive'. But for *Jude* 13, they prefer 'fruitless'.[267] The preferred translation depends upon our understanding of φθινοπωρινὰ (*phthinopōrina*)—its only occurrence in the NT. What season does this refer to?

Mayor devotes an appendix to understanding the derivation and meaning of *phthinopōrinos*.[268] Jude is referring to harvest-time: that time of autumn when the farmer would expect to pick ripe fruit from the trees. It should have been the time when, as the poet John Keats penned:

Season of mists and mellow fruitfulness,

Close bosom–friend of the maturing sun;

---

267. Zerwick and Grosvenor, *Grammatical Analysis*, 2:651, 740, 717, respectively.
268. See Mayor, *Epistle of St Jude*, 55–58.

> Conspiring with him how to load and bless
> With fruit the vines that round the thatch-eaves run.[269]

But the exact opposite happened as an outcome of the Intruders' efforts. Like the fig tree in Luke 13:6, this analysis holds that these trees were unfruitful when fruit should have been plentiful. This image would complement the previous picture of disappointment concerning the dry (unproductive) clouds. 'Unfruitful' seems a more appropriate description in the context of harvest-time. Just as the clouds disappointed, so did the trees. The only logical outcome is to dig them up and destroy them. Of relevance to these trees are the words of Jesus in Matthew 7:15–20; 12:33. Note that Jesus prefaces his comments about the fruit trees with a warning about false prophets. The reference to sheep is also interesting, considering the previous part of verse 12:

v. 15 'Beware of the *false prophets, who come to you in sheep's clothing*, but inwardly are ravenous wolves.

v. 16 '*You will know them by their fruits.* Grapes are not gathered from thorn bushes, nor figs from thistles, are they?

v. 17 'Even so, every good tree bears good fruit; but the rotten tree bears bad fruit.

v. 18 'A good tree cannot produce bad fruit, nor can a rotten tree produce good fruit.

v. 19 "*Every tree that does not bear good fruit is cut down* and thrown into the fire.

v. 20   'so then, you will know them by their fruits.'

Matthew 7:15–20 (emphases added)

These trees are described as having died twice (δὶς—*dis*). The Intruders are doubly dead through their unexpected lack of fruit and their being uprooted. Jude's 'uprooted' is a final

---

[269]. J. Keats, *To Autumn* (1820), *The Oxford Dictionary of Quotations* (Oxford: Oxford University Press, 1999), 430.

announcement of their inevitable fate (see Matt. 7:19; Luke 13:6).

Verse 13 in Detail

wild waves of the sea, tossing up (the) foam of their own shame κύματα ἄγρια θαλάσσης ἐπαφρίζοντα τὰς ἑαυτῶν αἰσχύνας Jude turns his attention from the worthlessness of the Intruders' deeds to their moral failure. He describes 'wild' (ἄγρια—*agria*) waves of the sea. The adjective *agria* literally means 'found in the open field' or 'wild'. Its only other use in the New Testament is to describe the 'wild honey' that fed John the Baptist (Matt. 3:4; Mark 1:6). Biblical writers had a general fear of the ocean; most references to the sea in Scripture have negative connotations: the dwelling place of monsters, the unknown, something beyond man's control. This ranged from the dreadful prospect of Israel being trapped by the Red Sea (Exod. 14:10–12) to fear during the fierce storm in Matthew 8:26. Paul personally experienced shipwreck on three occasions (Acts 27; 2 Cor. 11:25). Old Testament examples are the Book of Jonah and Zechariah 10:11. Jude follows this trend by referring to the Intruders as 'wild waves of the sea' (κύματα ἄγρια θαλάσσης—*kumata agria thalassēs*). His emphasis is on the restlessness and instability of the waves and, therefore, the conduct of the Intruders. Jude's brother, James, used the idea of restlessness as connoting disorder and evil (James 3:8, 16). The accepted OT reference to which Jude refers is Isaiah 57:20: 'But the wicked are like the tossing sea, for it cannot quiet, and its waters toss up refuse and mud.' The imagery of wild waves is also used by Paul, who applies it to false teachers in Ephesians 4:14.

Jude's image reminds me of our family's frequent holidays to Apollo Bay, Victoria, on the Great Southern Ocean. When we walked along the seashore after wild weather at sea, especially in winter, the receding tide left a filthy scum of bubbles and seaweed behind on the sand. In the same way, the consequence of the Intruders' behaviour is to leave behind a dirty and polluting influence on the congregation, which blemish remains after they have departed. This links nicely with the alternative blemish image with which the Intruders smear the *agapais*. Mayor puts it this way:

> The rare word ἐπαφρίζω is used of the sea in Moschus v. 5. It refers to the seaweed and other refuse borne on the crest of the waves and thrown up on the beach, to which are compared the overflowings of ungodliness (Psalm 17:4), the ῥυπαρία [*sic*] καὶ περισσεία [*sic*] κακίας condemned by James 1:21, where see my note. The libertines foam out their own shames by their swelling words (v. 16), while they turn the grace of God into a cloak for their licentiousness (v. 4). We may compare Philippians 3:19 ἡ δόξα ἐν τῇ αἰσχύνῃ αὐτῶν.[270]

It is notable that the phrase 'its waters toss up refuse and mud' is only extant in Hebrew versions of the OT, not the LXX (see NASB, Isa. 57:20). This further supports the view that Jude's OT references come from a Hebrew text. However, Jude changes the end of his quote from Isaiah, which refers to refuse and mud. Jude refers to the waves tossing up 'the foam of their own shame'. There is some academic dispute as to whether 'shame' refers to the words or deeds of the Intruders, or both. This is irrelevant because both would be shameful in God's eyes. The point is that
Jude's readers would have more information on this subject than Jude himself, who condemns all their activities. See 1 Corinthians 5:1–3 regarding shameful behaviour.

wandering stars | ἀστέρες πλανῆται

Having used images of air, land and sea, Jude now uses the heavens as illustrations of the sins of the Intruders. Bigg provides useful background information on earlier Jewish traditions that regarded the planets as wandering and wicked stars, although, by Jude's time, it was well recognised that the planets were heavenly bodies that moved in an orderly and predictable manner. Jude uses these earlier views, and possibly

---

[270] . Mayor, *Epistle of St Jude*, 43.

Isaiah 14:12–20, as background material for his allegations that the Intruders are untrustworthy, just as wandering stars would mislead a navigator at sea. Both Bauckham and Davids devote much analysis to the connection between Jude's comments and the stars of 1 Enoch 80, which suggest that Jude perceived that the fate of the good and bad angels in that text would be the outcome for faithful and unfaithful believers. This analysis is of historical interest, but our present knowledge of the galaxy renders much of Jude's argument redundant for modern readers. However, that does not imply that the content of his message is now irrelevant.

Jude's clever use of words can reveal double meanings, and he repeats this technique in his use of πλανῆται (*planētai*) to describe the stars (ἀστέρες—*asteres*) as 'wandering'. In verse 11, using a similarly spelt word, Jude referred to the error (τῇ πλάνη—*tē planē*) of Balaam. As Balaam erred (wandered) from the way of God, so these Intruders have done the same thing. This Greek word is used throughout the NT (Matt. 24:5, 11, 24; Rom. 1:27; 1 Thess. 2:3; 2 Pet. 3:17) to describe those whose wayward teaching or behaviour does not conform to the gospel. Paul's use of the word in Ephesians 4:14 is in a verse that also contains references to winds and the tossing sea—just like the phrasing in *Jude*.

for whom the gloom of darkness for the age has been reservedοἷς ὁ ζόφος τοῦ σκότους εἰς αἰῶνα τετήρηται

Just like the fate of the uprooted trees, the end of the Intruders is a foregone conclusion. In English, the phrase 'doom and gloom' denotes a grim destiny made dark or dreadful. Jude would find this a suitable equivalent to his description of the fate of the Intruders. This contrasts starkly with the brightness of stars.

Darkness frequently stands for judgement in both the OT (1 Sam. 2:9; Psalm 88:5–7; Jer. 13:16; Joel 2:1–2) and NT (Matt. 8:12; 22:13; 25:30; 2 Pet. 2:4; Rev. 16:10). Jude describes not only their fate but also its inevitability. It is 'reserved' (τετήρηται—*tetērētai*) for them. This word is derived from τηρέω (*tēreō*), meaning 'to keep' or 'to reserve'. It is used in opposite contexts in *Jude* for the faithful and the damned but, in each instance, its use emphasises the conviction that the outcome is certain. In verse 1, Jude used it to describe believers *kept safe* for Christ. [271] In verse 6, he referred to evil angels *kept* in darkness. Here, it is used to confirm the outcome of the Intruders.

---

[271] . See comments on vv. 1, 6, 21, 24.

The Prophecy of Enoch: An Example of Judgement

Verse 14   But Enoch, the seventh from Adam, also prophesied with reference to these men, saying, 'Look! The Lord is coming amidst myriads of his holy ones

Verse 15   to execute judgement against all and to convict all those ungodly (men) concerning all their works of ungodliness which they have done in an ungodly way and concerning all the harsh (things) that ungodly sinners have spoken against him.'

Verse 14 in Detail

But Enoch, the seventh from Adam, also prophesied with reference to these men, saying, 'Look! The Lord is coming amidst myriads of his holy ones

Προεφήτευσε δὲ καὶ τούτοις ἔβδομος ἀπὸ Ἀδὰμ Ἐνὼχ λέγων,
Ἰδοὺ ἦλθε Κύριος ἐν ἁγίαις μυριάσιν αὐτοῦ

The Greek words in the introduction to this verse do not make much sense if translated in their textual order into English.[272] The translation above attempts to convey Jude's meaning in modern English. As in the previous verse, Jude's target is clear. It is '*these* men' (τούτοις—*toutois*). Enoch did not prophesy about sinners in general, but men just like the Intruders. To confirm his condemnation of the Intruders Jude now quotes 1 Enoch 1:9 and introduces the speaker: Enoch, the seventh (ἔβδομος—*hebdomos*) man from Adam. This numbering is taken from Genesis 2, where we have the lineage of Adam. The order is Adam, Seth, Enosh, Kenan, Mahalalel, Jered, Enoch. (The numbering reflects the Semitic style of including the first and last person.) Seven has a special place in Jewish tradition, being the number of perfection.[273] Its significance can be seen throughout Scripture—from the seven days for creation in Genesis 1:1-2:3 to the frequent use of seven in the Book of Revelation.

---

[272] . See G. L. Green, *Jude and 2 Peter*, 101–108 for detailed comments on verses 14–15.

[273] . H. Lockyer Sr (ed.), 'Seven, Seventh', *The Hodder and Stoughton Illustrated*

The use of προεφήτευσε (*proethēteuse*—prophesied) gives an important clue as to Jude's understanding of, and respect for, 1 Enoch. To say that Enoch 'prophesied' is to attribute divine revelation to him and state that he is speaking God's words.[3]

This is the only direct quotation used by Jude and, therefore, deserves some attention. The use of λέγων (*legōn*) is the Greek equivalent of English quotation marks. Although Jude quotes 1 Enoch 1:9, he also alters the original text. This section deals only with the implications of verse 15 for both the Intruders and Jude's readers.

The quotation begins with the suddenness of ἰδού (*idou*), translated as 'Look!' (or 'Behold!'). The original text says that 'he' (i.e., God) will come, but Jude substitutes 'the Lord'.

> The term 'Lord' is not in any of the other [ancient original] versions, representing Jude's Christological interpretation of the judgment. In applying a text that referred to God's judgment to Christ, Jude followed the precedent of other NT writers (cf. 1 Thess. 3:13; 2 Thess. 1:7; Rev. 19:13, 15; 22:12).[4]

The initial description of God (probably for Jude, 'Christ') coming with a huge number of 'holy ones' probably comes from Deuteronomy 33:2: 'And He came from the midst of ten thousand holy ones.' Whether they are angels is questionable considering the subsequent verse in Deuteronomy, where the holy ones are

---

Bible Dictionary (Nashville: Thomas Nelson Publishers, 1986), 968.

3. For more background on this point, see J. D. Charles, 'Jude's Use of Pseude-pigraphical Source Material as Part of a Literary Strategy,' *New Testament Studies* 37:1 (1991): 130–145; J. D. Charles, 'Those and These: The Use of the OT in Jude,' *Journal for the Study of the New Testament* 38:12 (1990): 109–124, especially 112, 119–120, 120 n. 4; M. Black, 'The Maranatha Invocation and Jude 14, 15 (1 Enoch 1:9)' in *Christ and Spirit in the New Testament: Studies in Honour of C. F. D. Moule*, eds B. Lindars and S. S. Smalley (London: Cambridge University Press, 1973), 189–196; C. D. Osburn, 'The Christological Use of 1 Enoch 1:9 in Jude 14, 15,' *New Testament Studies* 23:3 (1977): 334–341.

4. Schreiner, *Jude*, 471–472.

described as the people God loves. Another possibility is Zechariah 14:5: 'Then the Lord, my God, will come, *and* all the holy ones with Him.' However, Jude would also be familiar with Jesus' references to himself and the angels, as in Matthew 16:27; 24:30–31; 25:31. Given the apocalyptic tendencies in *Jude*, it would not be surprising that both Jude and his readers had accustomed their thinking to a glorious return to earth by Christ Jesus rather than God (the Father). Jude's reference may be to Jesus rather than the Father, taking account of Jesus' own claims to return in glory.

Whereas 1 Enoch speaks of an accomplished event, Jude is clearly speaking of an expected (and certain) future event. Jude's conclusion is reflected in his choice of tense for ἦλθε (*ēlthe*). The Greek tense is aorist active indicative, which is literally translated 'came', indicating a past event.[274] However, in this case, '[t]he aorist indicative can be used to describe an event that is not yet past as though it were already completed...An author sometimes uses the aorist for the future to stress the certainty of the event. It involves a 'rhetorical transfer' of a future event as though it were past.'[275]

The most important feature of this use of the aorist active indicative is the certainty that attaches to the expectation of the Lord's coming with his hosts. The most appropriate translation is: 'The Lord is coming'.[276]

Verse 15 in Detail

to execute judgement against all and to convict all those ungodly (men) concerning all their works of ungodliness which they have done in an ungodly way and concerning all

---

[274]. See NASB, RSV.

[275]. D. B. Wallace, *Greek Grammar Beyond the Basics* (Grand Rapids, MI: Zondervan Publishing House, 1966), 563–564. See also Davids, *Handbook*, 24; Davids, 2 Peter, Jude, 79–80.

[276]. See NIV, Good News Bible.

the harsh (things) that ungodly sinners have spoken against him.'

ποιῆσαι κρίσιν κατὰ πάντων καὶ ἐλέγξαι πᾶσαν ψυχὴν περὶ πάντων τῶν ἔργων ἀσεβείας αὐτῶν ὧν ἠσέβησαν καὶ περὶ πάντων τῶν σκληρῶν ὧν ἐλάλησαν κατ' αὐτοῦ ἁμαρτωλοὶ ἀσεβεῖς.

The two ancient versions of 1 Enoch 1:9 that are relevant to Jude's quotation are provided below, quoting Davids' translations:[277]

Ethiopic/Greek	Aramaic
Behold, he [= God] will arrive with ten million of the holy ones in order to execute judgment upon all. He will destroy the wicked ones and censure [or rebuke] all flesh on account of everything that they have done, that which sinners and the wicked ones committed against him.	[when he comes with] the myriads of his holy ones [to carry out the sentence against everyone; and he will destroy all the wicked] [17] [and he will accuse all] flesh for all their [wicked deeds which they have committed by word and deed] [18] [and for all their] arrogant and wicked [words which wicked sinners have directed against him]

Lockett comments on another ancient version of the text as per the table below,[10] which raises the issue of whether the Intruders are to be destroyed or simply condemned with 'the ungodly'. This also relates to verses 22–23 as to whether the Intruders should be included amongst those who warrant mercy to be shown to them.

---

[277] . Davids, *2 Peter, Jude*, 78.

Jude vv. 14b-15	Greek 1 Enoch 1:9	Ethiopic 1 Enoch 1:9
ἰδοὺ ἦλθεν κύριος ἐν ἁγίαις μυριάσιν αὐτοῦ ποιῆσαι κρίσιν κατὰ πάντων…καὶ ἐλέγξαι πάντας τοὺς ἀσεβεῖς [πᾶσαν ψυχὴν] περὶ πάντων τῶν ἔργων ἀσεβείας αὐτῶν ὧν ἠσέβησαν καὶ περὶ πάντων τῶν σκληρῶν ὧν ἐλάλησαν κατ᾽ αὐτοῦ ἁμαρτωλοὶ ἀσεβεῖς	ὅτι ἔρχεται σὺν ταῖς μυριάσιν αὐτοῦ καὶ τοῖς ἁγίοις αὐτοῦ ποιῆσαι κρίσιν κατὰ πάντων, καὶ ἀπολέσει πάντας τοὺς ἀσεβεῖς καὶ ἐλέγξει πᾶσαν σάρκα περὶ πάντων ἔργων τῆς ἀσεβείας αὐτῶν ὧν ἠσέβησαν καὶ σκληρῶν ὧν κατελάλησαν κατ᾽ αὐτοῦ ἁμαρτωλοὶ ἀσεβεῖς	Behold, he will arrive with ten million of the holy ones in order to execute judgment upon all. He will destroy the wicked ones and censure all flesh on account of everything that they have done, that which the sinners and the wicked ones committed against him.

Jude contains only the first and third elements—judgment and conviction—leaving out any reference to the destruction of the ungodly (noted by the ellipsis in the Greek text on the following page). Thus, the first clear alteration is that Jude omits the reference to destruction (ἀπόλλυμι) present in the second clause of 1 Enoch 1:9. Davids notes that this "is a bit surprising since he mentions it elsewhere." [279]

Webb observes a second alteration of the 1 Enoch quotation. Where in 1 Enoch the scope of conviction is universal, 'all flesh' (πᾶσαν σάρκα, 1:9), Jude narrows the object of such censure to 'the ungodly'—the object of the verb 'convict' (ἐλέγξει) is πάντας τοὺς ἀσεβεῖς, not πᾶσαν σάρκα. Thus, Jude has not only omitted the reference to 'destruction' present in the second clause

[278] . This table is per D. Lockett, 'Objects of Mercy in *Jude: The Prophetic Background of Jude* 22–23,' Catholic Biblical Quarterly 77:2 (2015): 322–336, 330.
[279] . Davids, *Letters of 2 Peter and Jude*, 79 cited in Lockett, *Objects of Mercy*, 330.

of 1 Enoch but also has narrowed the object of the second line.[280]

The first thing that stands out in this verse is Jude's fourfold use of ἀσεβεῖς (*asebeis*—ungodly). This is the culmination of his initial use of this word in verse 4. He will use it again in verse 18. Jude clearly wants to drive home the fundamental characteristic of the Intruders. Every wrong thing that they do or say is derived from the basic condition of their own ungodliness. That, in turn, leads to acts that are ungodly. Of the seventeen occurrences of this word and its derivatives in the NT, six appear in *Jude*. Paul and Peter also used this word to describe opponents to the gospel (Rom. 1:18; 4:5; 5:6; 11:26; 1 Tim. 1:9; 2 Tim. 2:16; Ti. 2:12; 1 Pet. 4:18).

This emphasis reflects the purpose of the Lord's coming: to execute judgement against the wicked. Taken together, the words ποιῆσαι κρίσιν (*poiēsai krisin*) mean 'to execute judgement'. In verses 6 and 9 we have seen the use of *krisis*, noting its NT use as implying judgement by God. It is used here with the same meaning. As with poiēsai, Jude uses the aorist infinitive tense for ἐλέγξαι (*elegaxai*), meaning 'to convict'. This tense is used because Jude regards this future event as being beyond doubt; it is as if it has already occurred. The word is always used in the NT with the negative connotation of being found guilty of wrongdoing. In this case, it has the force used by Jude's brother in James 2:9 (emphasis added): '*convicted* by the law as transgressors'. In this case, God is both prosecutor and judge.

It is important to recognise that the Intruders will be convicted of two crimes: one done and one spoken. The first conviction concerns πάντων καὶ ἐλέγξαι πάντας τοὺς ἀσεβεῖς αὐτῶν περὶ πάντων τῶν ἔργων ἀσεβείας αὐτῶν ὧν ἠσέβησαν (*kai elegaxai pantas tous asebeias autōn peri pantōn tōn ergōn asebeias autōn hōn ēsebēsan*—all their works of ungodliness

---

[280] . R. L. Webb, 'The Eschatology of the Epistle of Jude and Its Rhetorical and Social Functions,' *Bulletin for Biblical Research* 6 (1996): 139-51 cited in Lockett, *Objects of Mercy*, 331.

168

which they have done in an ungodly way). This provides a salient reminder that what we do on earth matters. For the early believers, judgement against ungodly deeds was a critical part of Christ's return. Not only would he take the redeemed to his eternal kingdom, but also wrongs would be righted and divine justice would prevail.

The second conviction concerns πάντων τῶν σκληρῶν ὧν ἐλάλησαν κατ' αὐτοῦ ἁμαρτωλοὶ ἀσεβεῖς (*pantōn tōn sklērōn hōn elalēsav kat autou amartōloi asebeis*—all the harsh [things] that ungodly sinners have spoken against him [God]). To the extent that the Intruders have influence in the congregation(s), what they say matters and can be regarded as 'teaching'. Their words are leading people astray. The following verse gives more (generalised) details about their speech. Speaking harshly against God (by angels) is an ongoing theme of 1 Enoch 1:9; 5:4; 27:2; 101:3. In this context, 1 Enoch has described 'harsh things' (σκληρόι—*sklēroi*) as 'proud and hard words' (5:4), 'unseemly words' (27:2), and 'insolent words' (101:3)—cf. Matthew 25:24; Acts 26:14. Hard words are defiant words. This manner of speaking towards the ruler of the universe is grossly inappropriate. The Intruders' speech is completely unacceptable in the company of believers if it is of this type. Speaking harshly against God can be construed from two perspectives: how things are said, and what is said. Speaking in a defiant, rebellious, irreverent manner is clearly ungodly. However, even more egregious is *what* is said. Speaking harshly includes derogation of the authority of Scripture, the saving power of the gospel and the lordship of Christ over all creation. These are the essentials of 'the faith', which Jude is exhorting his readers to contend for and defend.[281] MacArthur comments:

> Hell is certainly not a popular concept in Western society. In an age of tolerance and acceptance, the topic of eternal punishment is taboo; the very mention of it is considered unloving. After all, postmodern culture believes that everyone is basically good and expects that

---

[281]. See Lawlor, *Translation and Exposition*, 112 n. 20, n. 22 for apt comments about today's apostates who cloak their deception in pious religiosity.

life after death (if the afterlife even exists) includes heaven for all but the most evil people.

Sadly, the political correctness and doctrinal ambiguity that characterises the world has also permeated the church. Even among those who call themselves evangelicals, hell is regarded as a theological embarrassment. Passages that teach eternal destruction are often explained away, arbitrarily softened, or ignored altogether. As a result, society's erroneous views about God's judgment are only reinforced.[282]

This condemnation is the conclusion of Jude's use of πάλαι (*palai*—long ago) in his overview in verse 4.

---

[282] . MacArthur, *Commentary*, 183–184. Pages 184–187 provide seven primary features of God's judgment.

Further Criticism of the Intruders

Verse 16 These men are grumblers, complainers, following after their own lusts and their mouths speak huge boasts, showing partiality to people for the sake of gain.

Verse 17 But you, beloved, remember the words having `been spoken beforehand through the apostles of our Lord Jesus Christ

Verse 18 that they said to you that in the last time there will be mockers following after their own passions of ungodlinesses.

Verse 19 These people are those causing divisions, worldly-minded, not having (the) Spirit.

It is correct to say that Jude is far more interested in the behaviour of the Intruders than in errors of doctrine; however, this should not diminish Jude's criticism of what they said. Their language as well as their actions provide guidance on whether these men possessed sound doctrine and the Spirit of God. Neyrey well summarises this issue of speech but appears to overstate its importance in Jude's overall condemnation of the Intruders.

> Jude criticises his opponents for many vices, but he levels his most emphatic censure for their sins of the mouth. From a social science perspective, we know that when the social organisations are strongly organised and classified, this sense of order and propriety tends to be replicated in the control of the physical body...According to Jude, then, they threaten the social boundaries and internal structure of the holy and orderly group. Correspondingly, Jude calls attention to their lack of bodily control, especially the polluting speech that creeps from their mouths. Social unrest is replicated in lack of bodily control.[283]

A lack of 'bodily control' involves much more than speech.

---

[283] . Neyrey, *2 Peter, Jude*, 78.

Jude's underlying complaint is about behaviour more than speech.

Grumblers and Complainers

Verse 16 in Detail

These men are grumblers

Οὗτοί εἰσι γογγυσταί

Again, there is the repeated reference to '*these* men'. Jude provides a list of their sins. First, they are grumblers; this is the only appearance of γογγυστής (*goggustēs*) in the NT, although other forms of the word do occur. Three other forms of this word occur in the LXX. In giving this description, Jude probably has in mind Exodus 15:24; 17:3; Numbers 14:2, 27, 29.[284] These three passages describe the grumbling of the Israelites in the wilderness. Both Exodus references concern grumbling against Moses, which resulted from the people's lack of drinking water. In the Numbers incident, the people had grumbled against God for so long that he announced the severe verdict that everyone of twenty years and older would not enter the promised land. These references can also incorporate the behaviour of Korah (v. 11). In 1 Corinthians 10:10, Paul uses a related word (γογγύζω— *gogguzō*) to refer to Korah. Although variants of this word are generally used with a negative connotation (Matt. 20:11; John 6:41–43; 1 Pet. 4:9), John 7:32 uses the word to refer to people who spoke favourably of Jesus.

By using *goggustai* Jude compares the complaints of the Israelites against adverse physical circumstances with the grumbling of the Intruders regarding God and the angels. There is a direct connection between the behaviour of Intruders and that of Korah (v. 11) and, to a lesser extent, that of verse 5. *Jude* insists that *these* men are repeating behaviour that has been evident for millennia. It still goes on today in the church. *Jude*

---

[284] . Other OT references for grumbling against Moses are Exod. 16:2, 8; Num. 11:1; 14:2, 27, 29, 36; 16:41; 17:5. OT references for grumbling against God are Exod. 16:8; Num. 11:1; 16:11; 17:10; Deut. 1:27; Psalm 106:25.

warns that the same fate is ever present for those who grumble against God.

complainers

μεμψίμοιροι

The word means 'complainers'. A related word is found in Colossians 3:13. However, it is not found in the LXX. While the two words are similar in meaning, complaining is more than grumbling (being discontented, murmuring) because complaining is the articulation of an express dissatisfaction with a situation. Note that this word comes closely after those who said harsh things against God (v. 15). The Intruders have caused disquiet among the congregation and also directed vocal criticism (about angels, if nothing else). Two uses of the related verb are found in Romans 9:19 and Hebrews 8:8.

These two descriptions are particularly relevant to much of the Western church in the twenty-first century. Many who claim to be Christians (including prominent church leaders) are now willing to pick and choose what bits of Jesus' (and the Bible's) teaching with which they will comply. They grumble and complain that some of Scripture is no longer relevant to modern times. They complain that some parts of the Bible are no longer relevant to the modern era (e.g., teaching about homosexuality, same-sex 'marriage' or other gender issues) and should be ignored. They give no basis for their discrimination between acceptance and rejection of particular teachings, other than to say that it suits their opinion or interpretation of Scripture, which, on careful examination, is always the most liberal understanding possible. The truth of Romans 1:18-32 is anathema to them.[285] Hard, tough obedience to God's Word is beyond the endurance of such people, whose opinions should be shunned by orthodox Christians.

following after their own lusts κατὰ τὰς ἐπιθυμίας ἑαυτῶν πορευόμενοι

---

[285] . Note that sexual sin is the first evil highlighted by Paul in a long list of sins.

There is a constant linkage in *Jude* between the behaviour of the Intruders and that of the ancient examples enumerated in the text. Here, Jude uses πορεύομαι (*poreuomai*), which, when taken with κατά (*kata*), means 'follow'. It also appears in verse 18. This verb is related to the one used in verse 11 for 'walking in the way of' Cain. Just as Cain was reputed to follow *his own* desires, so the Intruders have rejected accepted Christian/Jewish morality and, instead, followed *their own* lusts (ἐπιθυμία— *epithumia*) or evil desires. Of its thirty-eight appearances in the NT, the occurrence of *epithumia*, with three exceptions, refers to sinful desire. The exceptions are Luke 22:15, Philippians 1:23, and 1 Thessalonians 2:17. Each use expresses the intensity of the desire. This word is used by Jesus in the parable of the sower (Mark 4:19) to describe those things that 'choke the word and it becomes unfruitful' (cf. *Jude* 12). The Intruders are intentionally focused on meeting their own (physical) needs before looking after others (physically and spiritually): shepherds who feed themselves (v. 12). The specific description of these desires is not as important as the recognition of their evil nature.

and their mouths speak huge boasts

καὶ τὸ στόμα αὐτῶν λαλεῖ ὑπέρογκα

Although τὸ στόμα (*to stoma*) literally means 'the mouth', Jude employs the singular in such a way as to imply the plural to express the English equivalent of 'their mouths'. It is as if the Intruders 'speak with one voice' in their defiance of accepted belief and behaviour in the early Jesus movement. But about what or whom are the words spoken? The use of ὑπέρογκος (*huperogkos*) should be noted. For large things, *koinē* Greek generally uses μέγα (*mega*), meaning 'great'; but here, the inclusion of ὑπέρ (*huper*—huge) at the beginning of the word (and many other Greek words) indicates an exaggerated size. We might presume that the huge words uttered by the Intruders are about themselves, but this meaning does not sit comfortably with the use of *huperogkos* in 1 Enoch 5:4; 101:3; the LXX (Dan. 7:8, 20) or Jude's earlier comments in verses 4, 8, 11. The Intruders might be boasting about themselves, but, ultimately, their words are so 'big' that they are expressing contempt for God's moral authority over them. This is exactly the opposite of the attitude required by Christ (Matt. 5:5; 11:29). Contempt for God's ways is increasingly displayed by modern society. Humility before God is an essential aspect of holiness.

showing partiality to people for the sake of gain

θαυμάζοντες πρόσωπα ὠφελείας χάριν

The final criticism is that the Intruders show partiality to people for the sake of gain. The combination of θαυμάζοντες πρόσωπα (*thaumazontes prosōpa*) means showing favour or partiality to people. The word πρόσωπον (*prosōpon*) is used in Galatians 2:6 where God shows no partiality. Its original meaning was the mask of an actor, 'hence the face one presents to the world, outward circumstances or position'.[286] Paul used it in the context of not judging people by their external appearances. Clearly, some in the congregation(s) to which Jude wrote were fooled in this way. The object of this show of favouritism by the Intruders is not mere self-aggrandisement but gain for their own 'advantage' (ὠφελεια—*ōpheleia*), probably money. This expression is used in the OT with reference to taking bribes in the administration of 'justice' (e.g., Lev. 19:15; Deut. 1:17; 10:17; 16:19; 2 Chron. 19:7; Job 13:10; Prov. 28:21). Relevant NT references are 1 Timothy 3:8 (see v. 11 above) and James 2:1. This description summarises the Intruders' behaviour described earlier in verses 8, 11, and 12.

This section of *Jude* demonstrates the applicability of the quotation from 1 Enoch. As prophesied long ago, the Intruders fit Enoch's description exactly.

---

286. Zerwick and Grosvenor, *Grammatical Analysis*, 2:566.

Remember Apostolic Prophecy

Verse 17 in Detail

But you, beloved, remember the words having been spoken beforehand through the apostles of our Lord Jesus Christ Ὑμεῖς δέ, ἀγαπητοί, μνήσθητε τῶν ῥημάτων τῶν προειρημένων ὑπὸ τῶν ἀποστόλων τοῦ κυρίου ἡμῶν Ἰησοῦ Χριστοῦ

We have become accustomed to Jude's use of *de* when contrasting people or events and his emphatic use of *houtoi* to distinguish the Intruders. On this occasion, he turns this technique against his readers: 'But you!' (Ὑμεῖς δέ—*humeis de!*; cf. *Jude* 20). His readers are to be quite different! But this is not a turning point in the letter. Jude still has more to say about the Intruders. There must be a distinct and noticeable contrast between the behaviour (and ideas) of Jude's true believers and those of the Intruders. Having mentioned his readers (last addressed in v. 5), Jude uses the term that unites them in Christ: *agapētoi*—the same intimate connection used in verse 3, which reminds these believers that they and Jude are all part of one cause based on a solid foundation, the love of God in Christ Jesus. Jude calls on them to *remember* (μιμνήσκομαι—*mimnēskomai*). He had previously acknowledged (v. 5) his readers' understanding of the matters (OT and Jewish writings) contained in verses 5–15, but he reinforces this by also acknowledging that they also knew what the apostles taught them. [287] They must remember the words (τά ῥημάτα—*ta rhēmata*) of the apostles. What was once contemplated is now coming to pass. Again, this suggests an earlier date for *Jude*.

The need for the readers to remember highlights several important issues. First, remembrance is required because they have nothing in writing; otherwise, they would have been directed to *read* what had been provided to them for instruction. In this context, remembrance is necessary because there is no other method to relate the apostles' words. The believers had received an oral tradition from some 'apostles' in the early Jesus

---

[287] . You can only *remember* something that you were previously told.

176

movement. Jude's letter may well have been the first written instruction that they had ever received. Second, the need to remember reinforces our earlier conclusion that 'the faith' (v. 3) was (currently) more comparable to an orally transmitted gospel than to a written code. Third, the lack of documentation in the hands of the believers argues for an earlier, rather than later, date for *Jude*. It seems clear that these believers had not seen anything in writing.

Verse 17 contains important text which has led to a debate regarding the letter's date of composition (see Introduction). It concerns the words τῶν ῥημάτων τῶν προειρημένων ὑπὸ τῶν ἀποστόλων (*tōn rhēmatōn tōn proeirēmenōn hupo tōn apostolōn*—the words having been spoken beforehand by the apostles). It is also legitimate to translate ὑπὸ (*hupo*) as 'through'. This word conveys the important truth that the gospel was not an invention of the apostles but specially delivered *through* them by the Holy Spirit. This use of *hupo* emphasises even more strongly the authoritative message they have heard. It originates with God himself. Jude asks, how then can the Intruders' message have any validity or credibility at all when it stands against the divine word?

The use of ῥημά (*rhēma*—word) in the NT seems to refer most frequently to spoken, rather than written, words.[288] This strengthens the argument that these believers first received the gospel in an oral form. These words had been spoken beforehand (προειρημένων—*proeirēmenōn*). This word is derived from προλέγω—*prolegō,* meaning 'to say something previously'. The extent to which the past event (speaking) precedes the current event (remembering) in *Jude* is a matter of uncertainty. The word is used in the NT to refer back to ancient events (Acts 1:16; Rom. 9:29) as well as relatively contemporary events (2 Cor. 13:2; 1 Thess. 4:6). It does not contain any implications for the effluxion of time. Its use in verse 17 is poor evidence in the attempt to give Jude a late or early date of composition, but it does nothing to weaken the conclusion of an early date.

---

[288] . Kohlenberger, *Greek English Concordance*, 675, 4839.

Who are the 'apostles'? The noun 'apostles' in verse 17 need not be a reference to the Twelve. 'Apostle' had a wider meaning in the early Jesus movement. Paul was an apostle, and it is significant in Romans 16:7 that he commends 'Andronicus and Junias, my kinsmen, and my fellow-prisoners, who are outstanding among the apostles, who also were in Christ before me.' [289] 'Apostle' in *koine* Greek meant no more than 'messenger' or 'sent one' (Matt. 28:16–20). Paul uses the word in this way in 2 Corinthians 8:23. The particular apostles who delivered the gospel to Jude's readers cannot be identified— there may have been only one person (apostle) who presented the gospel to them. If, in fact, Antioch was the destination of the letter, Paul himself had been a member of that church. However, Jude describes them as 'the apostles of our Lord Jesus Christ'. This description uses the same style that Jude uses of himself in verse 1 (a slave of Jesus Christ) and his readers (kept safe for Jesus Christ). The apostles, Jude, and his readers are all one in Christ (cf. Rom. 16:3, 7, 8, 9). Together, they represent a united opposition to the Intruders.

It was noted earlier that the apostles 'had spoken beforehand'. It is also reasonable to say that the apostles had *foretold* these events. In understanding the import of this word, it is important to focus on Jude's emphasis on prophetic revelation throughout his letter. If he relies on the prophetic authenticity of 1 Enoch, how much more should we expect Jude to attribute prophetic utterances to the apostles of Jesus Christ, who were inspired by the Holy Spirit? In other words, by remembering the apostolic message, the believers should not be surprised that what was predicted (foretold) has now occurred in their midst.

---

[289] . See Cranfield, *Romans*, 2:788–790 regarding the nature of an apostle. Interested readers are particularly referred to L. Belleville, Ἰουνιαν ... ἐπίσημοι ἐν τοῖς ἀποστόλοις: A Re-examination of Romans 16:7 in Light of Primary Source Materials,' *New Testament Studies* 51:2 (2005): 231–249.

Mockers

Verse 18 in Detail

that they said to you in the last time there will be mockers following after their own passions of ungodlinesses. ὅτι ἔλεγον ὑμῖν ὅτι ἐν ἐσχάτῳ [τοῦ] χρόνῳ ἔσονται ἐμπαῖκται κατὰ τὰς ἑαυτῶν ἐπιθυμίας πορευόμενοι τῶν ἀσεβειῶν.

It is relevant to note Mayor's comment regarding ὅτι ἔλεγον ὑμῖν (*hoti elegon humin*—that they said to you): these words 'imply that *the warning was spoken, not written*, and that it was often repeated.'[290] This is an important clue to the dating of Jude. If Jude is writing to people to whom the apostles spoke personally, that would indicate an early date for his letter. Jude reminds his readers that the apostles' words were said *to them*. They were not directed to the world in general but to believers in Jesus. Sometimes regular churchgoers complain that a minister's sermons contain little that is 'new' or 'interesting' and that the same themes are constantly repeated. Sermons are not provided to congregations for entertainment or the propagation of novel ideas. *Their purpose is*, as Jude writes, *to remind* modern-day listeners of 'the faith once for all time entrusted to the saints' (v. 3), so that they will remain faithful to Christ, avoid ungodliness (especially in the form of beliefs and behaviour contrary to the gospel) and know what to entrust to the next generation.

Many commentators have noted that, despite his familial relationship with Jesus, Jude does not include himself as an apostle. This may reflect his acknowledgement that he did not recognise Jesus as the Christ until after the resurrection; or, perhaps, that he (even if he was regarded by some believers as an apostle) did not deliver the gospel to this congregation(s). His reticence in this respect also adds to the authority of what these apostles did say. Jude is placing himself alongside his readers as one who is equally bound by the authority of this apostolic teaching. He is as one with his readers in needing to remember the unchanging message of the gospel.

---

290 . Mayor, *Epistle of St Jude*, 46 (emphasis added).

The prophetic message concerned the ἔσχατος χρόνος (*eschatos chronos*—last time), a phrase that would resonate with the readers. It is comparable to Paul's use of ἐν ἐσχάταις ἡμέραις (*en eschatais hēmerais*—in the last days) in 2 Timothy 3:1. Jesus himself refers to 'the last day' four times (John 6:39, 40, 44, 54). All the members of the early Jesus movement would have recognised this reference to the approaching end time (e.g., Matt. 28:20). From Jude's perspective, he sees himself as living in 'the last time', which commenced with the birth of Christ. It is happening as he writes.

Martin describes it this way:

> The same Greek word for 'mockers, scoffers' in both Jude and 2 Peter indicates that the point of issue was eschatological, a fact of some theological significance. In Jude the teachers denied the reality of judgment, in 2 Peter they questioned on other grounds (3:4) the delay of the final advent: 'What has become of the promise of his coming?' The same appeal is made in both documents to the teaching of the apostles as the fountainhead of authority. We find here an allegation that the teachers were deemed to have set themselves up as rival authorities who sought to undermine Jude's adherence to what he believed to be pure doctrine, handed down from a venerable source. Jude does not align himself directly with the apostles; rather he makes an appeal to them as authority figures who ought to be recognised by the congregation.[291]

The Intruders are called ἐμπαῖκτης (*empaiktēs*—mockers/scoffers) (cf. 2 Pet. 3:3). This term carried much more weight in the first century than it does today. G. L. Green explains its significance for Jude's readers (and their impression of the Intruders). This word is used in 2 Chronicles 36:16 (LXX) to describe the treatment of messengers of God. These scoffers are strongly motivated, following their own 'passions/evil desires' (ἐπιθυμία—*epithumia*), a word which carries the sense of a strong desire. Its use in the NT, especially in the Pauline and

---

[291] . Martin, *Theology of Jude*, 72.

pastoral letters, almost always has the connotation of evil desires.

Jude has become so angered by the waywardness of the Intruders that he uses the extreme word 'ungodlinesses' (my best attempt at an English word!) to describe their passions.[292] Jude writes that in the last days there will be mockers of God's authority and his people. The Intruders were so self-consumed by evil that they were κατὰ τὰς ἑαυτῶν ἐπιθυμίας πορευόμενοι τῶν ἀσεβειῶν (*kata tas heautōn epithymias poreuomenoi tōn asebeiōn*—following after their own passions of ungodlinesses).

Mockers now prevail in Western society. It is now fashionable among the intellectual elites in Western society (and the *hoi polloi*!) to actively mock Christian faith and values. *The Australian Financial Review,* for example, does not hesitate to publish cartoons that blaspheme Christ; even the Lord's Supper has been used in the context of mocking politicians.[293] These people are not merely mocking Christianity but pouring scorn on it. This tactic has been renewed with vigour by left-wing political activists in Western society in the twenty-first century. They are not prepared to engage Christians in rational debate but respond with scorn and, if needed, violence. It is also noteworthy that most newspapers and the media generally never have the courage to print comparable blasphemies against Islam, Buddhism, Hinduism, etc., but Christians are 'fair game' at any time and in any way. This prophecy of the apostles and Jude himself is again being fulfilled in the present time. It should not come as a surprise. This is the status quo for followers of Jesus (1 Cor. 1:23). The mockery of Jude's Intruders exactly describes twenty-first-century attitudes to the gospel in the 'sophisticated' Western world (cf. 1 Cor. 1:26–29; 2:6–8).

---

[292] . This word is not mere hyperbole. Jude could not be more serious about the gross sins of the Intruders.

[293] . See editorial cartoon in *The Australian Financial Review*, 3 June 2015.

Causing Divisions, Not Having the Spirit

Verse 19 in Detail

These people are those causing divisions, worldly-minded, not having (the) Spirit.

Οὗτοί εἰσιν οἱ ἀποδιορίζοντες, ψυχικοί, Πνεῦμα μὴ ἔχοντες.

Jude's ongoing style of reference to the Intruders ends with this final use of *houtoi*. Further adverse generalisations follow to sum up their evil character. First, they are οἱ ἀποδιορίζοντες (*hoi apodiorizontes*—those who cause divisions); a word occurring in the New Testament only here. But what sort of divisions arose? Mayor notes that 'this rare word is used of logical distinctions in Arist *Pol* 4.48…and I believe in every other passage in which it is known to occur.'[294] This clarifies the position, showing that the divisions arose mainly out of behavioural (and hence doctrinal) distinctions between the Intruders and the orthodox believers, rather than primarily out of social tensions between the rich and poor, or educated and uneducated.

This type of division also explains why *Jude* concentrates on gospel issues and the foundation of beliefs adopted from the apostles' teaching. While the behaviour of the Intruders (especially at the *agapais*) may have aroused bitterness, envy and social friction in the congregation(s) (almost a certainty), the much more fundamental point, from Jude's perspective, was that their behaviour threatened to undermine the gospel foundation on which these congregations were established in the first place. Paul's rebuke in 1 Corinthians 1:10–11 is noteworthy because his emphasis is on gospel issues rather than social disharmony *per se*. As noted in the Introduction, the divisions caused by factionalism were one of the Corinthian church's fundamental problems. Both Paul and Jude wrote their letters to resolve divisions, which attack the heart of a congregation. Solve the fundamental issues of 'the faith' and put them into practice: then

---

[294] . Mayor, *Epistle of St Jude*, clxxxvi. The same text is printed in Mayor, 47, but the reference there is 4.43.

social tensions within the church will begin to resolve themselves.

The tenacity of Christians throughout the centuries to hold fast to 'the faith' has caused much division—some good and some bad—but, as Lawlor notes, there is:

> no question that the widespread departure from the faith in modern times, and the increasing advance of destructive heresies have forced true Christians into divisions and separations that have led to the necessary establishment of new churches and new associations of churches, which stand unitedly for the truth and contend earnestly for the faith.[295]

Secondly, the Intruders are ψυχικοί (*psuchikoi*): worldly-minded; people who concentrated on worldly matters. They have no interest in the things of God. The NIV translates this description as those who 'follow mere natural instincts' but this seems to understate their active opposition to the gospel.

Lawlor comments at length that the appearance of apparent morality, personable appearance, clerical garb, or eloquent speech and mannerisms cannot regenerate the lives of purported Christians, particularly those who are the 'heads of denominations, councils, and conventions.'[296] Only the Holy Spirit can do that. Paul uses *psuchikoi* four times in 1 Corinthians (2:14; 15:44 [twice]; 15:46) to describe people who have their minds on this world, not the world to come, who cannot discern between 'natural' and 'spiritual' matters. It is also used in James 3:15 to describe people as unspiritual.

Thirdly, the logical consequence of the preceding descriptions is that they are Πνεῦμα μὴ ἔχοντες (*Pneuma mē echontes*—not having the Spirit). This is the third part of another of Jude's triplets. It is not an attack on the Intruders only. The emphasis here is that the Intruders belong to a class of people not having the Spirit. It just happens that, of this wide group of people throughout the world, these individuals have infiltrated

---

[295] . Lawlor, *Translation and Exposition*, 123 n. 17.
[296] . Lawlor, *Translation and Exposition*, 121.

this particular congregation. The Spirit is mentioned only here and verse 20 in *Jude*. But it is telling that he mentions the Holy Spirit at all. In this letter, Jude has written of God (the Father), the Son and the Spirit, the essence of Trinitarian doctrine. The possession of the Holy Spirit is critical, without whom people cannot be redeemed (Rom. 8:9b; 1 Cor. 12:3b).

> Here lay the foundation of the Christian Church. The Lord Christ had called his apostles to the great work of building his Church, and propagating his gospel in the world; for which, in themselves, they were evidently defective in all needful qualifications. But whatever was wanting, in wisdom, utterance, or courage, he promised to supply. And this he would do, only by the Holy Ghost; on whose assistance the whole success of their ministry depended. Hence, when he was about to leave them, after his resurrection, he ordered them to sit still and do nothing in the public work of building his Church, till the promise of the Spirit were actually accomplished. 'He commended them that they should not depart from Jerusalem, but wait for the promise of the Father.—Ye shall receive power after the Holy Spirit is come upon you, and ye shall be witnesses unto me in Jerusalem, Judea, Samaria, and to the utmost parts of the earth,' Acts 1:4, 8. In this promise he founded the Church itself, and by it he builded it up. And this is the hinge on which the whole weight of it turns to this day. Take this away; suppose it to cease, as to actual accomplishment, and there is an end of the Church of Christ in this world. No dispensation of the Spirit, no Church.[297]

This is the climax of Jude's condemnation of the Intruders: no Spirit equals no life. No worse fate could befall these disturbers of God's people.

---

[297] . J. Owen, *The Holy Spirit: His Gifts and Power* (Grand Rapids, MI: Kregel Publications, 1973), 109.

Exhortations to the Faithful

Verse 20   But you, beloved, building yourselves up in your most holy faith, praying in the Holy Spirit

Verse 21   keep yourselves in (the) love of God, eagerly awaiting the mercy of our Lord Jesus Christ unto life eternal.

Verse 22   And have mercy on some, who are doubting;

Verse 23   save others, snatching them out of the fire; and on some have mercy with fear, hating even the garment polluted by the flesh.

Build Yourselves Up, and Pray

Verse 20 in Detail

But you, beloved, building yourselves up in your most holy faith, praying in the Holy Spirit

ὑμεῖς δέ, ἀγαπητοί, ἐποικοδομοῦντες ἑαυτοὺς τῇ ἁγιωτάτῃ ὑμῶν πίστει, ἐν πνεύματι ἁγίῳ προσευχόμενοι

As he does in verse 17, Jude begins the ending of his letter with the words *humeis de, agapētoi*: 'But you, beloved'. The readers are to be quite different! Verse 3 contains the general instruction to 'contend earnestly for the faith'. Although brief in the context of the whole of *Jude*, verses 20–23 contain the most important part of Jude's message. Jude instructs his readers that 'contending earnestly' comprises more than just combatting opponents of the gospel. Jude's central idea here is that they should also keep themselves in the love of God (v. 21), so he provides three means of achieving this. They are to keep on building themselves up. The present active participle ἐποικοδομοῦντες (*epoikodomountes*) has the sense of 'completing or adding to a constructed building', particularly a temple, in the context of the NT. This tense refers to an ongoing process that the believers must continue forever. The analogy of comparing a congregation to a building is a common theme in the Pauline Epistles, but Jude's use of the term does not imply his reliance on Paul. The concept of the people of God as a structure finds its peak in 1 Peter 2:5, where believers 'as living

185

stones, are being built up as a spiritual house for a holy priesthood'.

Importantly, the NT writers never use this concept to refer to a physical structure. There can be no implication that Jude is referring to the establishment of some building programme. In Ephesians 2:20 and Colossians 2:7, Paul's reference is to something being accomplished (if not already completed), but here it clearly denotes a current need and future activity. This is not a call for individualism, such as pulling oneself up by one's bootstraps. The emphasis is on community action. For the sake of cohesion and unity, the whole congregation must be involved in this activity. Through a joint effort, individuals as well as the church body will gain spiritual benefit and encouragement. The focus is on the congregation and what members should do among themselves, not what they should do to the Intruders.

The readers are encouraged to keep on strengthening their fellowship τῇ ἁγιωτάτῃ ὑμῶν πίστει (*tē hagiōtatē humōn pistei*—in *your* most holy faith). Note that Jude uses the superlative adjective ἁγιωτάτῃ (*hagiōtatē*—most holy) to describe *their* faith. Whereas it was the faith entrusted to the saints (v. 3) and words spoken by apostles (v. 17), Jude now reminds his readers that 'the faith' is not some vague generalisation but *their* faith: a most holy (separated) faith. It is most holy because it comes from God (1 John 1:4, 5), unlike the rubbish that comes from the Intruders. We need to contrast Jude's statements about '*the* faith' (v. 3) with his directions to the believers about what he calls '*your* faith'. His earlier comments refer to the principles of belief laid down by the apostles, but here the reference is to individual faith (trust) in Christ for salvation. This personal trust is required of each believer and its value to each of the readers is emphasised in the use of *hagiōtatē*.

Jude's readers (and all believers) will strengthen their faith by keeping on ἐν πνεύματι ἁγίῳ προσευχόμενοι (*en pneumati hagiō proseuchomenoi*—praying in the Holy Spirit), thereby keeping themselves in God's love. *Jude* has a primary focus on the Holy Spirit as the centre of their actions. Exegesis of this phrase can be subject to denominational bias. At one end of the spectrum, Pentecostals will insist that it must refer to speaking in tongues (glossolalia): 'From a Pentecostal perspective, the injunction to 'pray in the Holy Spirit' (v. 20) should have special significance. Meaning to pray 'in the control of the Spirit' or 'under the inspiration of the Spirit', it likely refers to glossolalia.'[298]

At the other end of the spectrum, it will be emphasised that 'in the Spirit' just means 'with the Spirit's help'. The reality is (as usual) somewhere nearer to the middle. To attempt a better understanding of Jude's use of the term *in the middle of the first century ad*, it is helpful to turn to Paul's usage and to incidents in Acts, which must reflect the broad understanding of the Jesus movement *at that time*. In 1 Corinthians 14:15 Paul draws a distinction between praying *with* the Spirit' (τῷ πνεύματι—*tō pneumati*) and *with* the mind' (τῷ voΐ—*tō noi*). In this passage about speaking in tongues, Paul does not use ἐν πνεύματι (*en pneumati—in* the Spirit). When Paul does use these words in Ephesians 6:18, the context is broader than the same words used in *Jude*. Ephesians 6:18 says, 'With all prayer and petition pray *at all times in the Spirit*, and with this in view, be on the alert with all perseverance and petition for all the saints.' Given Paul's reference to different types of praying, it is illogical to impute a requirement for glossolalia to occur in every reference to praying in the Spirit, because Paul urges the Ephesians to pray in the Spirit *at all times* (ἐν παντὶ καιρῷ—*en panti kairō*).

It is highly likely that at least some of Jude's readers spoke in tongues because this seems to have been the experience of many converts at this early time of evangelism. It is reasonable to expect that Jude's command to pray in the Spirit would include that experience, but it is going too far to insist that this particular instruction must include glossolalia. A middle position seems to be that of Dunn, who does not reach a dogmatic conclusion on this point: 'A reference to charismatic prayer, *including glossolalic prayer*, may therefore be presumed for

---

[298] . R. Dutcher, 'An Unorthodox Argument and Jude's Non-Canonical Sources,' *Asian Journal of Pentecostal Studies* 11:1–2 (2008): 33–43, 40.

Jude 20.'[299] Both Schreiner[300] and G. L. Green[301] correctly hold the view that this command of Jude does not insist on glossolalic prayer.

Keep in the Love of God

Verse 21 in Detail

keep yourselves in (the) love of God, eagerly awaiting the mercy of our Lord Jesus Christ unto life eternal.

ἑαυτοὺς ἐν ἀγάπῃ θεοῦ τηρήσατε, προσδεχόμενοι τὸ ἔλεος τοῦ κυρίου ἡμῶν Ἰησοῦ Χριστοῦ εἰς ζωὴν αἰώνιον

The point of following the instructions in verse 20 is that the readers will keep themselves in the love of God (ἐν ἀγάπῃ θεοῦ—*en agapē Theou*). Here, the use of τηρήσατε (*tērēsate*—keep) refers us to verses 1, 6, 13, and 24. In each case, it is used with a sense of finality, in terms of outcome. On this occasion, however, its strength depends on the readers' actions. *Jude issues a command.* In verse 1, Jude uses the passive tense to describe the readers as those who are kept by God, but here he uses the active tense (in an unusual order of words) to remind the readers that *they have to keep themselves* in God's love (cf. James 1:27; Phil. 2:12). The aorist imperative is used to express urgency. In verse 2, Jude invokes a divine blessing on his readers, but here he instructs them to ensure that they hold on to its benefits. The certainty of God's love is beyond dispute (v. 1), but the believers need to work hard to remain in his safekeeping. The tone of this verse is similar to John 15:9–10, where Jesus tells his disciples to remain in his love, just as he remains in the Father's love. Their continuance in that state is subject to their obeying Christ's commandments. Some action is required by Jesus' hearers. In verse 10, John uses τηρήσητε (*tērēsēte*) for 'if you keep my commands', the same word used in *Jude*. The verb 'keep' ought

---

[299] . J. D. G. Dunn, *Jesus and the Spirit* (London: SCM Press, 1975), 245–46 (emphasis added). Bauckham, *Jude, 2 Peter*, 113, and Davids, *2 Peter, Jude*, 95 agree with this conclusion.

[300] . Schreiner, *Jude*, 483.

[301] . G. L. Green, *Jude and 2 Peter*, 121.

to be seen as referring to all of 'building yourself up' and 'praying' (v. 20) and 'staying in the love of God' (v. 21).

The meaning of *en agapē Theou* should be clarified. It refers not to the Christian's love for God but God's love for us. Christians are to keep close to the love with which God blesses and protects his people. There is a close connection between the descriptions of God's love in verse 1 (*en Theou patri ēgapēmenois*) and this verse. In each case (from the beginning of his letter to the end), Jude reminds his readers that God's love surrounds (keeps) them.

Jude's readers need both resilience to keep themselves in God's love and patience to wait for Christ's mercy. This is an important example of the tension between human responsibility and God's sovereignty—a tension which appears throughout the Bible. Of course, God must, and will, have the final say. However, human responsibility and God's sovereignty both must be at work in the divine plan for salvation. The key word here is 'mercy' (τὸ ἔλεος—*to eleos*), which is synonymous with 'redemption' (1 Enoch 1:8; 5:6; 27:4; Matt. 5:7; 2 Tim. 1:18). This word occurred in verse 1; it was the first divine blessing invoked towards Jude's readers. Now it is an integral part of the end of this letter. The readers are to wait eagerly for Christ's mercy. The verb προσδέχομαι (*prosdechomai*) means 'to wait for something with an expectation of its fulfilment' (Mark 15:43; Luke 2:25, 38). 'Waiting' has always been an integral component of the obedience of God's people. Growing impatient with God's timing has caused significant human disasters, not the least of which was the impatience of Abraham and Sarah (Gen. 12–18; 21). The ongoing conflict between Jews and Arabs in the Middle East thousands of years later is testament to the legacy of that impatience.

Waiting in and of itself does not show sufficient obedience to this command. Waiting must be accompanied by hope. Waiting is the climax of eschatological expectation and can only look forward to realisation when the believer has hope. 'To hope means to look forward expectantly for God's future activity...In community with others, he [the believer] experiences the Spirit as a foretaste of the eschatological kingdom (2 Cor. 1:22).'[302] Without the benefit of the revelation of Jesus Christ, the waiting (with hope) of the OT prophets is to be greatly admired (Isa. 30:18; 49:23; 51:5; 60:9; 64:4; Dan. 12:2; Mic. 7:7; Hab. 2:3; Zeph. 3:8). The same theme is repeated in Paul's letters (Rom. 8:23; 1 Cor. 1:7; Gal. 5:5; Phil. 3:20; 1 Thess. 1:10; Ti. 2:13) and Hebrews 9:28. Notably, the NT makes frequent references to waiting *eagerly*.

Jude's readers are to wait for the mercy of Jesus Christ. This is an unusual phrase. Generally, the NT writers refer to the mercy of God (the Father), but there is the case of Onesiphorus in 2 Timothy 1:18, where Paul twice seeks 'mercy from the Lord' (ἔλεος παρὰ κυρίου—*eleos para kuriou*) to fall upon this faithful worker and his household. In this case, it is unclear whether Paul's use of 'Lord' refers to the Father or the Son, but, given his audience, the Son seems more likely. Also, the early Jesus movement understood that the Father had committed the judgement of the last day to the Son (John 5:22), making it quite appropriate for Jude to refer to Christ's mercy towards his people at the end of the age. This linking of ideas about the Father and the Son is further evidence for Jude's conviction of the divinity of Jesus and gives a glimpse that Trinitarian theology was already present in the earliest part of the Jesus movement (even if it was not recognised as such at that time). This expectation of Christ's mercy is to last 'unto life eternal' (εἰς ζωὴν αἰώνιον— *eis zōēn aiōnion*). The less literal NIV translation 'to bring you to eternal life' better describes what Jude is encouraging his readers to wait for. Jude is saying exactly what Jesus instructed his disciples to do in John 15:9–10. It is that important pinnacle of the triangle whose sides represent God's unfailing love, the ongoing faith and hope ('waiting') of believers, and Christ's victory on the cross (the latter, of course, being the base of the triangle).

The fullness of Jude's description of the need to keep in the love of God while waiting for Christ's mercy on the last day is

---

[302] . S H Travis, 'Hope,' in *New Dictionary of Theology*, eds S. B. Ferguson and D.

to emphasise the emptiness of the position facing the Intruders. Through their disobedience, they have not kept themselves in the love of God. There is no way that they can expect to be spared from God's wrath and, therefore, to be rescued by the mercy of

---

F. Wright (Leicester, UK: Inter-Varsity Press, 1988), 321–322.

Christ. They face only condemnation and destruction. They do not have the Spirit (v. 19)!

Have Mercy on Some, and Save Others

Verse 22 in Detail

And have mercy on some, who are doubting

καὶ οὓς μὲν ἐλεᾶτε διακρινομένους

All commentators on *Jude* agree that the original text of verses 22–23 is quite uncertain.[303] The NASB translation for these verses follows. It captures Jude's ongoing use of triplets and does not contradict the sense of the remainder of the letter:

v. 22   And have mercy on some, who are doubting;

v. 23 save others, snatching them out of the fire; and on some have mercy with fear, hating even the garment polluted by the   flesh.

Just as Jude tells his readers to look expectantly for Christ's mercy on the last day (having already received mercy through the forgiveness of sins), so does he instruct them to keep themselves in God's love (v. 21) and to have mercy (v. 22). All

---

[303] . For a detailed examination of these verses, see C. D. Osburn, 'Text of Jude 22–23,' *Zeitschrift fur die neutestamentliche Wissenschaft* 63 (1972): 139–144. A. Robinson, S. Llewelyn and B. Wassell, 'Showing Mercy to the Ungodly and the Inversion of Invective in Jude,' *NTS* 64:2 (2018): 194-212 regard their paper as a 'new interpretation' of Jude 22–23 but it reflects what Lockett, *Objects of Mercy*, 332 describes as '[t]he traditional understanding of Jude 22-23 is that the author exhorts his audience to extend mercy to members of the community who are wavering in their faith due to the influence of the intruders.'

these instructions are imperative verbs. Jude commands his readers to have mercy on others.

The meaning that Jude attributes to διακρινόμενους (*diakrinomenous*—those who doubt) is difficult to discern. There are nineteen words in the NT derived from the root word διακρίνω (*diakrinō*). One occurs in verse 9, which, in the context used, has been translated as 'dispute'. Its use there relates to Zechariah 3:1–2 and *Jude* 23 leaves no doubt that this OT reference is particularly significant here. To that extent, 'dispute' in verse 9 appears to be an appropriate translation. The NIV variously translates the word as 'doubt' (Matt. 21:21; Rom. 14:23); 'judge a dispute' (1 Cor. 6:5); 'weigh carefully' (1 Cor. 14:29); and 'hesitate' (Acts 10:20). On Romans 4:20, Cranfield comments:

> The reference to the divine promise at this point is vitally important. It makes clear that the faith with which Paul is concerned is not belief in the impossible simply because it is impossible (as though faith and paradox were interchangeable concepts), nor any other anthropocentric mental stance of man, but is wholly based on, and controlled by, the divine promise. It is the promise on which it rests which is its power. It exists because a man has been overpowered, held and sustained by God's promise. For the use of διακρίνεσθαι in the sense 'be divided within oneself', 'waver', 'doubt' (the NT provides the earliest known examples of it) compare [Rom.] 14:23; also Matt. 21:21; Mark 11:23; Acts 10:20; James 1:6; 2:4; *Jude* 22.'[304]

The people to whom Jude refers are not the Intruders but their followers (or potential followers) in the congregation(s).[305] Having delivered such a strong condemnation against the Intruders, it seems clear that Jude is convinced that they are beyond redemption; but, perhaps, others, even their followers, can still find redemption. These followers, actual or potential, are those who have varying degrees of uncertainty about the

---

[304] . Cranfield, *Romans*, 1:248.
[305] . See comments on v. 15 above.

Intruders' behaviour and opinions. As to the fate of the Intruders, Lockett (and Reese) have less condemnatory views:

> The foregoing argument demonstrates how Jude, viewed as a "prophetic discourse," indicates a concern for mercy alongside the letter's clear focus on judgment. The quotation of 1 Enoch 1:9 and allusions to Zechariah 3 provide the prophetic context of mercy in the midst of judgment. Here it is especially important to note what the letter fails to say. The muted judgment from 1 Enoch along with the pressure for mercy and restoration exerted by the allusions to Zechariah together are less than an announcement of the sure and final destruction of the intruders that commentators often find. Though judgment is clearly sounded throughout vv. 5-19, the letter's omission of clear and definitive condemnation should keep interpreters from assuming that the "others" in Jude 22-23 could not be the intruders themselves…Jude's message, then, suggests that readers—both ancient and modern—should heed the command to show mercy in the context of God's judgment. Calling attention to this feature of Jude furthermore suggests a common concern shared between Jude and his brother James, namely, that "mercy triumphs over judgment" (Jas 2:13b).[306]

However, the arguments of Schreiner[307], Bauckham[308] and G. L. Green[309] advocating the complete destruction of the Intruders are more convincing (cf. 2 Thess. 1:7–10).

At one end of the spectrum, there are 'doubters' who are unsure about the truth of the gospel; at the other are those 'disputers' more strongly committed to false ideas and values than the truth of the gospel. Jude suggests that initially, at least, it is better to have mercy on these people so that they may repent and believe the truth. A broader meaning for the word is

---

[306] . Lockett, *Objects of Mercy*, 336. See R. A. Reese, *2 Peter and Jude*, 72.
[307] . Schreiner, *1, 2 Peter, Jude*, 438–439.
[308] . Bauckham, *Jude, 2 Peter*, 37.
[309] . G. L. Green, *Jude and 2 Peter*, 58.

preferred to take account of the likely breadth of opinions of those who could not be counted as Jude's supporters. 'Doubt' is used because it encompasses that broad range of opinions from those who hesitate to those who dispute (with varying degrees of aggression).

Jude's comments have changed my own attitude on how to frame an appropriate response to false teaching in the Christian community. 'Kick the heretics out!' would have been my previous response, with a view to eliminating troublesome falsehoods.

However, *Jude* has caused me to adopt a less strident position. By all means, remove the rebellious, unrepentant troublemakers (1 Cor. 5:11–13), but deal more gently with those who might be rescued from error. In such circumstances, mercy and grace can be even stronger than judgement (Psalm 103):

> Given the character of invective, one would expect the writer to instruct the beloved to expel the ungodly from the community. Instead, Jude commands the beloved to 'show mercy' to the very ones with whom they contend (*Jude* 22), a profound reflection of Jude's understanding of mercy and faith.[310]

Unsurprisingly, this reflects Jesus' own preference for repentance and God's mercy over judgement (e.g., Matt. 11:20; 18:33).

Verse 23 in Detail

save others, snatching them out of the fire
οὓς δὲ σῴζετε ἐκ πυρὸς ἁρπάζοντες

Jude uses the imperative σῴζετε (*sōzete*—save) to emphasise that time is of the essence in this rescue operation. Of course, it is only God who can save; but, here, Jude refers to the person who is the instrument of God's will and power.

---

[310] . See A. Robinson et al., *Showing Mercy*, 194.

The references to Zechariah 3:1–2 in verses 9 and 22 are now widened to 3:1–5 of that Old Testament book:

v. 1 Then he showed me Joshua the high priest standing before the angel of the Lord, and Satan standing at his right hand to   accuse him.

v. 2 And the Lord said to Satan, 'The Lord rebuke you, Satan! Indeed, the Lord who has chosen Jerusalem rebuke you! Is this not a brand plucked from the fire?'

v. 3 Now Joshua was clothed with filthy garments and standing before the angel.

v. 4 And he spoke and said to those who were standing before him saying, 'Remove the filthy garments from him.' Again he said to him, 'see, I have taken your iniquity away from you and will clothe you with festal robes.'

v. 5 Then I said, 'Let them put a clean turban on his head.' So they put a clean turban on his head and clothed him with garments, while the angel of the Lord was standing by.

Zechariah 3:1–5

As with the previous verse, Jude continues using imperative verbs to command his readers to act. This part of the verse is more applicable to disputers, rather than the hesitaters and doubters at its beginning. The situation is urgent, and there is no time to lose if disputers are to be saved from the wrath to come. These are not suggestions from Jude *but instructions* about what is needed quickly if forgiveness and salvation are to remain on these people. In the NT, the verb ἁρπάζοντες (*harpazontes*— snatch) always has a sense of suddenness associated with it (e.g., Matt. 13:19; Acts 8:39). Those in danger must be snatched out of the fire (ἐκ τοῦ πυρὸς—*ek tou puros*). As usual, Jude associates fire with the final judgement or punishment to be meted out after condemnation. By the time this letter was written the early Jesus movement was well acquainted with this association. Not only were there numerous OT passages linking fire with God's ending of the world, but there were also the words of John the Baptist (Matt. 3:10), Jesus himself (Matt. 5:22; 13:40–42; 18:8–9), and NT writers (1 Cor. 3:13 [an idea rarely

195

used by Paul]; Heb. 10:27; Rev. 20:14–15). Without urgent repentance, the fate of these people will match that of the Intruders.

The reference in Zechariah (and Amos, see below) pictures a just-in-time rescue that is, hopefully, to be replicated in this situation. The Amos text is associated with Jude's reference to Sodom (v. 7), and the Zechariah text takes up the theme of filthy clothes. Fire is also associated with the demise of Korah (see v. 11). The phrase 'a brand plucked from the burning' was used by Susannah Wesley to describe the nearly miraculous rescue of her five-year-old son, John, from their burning home on the night of 9 February 1705. Wesley himself used the same description throughout his life. [311] Although not considered by some commentators to be part of Jude's inspiration for the text, another relevant OT passage is Amos 4:11: "I overthrew you as God overthrew Sodom and Gomorrah, and you were like a firebrand snatched from a blaze; yet you have not returned to Me', declares the Lord.' Given Jude's earlier reference to Sodom and Gomorrah (v. 7), this verse probably did play a part in his thinking. However, the Zechariah reference is more relevant to Jude's situation than the Amos passage because it deals with a godly man accused by Satan. The Lord is more concerned with mercy and repentance (giving him clean clothes) than with condemnation and judgement. Satan is trying to have Joshua thrown into hell, whereas the Lord wishes to save him from that fate.

and on some have mercy with fear

οὓς δὲ ἐλεᾶτε ἐν φόβῳ,

Who 'the others' are is unclear; however, given the increasing degree of recalcitrance implied in Jude's list, these people may have been so close to the edge of the abyss that any mercy shown to them would have to be accompanied by some type of fear. It may be that Jude is urging his readers to show mercy, rather than condemnation, to those who are so close to perishing, in a last-

---

[311]. See R. Hattersley, *The Life of John Wesley: A Brand From the Burning* (New York: Doubleday, 2003).

gasp hope that this might persuade them to repent. In verse 12, Jude describes the Intruders as being without fear (ἀφόβως— *aphobōs*) when looking after themselves. In that context, the Intruders showed no fear of God's judgement. That same fear is most likely the one described here. Jude is probably referring to the issue of becoming entrapped in sin while on the rescue mission; nevertheless, the warning about fear of God's wrath should not be underestimated.

hating even the garment polluted by the flesh.

μισοῦντες καὶ τὸν ἀπὸ τῆς σαρκὸς ἐσπιλωμένον χιτῶνα.

It is most likely that this phrase contains both spiritual warnings and common medical prejudices of the first century ad. Even in the twenty-first century, the spiritual warnings remain valid. Jude uses the very strong word μισέω (*miseō*—to hate) in this instruction. This verb is used forty times in the NT, often incorporating a sense of sinners hating God, goodness or purity. Whenever used, the word always invokes strong feelings. This is the way Jude's readers must detest the evil practices of the Intruders and their followers, lest they (his readers) become infected. Jude's use of σπιλόω (*spiloō*) takes us back to the controversy surrounding the meaning of *spilades* in verse 12. The meaning here is clear: the garment has a blemish on it. Relevant OT passages that may have influenced Jude are Leviticus 15:7 and Zechariah 3:4. Jude has already laid emphasis on purity regarding the Lord's Supper.

Leviticus 13:47–59 states that garments worn by lepers must be burned by fire: there could then be no possibility of the garment polluting others. However, note that Leviticus 13:56 is comparable to 'snatching from the fire'. Whether Jude's use of this word here has implications for the translation of verse 12 is impossible to say.

The clothing referred to is a chiton (χιτών—*chitōn*), which is described in John 19:23–24. It was an undergarment worn next to the skin, like a singlet. It could, therefore, be stained by perspiration, etc. Obviously, the Intruders (and everyone else!) wore one, so Jude's comment has nothing to do with physical cleanliness; it is a metaphor for spiritual purity. 'They were to fear contamination from too-close contact with them. Just as leprosy can be spread by an infected garment, so, Jude implies, too-close contact with the heretics could spread their contagion.'[312] Revelation 3:4 speaks of 'a few people in Sardis who have not soiled their garments'; but the word there is ἱμάτιον (*himation*), meaning 'outer clothes'. Nevertheless, the metaphorical meaning is the same: the clothing is contaminated by the body in the same way that people are contaminated by sin. Throughout the NT, σάρξ (*sarx*—flesh) has a dual meaning: the physical sense of 'human skin/body' (e.g., John 3:6) and the spiritual undertone of the 'sinful human nature' (e.g., Rom. 8:3–8).

This curious phrase speaks of the staining of an inner garment as it is brought into contact with dirt. The human body is affected as well. Jude uses the vivid imagery to demonstrate the way moral evil has power to contaminate once its influence is left unchecked. The line of thought is parallel with 1 Corinthians 5 where Paul calls for a drastic handling of a moral situation and 'separation' from evil.[313]

Verse 23 ends Jude's instructions to his readers.

---

[312] . Hamann, *Chi Rho Commentary*, 102.
[313] . Martin, *Theology of Jude*, 70.

Doxology

Verse 24 But to him being able to keep you from stumbling and to present (you) in the presence of his glory, without blemish with exaltation

Verse 25 to (the) only God our Saviour through Jesus Christ our Lord: glory, majesty, dominion and authority before all the ages and now and to all the ages.
Amen.

Jude completes his letter with a doxology. This is a form of prayer or praise to a god. It sometimes ended Greek and Roman letters in the first century. It is not a specifically Christian formulation. This type of ending substitutes for the more normal greeting or salutation that concludes most NT letters, which were addressed to specific groups or individuals. The absence of a greeting from a writer who knows and is known by his readers may indicate that there were too many to name or that multiple congregations were the recipients. Jude has instructed his readers about the sins of the Intruders and how they, as believers, were to respond to the behaviour and words of these sinners and the threats to 'the faith' that they represented. He has challenged his readers to rescue those who are in danger of falling into the eternal fires of destruction. He now points to the One who will keep *them* (his readers) from falling.

Although Paul always ends his letters with a greeting (cf. 2 Thess. 3:17), he also includes doxologies in the text of some of his letters (the beginning, the end, and the middle). We can describe the content of Pauline (and other NT) doxologies. Unsurprisingly, given its content, the largest number are found in the Book of Revelation. All follow a standard formula derived from the OT.[314]

---

[314] . For an excellent analysis of doxologies in the Bible, see R. Deichgräber, *Gotteshymnus und Christushymnus in der frühen Christenheit* (Göttingen: Vandenhoeck and Ruprecht, 1967).

The typical formulation of NT doxologies is founded upon the rather lengthy example in 1 Chronicles 29:10–13. There are also doxologies in some psalms (e.g., Psalm 72:19; 106:48). A list of NT doxologies appears below, and it is evident that, while more elaborate than most, verses 24–25 of *Jude* fit the traditional pattern:

Text	Addresse	Honour	Duration	Response
Rom. 1:25	The Creator	who is	forever	Amen
Rom. 9:5	God			Amen
Rom. 11:36	To Him	blessed	forever	Amen
Rom. 16:25-27	Now to Him who is able to establish you according to my gospel... to the only wise God, through Jesus Christ	blessed be the glory be	forever forever	Amen
Gal. 1:5	To whom	the glory be	forevermore	Amen
Eph. 3:20-21	[God and Father] to	the glory	forever and ever	Amen
Phil. 4:20	Him [God]	be the glory to	forever and ever	Amen
1 Tim. 1:17	Now to our God and Father	all generations be the glory	forever and ever	Amen
1 Tim. 6:16	Now to the King eternal, immortal, invisible, the only God	be honour and glory	[eternity]	Amen
2 Tim. 4:18	To Him [our Lord Jesus Christ]	be honour and eternal dominion	forever and ever	Amen
	To Him [the Lord]	be the glory		

Text	Addresse	Honour	Duration	Response
Heb. 13:21	To Jesus Christ	be the glory	forever and ever	Amen
1 Pet. 4:11	Jesus Christ	to whom belongs the glory and dominion	forever and ever	Amen
1 Pet. 5:11	To Him [the God of all grace]	be dominion	forever and ever	Amen
2 Pet. 3:18	To Him [our Lord and Saviour Jesus Christ]	be the glory	both now and to the day of eternity	Amen
Jude 24-25	Now to Him who is able... to the only God our Saviour, through Jesus Christ our Lord	be glory, majesty, dominion and authority	before all time and now and forever	Amen
Rev. 1:5-6	To Him who loves us...	be the glory and the dominion	forever and ever	Amen
Rev. 5:13	To Him who sits on the throne, and to the Lamb	be blessing and honour and glory and dominion	forever and ever	Amen
Rev. 7:10	To our God who sits on the throne, and	salvation		Amen
Rev. 7:12	To the Lamb		forever and ever	Amen
	To our God	be blessing and		

glory and
wisdom and
thanksgiving

Text	Addresse	Honour	Duration	Response
Rev. 19:1	To our God	belong salva-		Amen

tion and glory   Hallelujah and
power

Verse 24 in Detail

But to him being able to keep you from stumbling
Τῷ δὲ δυναμένῳ φυλάξαι ὑμᾶς ἀπταίστους
Jude's favourite linking word is δὲ (*de*—but).[315] God's power
to effect his will is undoubted, so Jude uses 'able' (δύναμαι—
dunamai, from which the English words 'dynamo' and
'dynamite' are derived) to describe the *certainty and power* (cf.
Rom. 16:25; Eph. 3:20) of God's ability to keep us from
falling. Unlike verses 1, 6, 13, and 21, in this verse Jude does
not use *tēreō* for 'keep' but φυλάσσω (*phulassō*), which has a
comparable, but stronger, meaning.[316] Earlier, Jude wrote that
people were kept (held), but φυλακή (*phulakē*, a cognate of the
word used in this verse) is used throughout the NT primarily
to refer to imprisonment (e.g., John 3:24). It is an even stronger
sense of being held securely, as in John 10:28 and 2
Thessalonians 3:3. It reflects a tenacious God who will never
let his people go.

God will ensure that Jude's readers do not 'stumble' or
'fall'. It is a matter of debate as to which English word is the
preferred translation. Both meanings are ascribed to
ἄπταιστος—*aptaistos*), its only occurrence in the NT. The text
of Proverbs generally renders 'stumble' as an appropriate
translation, and 'stumble' better fits *Jude*.[317]

and to present (you) in the presence of his glory, without
blemish with exaltation καὶ στῆσαι κατενώπιον τῆς δόξης
αὐτοῦ ἀμώμους ἐν ἀγαλλιάσει, Having been kept from

---

[315] . Both Romans 16:25 and Ephesians 3:20 begin with Τῷ δὲ (*Tō de*—But to
him).
[316] . The word might be better translated 'guard'. See comments on vv. 1, 6, 13,
21.
[317] . Prov. 3:23; 4:12, 19; 24:17.

stumbling, the readers of Jude's letter will eventually be presented before God himself. Commentators emphasise the (spiritual) state of those brought before the throne but generally overlook the significance of 'to present' (ἵστημι— *histēmi*). It is used twenty-one times in Revelation, sometimes reflecting the occasion here mentioned. This term should reflect the protocol of a person appearing before royalty. You do not just arrive at Buckingham Palace to see Queen Elizabeth ii; rather, you are 'presented' to her. Formalities are followed. You are instructed on how to address Her Majesty and how to behave in her presence; your clothes are scrutinised for their appropriateness. So it will be when the redeemed stand before the throne of glory and are presented to the Lord God Almighty. The verb *stēsai* is translated 'to present' rather than 'to stand' (its literal meaning), because it reflects the formality of the occasion. This Greek word is also used in this context in Ephesians 6:11, 13, 14, but not with the same degree of dignity attached to it.

The redeemed will be 'in the presence of his glory' (κατενώπιον τῆς δόξης αὐτοῦ—*katenōpion tēs doxēs autou*). In the other two uses of *katenōpion* in the NT (Eph. 1:4; Col. 1:22) it has the meaning of 'in the sight of' with reference to God. This word also appears in the LXX in Leviticus 4:17; Joshua 1:5. The implication is clear that they will see God as he really is, in all his glory, holiness, majesty and power. Standing before God's glory (δόξα—*doxa*) is to stand in front of God. The glory of God is discussed below.

There will be extremely strict dress requirements (figuratively speaking) for those presented to God. Given God's holiness, the clothing must be 'without blemish' (ἄμωμος— *amōmos*) because God cannot look upon sin (Hab. 1:13). This word has the connotation of being blameless and without fault (cf. Rev. 14:5). This word refers to the sacrificing of animals in an OT context. In the OT, God is particularly specific about the type of sacrifice that he will accept: animals without defect or blemish (Exod. 29:1; Lev. 1:3, 10; 3:1; Num. 6:14). Similarly, the people who worship God must be pure in thought and deed

(Psalm 15; 24:3–5). This concept is extended to the NT, where the most perfect sacrifice is Christ himself (Heb. 9:14; 1 Pet. 1:19). Of course, believers in Jesus are expected to present themselves before the throne of grace appropriately (Eph. 5:27; Col. 1:22; 1 Thess. 3:13).

The redeemed will be presented before the throne of God with exaltation (ἀγαλλίασις—*agalliasis*). The word occurs in 1 Enoch 5:9. This is not an individual matter but must be seen as a public proclamation of great joy (Isa. 12:6; 25:9; Jer. 31:7–8; Rev. 19:6–7). The most familiar modern equivalent of this type of exaltation is probably the roar of the crowd (of supporters!) when their team wins the football grand final (cf. Psalm 42:4).

Verse 25 in Detail to (the)

only   God   our   Saviour

μόνῳ θεῷ σωτῆρι ἡμῶν

In verse 4, Jude refers to 'the only God' (τὸν μόνον δεσπότην— *ton monon despotēn*), but here uses 'to (the) only God our Saviour' (μόνῳ θεῷ σωτῆρι ἡμῶν—*monō Theō sōtēsi hēmōn*). 'Saviour' is not commonly used to refer to God in the OT, but it occurs in some psalms[318] and Isaiah 45:15. In the NT, see Luke 1:47, 1 Timothy 1:1; 2:3; 4:10, and Titus 1:3; 2:10; 3:4. However, the NT invariably refers to Jesus as 'Saviour'. Paul's letter to Titus (1:3–4; 2:10–13; 3:4–6) provides an interesting alternative: referring to both God *and* Jesus as Saviour whenever that description is used. Also, although 2 Peter follows *Jude* chronologically and uses some extracts from *Jude*, 2 Peter never refers to God as 'Saviour'.

The use of 'only' (μόνῳ—*monō*) stands in stark contrast to both ancient and modern concepts of God. When Jude wrote, polytheism was widespread among virtually all cultures (with Judaism singularly different); obviously, the concept of

---

[318] . 'God of salvation' is a close equivalent. See Psalm 17:7; 18:2, 46; 24:5; 25:5; 27:9; 38:22; 51:14; 65:5; 68:19; 79:9; 85:4; 88:1; 91:16; 106:21; 149:4.

monotheism was a peculiarity (cf. Acts 17:23). However, it has always been the case that Israel knows only one God, who has himself declared this fact (Deut. 32:39) and is acknowledged to be so by his people (Psalm 83:18; 86:8–10). In today's world, it is a widely accepted concept that 'all paths lead to God', so whichever god one chooses to follow does not matter because, if they are a 'good' person, they will end up in the same place as all other good people (presumably, heaven). As both a Jew and a follower of Jesus, Jude will have none of this. His 'only' replicates Jesus' insistence that He is the *only* way to God (John 14:6). The God and Father of our Lord Jesus Christ is the *only* God and Saviour. Jude's insistence on this point stands in opposition to the Intruders, who 'deny our *only* Sovereign and Lord, Jesus Christ' (v. 4).

Many manuscripts have inserted 'to the only *wise* God' (emphasis added), but 'wise' should be omitted. It is not in the earliest documents. Its later insertion was probably influenced by Romans 16:27.[319]

through Jesus Christ our Lord
διὰ Ἰησοῦ Χριστοῦ τοῦ κυρίου
ἡμῶν

All the characteristics and attributes of God are to be ascribed to him through Jesus Christ our Lord. As in Romans 16:27, praise is rendered to the Father through the Son. This is only possible because Jesus Christ is the image of the invisible God (Col. 1:15).
Both share the same glory and warrant the same praise.

glory
δόξα

Glory is the most basic characteristic of God. It is displayed through God's creation of, and presence in, the universe (1

---

[319] . See Cranfield, *Jude*, 171.

Chron. 29:11; Isa. 6:3); his boundless grace towards and sustenance of everything (Exod. 16:7; Isa. 44:23); and, finally, in the person of Jesus Christ (John 13:31–32; 2 Cor. 4:4; Heb. 1:3).

Many translations insert the word 'be' before 'glory'. The verb does not appear in the Greek text. This is not a mere omission on the part of Jude. It reflects the nature of God. Plummer makes the absence of the verb clearer in relation to God's attributes:

> They belong to him. This seems to be the meaning rather than that they are ascribed to Him. No verb is given in the Greek; neither 'is' as in 1 Peter 4:11 (ᾧ ἐστιν ἡ δόξα καὶ τὸ κράτος), nor 'be' (ἔστω), which in most doxologies may be understood. 'To Him be glory before all time' is scarcely sense, for our wishes cannot influence the past. 'To Him belongs glory before all time' is the statement of a simple fact.[320]

God's glory can also be displayed and perceived through nature (Psalm 19:1) and his people (2 Cor. 3:18). Doxologies in the NT are *the means by which we acknowledge God's glory in worship.* A reference to God's glory is a reference to God himself, and the occurrence of the word 'glory' in 1 Enoch 27:2; 63:5; 102:3; 104:1 may have influenced Jude's choice of this first attribute of God.

> All serious Christian thinkers acknowledge that glorifying God is at once man's divine calling and his highest joy, both here and hereafter. Reformed theology goes beyond other views, however, in emphasising these three truths.
>
> 1. God's goal in all that he does is his glory, in the sense of displaying his moral excellence to his

---

[320] . A. Plummer, *The Epistle of St Jude.* Ellicott's Commentary, vol. 8 (Grand Rapids, MI: Zondervan Publishing House, 1943), 668.

creatures and evoking their praise for what they see
and for the benefit it brings them (cf. Eph. 1:3).

2. Man's goal in all his actions must be God's glory
    in the sense of doxology by word and deed.

3. God so made us that we find the duty of doxology
    to be our supreme delight, and in that way the
    furthering of our own highest good.

This coinciding of duty with interest and devotion with
fulfilment was classically formulated in the first answer
to the Westminster Shorter Catechism: 'Man's chief end
is to glorify God, and to enjoy him for ever'.[321]

Given this understanding, it is inappropriate for people to try to
'give glory to God'. God, in himself, contains all the glory that
it is possible to possess. No one can add to it or subtract from it.

A preferable form of reference might be to say that Christians
acknowledge or praise God's glory through their worship.

majesty

μεγαλωσύνη

Majesty is an expected attribute of one who possesses glory,
especially a king. It is a word that was familiar to people across
the Greek-speaking world of the first century ad, used regarding
deities. It is used in Acts 19:27 with reference to Paul's adverse
impact in Ephesus on the trade in statues of the goddess Artemis.
Paul was accused of impugning her divine majesty. In Daniel
4:22, it is used to describe King Nebuchadnezzar; the king uses
it of himself in 4:36; 5:18. Daniel declares that God has given
this attribute to the king. The word is used in 2 Peter 1:16 to
describe the majesty of Jesus while on earth. In the
Commonwealth of Nations, the sovereign, Queen Elizabeth ii, is
designated 'Her Majesty'. It is the highest honorific we know.
Appropriately, Jude attributes this title to God through Jesus

[321] . J. I. Packer, 'The Glory of God,' in *New Dictionary of Theology*, eds S. B.
Ferguson and D. F. Wright (Leicester, UK: Inter-Varsity Press, 1988), 272.

Christ. Majesty is not the same as glory. In Christian usage, 'majesty' is more an attribute of God, whereas 'glory' is a description of his being. Observing the difference between the two terms allows for their appropriate usage.

dominion

κράτος

This word denotes power in action. The OT is familiar with God's power (Exod. 3:20; Deut. 9:3). Throughout the NT, this word refers to the accomplishment of great deeds, especially by God (Luke 1:51; Eph. 1:19). This power is not a theoretical construct like the power inherent in legislation, which permits a government to act. It is the actualisation of power by the one who possesses it. Jude is acknowledging that the ultimate power to do things and cause events to occur in the universe lies in God our Saviour, who created, owns and sustains everything by his word and power.

and authority

καὶ ἐξουσία

It is one thing to possess power but another to have the *authority* to exercise it. God has authority to exercise power in his creation because he made and owns it. He granted his authority to his Son on earth (Matt. 9:6; 28:18; John 5:27; 10:18) and in eternity (Rev. 12:10). The possession of both power and authority means that the Triune God can and will determine whatever pleases his will for things, individuals and nations, consistent with his other attributes such as mercy, love and holiness.

πρὸ παντὸς τοῦ αἰῶνος καὶ νῦν καὶ εἰς πάντας τοὺς αἰῶνας:

before all the ages and now and to all the ages.

Jude's doxology is not only the longest in the NT but also the most comprehensive in terms of its span of time (cf. Heb. 13:8) concerning God's existence.

Amen.

ἀμήν

'Amen' is a Jewish finale to Jude's Greek document. His primarily Jewish readership will automatically recognise this ancient acknowledgement of 'so be it!' or 'truly!' that was taken by the Jesus movement from Judaism. When the letter was read aloud (as were all such documents), everyone would have responded with 'Amen!' at its conclusion.

While this doxology is primarily a paean to the holiness of God (in its broadest concept); it is also a final denunciation of the Intruders. Every attribute that God possesses is lacking in the Intruders. They do not have glory but display their shame like scum on a beach (v. 13). They do not have majesty but revile heavenly majesties (v. 8). They will be condemned for ungodliness (vv. 4, 15). They do not have dominion over spiritual matters but are subject to eternal punishment (v. 13). They have no spiritual power because they do not have the Holy Spirit (v. 19).

The message of *Jude* is a stark warning and should be a wakeup call to all Christians. Belief and faith matter. There is a gospel proclaimed by Jesus and amply described in the NT. It is a simple idea. By grace alone, Jesus Christ (God himself, the Creator of the universe) became human and lived among people. He died on a cross so that, by the shedding of his blood, the sins of all will be forgiven if they have faith in Christ's atoning sacrifice and resurrection (Rom. 8:11; Heb. 9:22). Jesus rose from the dead to show that he has power over our greatest enemy, death. A person's eternal relationship with God is achieved solely by trusting that Christ died for them, despite everything that they were or are. There is only one 'faith', and any other teaching is to be rejected. In these latter days we have the advantage of possessing The Bible; God's complete authoritative Word to humanity. There is no excuse for not knowing who God is and what he requires of everyone.

The letter also emphasises that behaviour matters. Like James, *Jude* emphasises that faith alone is pointless, unless it is accompanied by behaviour and speech that conform to Jesus' teaching and example (James 1:22–25).

Relating Jude to the Twenty-First-Century Church

This commentary has examined the text of a letter written by Jude, a brother of Christ Jesus and James, around the middle part of the first century ad. Although Jewish, Jude had a good command of Greek language and style. He wrote to a congregation(s) of the early Jesus movement that were probably located in Palestine (possibly in Antioch), warning of the danger posed by Intruders, who were trying to lead people from 'the faith' by ungodly, sophistic behaviour (leading to factionalism) and boasting about their own spiritual superiority. It is argued that the Intruders may have been strongly influenced by similar (unacceptable) behaviour in the early church in Corinth, which Paul had strongly condemned previously in 1 and 2 Corinthians.

Yet we know that the Intruders were not Gnostics, who emerged in the second century. Jude uses particularly strong language (almost unparalleled in the NT) to condemn the behaviour and attitudes of these Intruders. In much of his letter, Jude draws on examples from the OT and Jewish sacred writings to illustrate the fate awaiting the Intruders, regarding their doom as being as certain as the return of Christ.

Jude ends his letter by urging believers (his readers) to take action against the Intruders and those coming under their sway. He demands action, not sentiment. The conclusion of *Jude* ends in such glorious praise of the unshakeably reliable God and Father of our Lord Jesus Christ that it has become part of the liturgy of much of the church through two subsequent millennia. But how does the Letter of Jude concern the Christian church in the twenty-first century?

The answer lies in two parts. First, Jude speaks to attitudes and behaviour that always have been, and always will be, part of the make-up of congregations that comprise the body of Christ on earth. That is because this body is comprised of sinful human beings. Like the human body, the body of Christ constantly suffers from germs, colds and minor ailments, all of which are relatively easy to cure if tackled quickly. They are the constant irritations that the human body must combat. Thus, in the church, minor issues are constantly attended to so that unity is maintained and people grow into the likeness of Christ.

More importantly, though, for the twenty-first century, the Letter of Jude speaks about a cancer that is ravaging the body of Christ. As with cancer in a human body, the cancer of liberal morality, theology and doctrine, based on a repudiation of the truth and validity of the Bible, must be identified and then excised ruthlessly with the sword of the Word of God. This is the only way that the body can be restored to health. Otherwise, the body of Christ will survive (John 10:28) only as a broken reed (Isa. 42:3), rather than a tree firmly planted by streams of living water (Psalm 1:3). The church in the West is at a stage where radical surgery is essential. Even amputations may be necessary if the body is to survive.

Secondly, the Letter of Jude demonstrates the indisputable link between attitudes and behaviour on the one hand and orthodox doctrine on the other. The behaviour of the Intruders led some believers astray. Today, the behaviour and attitudes of some so-called Christian leaders betray their belief that society knows better than God about morality and ethics. The list of gross sin in our society grows week by week. Increasingly and disturbingly, it is foisted on people by governments. Yet Christian leaders in the church, society and politics generally stay silent on such matters. Consider the issues listed below, which beset individual Christians, churches and denominations, especially in Western countries. If Jude was presented with the following facts, imagine his response if you told him about:

- 'megachurches' that put fame, popularity and money first, using the name of Christ for profit.
- homosexual and lesbian behaviour accepted by some clergy, some of whom practise this behaviour.
- same-sex unions (called 'marriage' by government decree) increasingly accepted by Christians and churches.

- child abuse committed by some clergy and church workers, which is covered up by churches.

- gender politics, where God's intentions for men and women are disregarded by state and society, yet endorsed by some Christians and churches.[322]

- gross misbehaviour and corruption by politicians, 'celebrities', and leaders of big business and unions, many of whom call themselves 'Christian'.

- legislation for abortion, euthanasia and sexual deviancy enacted by politicians (some of whom claim to be 'Christian'), which is passed by governments without much adverse comment from some Christian denominations and many nominal Christians.

These are issues that the gospel and *Jude* address head-on. They would be useful subjects for discussion in Bible study groups that want to apply God's Word to their everyday lives. Jude would have had uncompromising condemnation for all these issues because the behavioural characteristics of them pervert the truth of the gospel.

It is time for Christians, particularly those who call themselves biblical, to stand up *and speak up*. People can no longer be satisfied with keeping their views to themselves! They need to write to newspapers, politicians and social media, and discuss these issues with those who will listen. Silence and acceptance of sin was never the way of Christ. The history of martyrs through the centuries displays the courage that is essential *today* for the gospel to be proclaimed in its fullness. Unless this occurs in a relevant way for people in the twenty-first century, our societies will increasingly slide down the hill to a godless, nihilistic end. The people of Israel in the OT just did not get it. They persisted in rebelling against God's ways for humanity for hundreds of years and, finally, came to catastrophic ends: first the exile in Babylon around 600 bc and then at the hands of the Romans in the first century ad.

---

[322] . For a biblical view of male and female relationships, see G. Manuell, *Gender Wars in Christianity* (Brisbane, Australia: Connor Court, 2018).

People in the West seem to think that the present prosperity of their countries will continue unabated, regardless of how society functions. This is a head-in-the-sand mentality. A simple example from my own country 130 years ago makes the point. In the 1890s, the two most prosperous nations in the world were Australia and Argentina because they did the same things: exported meat (beef and lamb), wool, and minerals to the world. That is why so many beautiful buildings were constructed in Adelaide, Melbourne and Sydney at that time. Nowadays, no one takes Argentina seriously as one of the world's most prosperous and well-governed nations—in fact, the very opposite would be the reaction. By world comparison, Australia's standard of living is not what it was then. However, it is considered inconceivable (in Australia, at least!) that Australia could become another Argentina, economically and politically. But why not?

In a book written about thirty-five years ago, I referred to the need for 'moral management' in business and society, quoting Proverbs 14:31–35:[323]

v. 31   He who oppresses the poor reproaches his Maker,
But he who is gracious to the needy honours Him. v. 32
The wicked is thrust down by his wrong–doing,   But the
righteous has a refuge when he dies.

v. 33   Wisdom rests in the heart of one who has understanding,
But that which is in the midst of fools is made known. v. 34
Righteousness exalts a nation,   But sin is a disgrace to any
people.

v. 35   The king's favour is toward a servant who acts wisely,
But his anger is toward him who acts shamefully.

At that time this comment was ridiculed as an inappropriate attack on society in a book on finance; however, this call from Scripture is now even more urgent for the retention of Christianity in Western civilisation. Things moral, political, economic and cultural have all slid further downhill in the

---

[323] . G. Manuell, *Floating Down Under: Foreign Exchange in Australia* (Sydney: Law Book Company, 1986), ix.

meantime. The pace of decline seems to be accelerating. Jude's call for action has even greater urgency today: revival is critical for the church to grow. Why should Western countries be immune from the wrath of God, now and in the future, when so many churches are infiltrated by the equivalent of Jude's Intruders? Peter's warning cannot be ignored:

> For it is time for judgment to begin with household of God; and if it begins with us first, what will be the outcome for those who do the not obey the gospel of God?

> (1 Peter 4:17)

The reality is that many countries in the Western world are in economic and, particularly, cultural decline. The COVID-19 pandemic of 2020/21 has only worsened the situation. This was particularly reflected in the deep divisions in American society leading up to the 2020 presidential election. Its aftermath is a deeply divided United(?) States of America. With the election result being so close, America is facing a civilian war where the country is nearly equally divided between left and right political sympathies. There ought to be a growing concern among Christians (and conservatives generally) that waves from the upheavals in the United States are reaching the shores of other (mainly Western) countries. Government and civilian chaos are evident in Europe where Islamic extremists act with relative impunity and Judeo/Christian values are treated with contempt by social and political elites. Australia is suffering a severe cultural decline where political correctness and left-wing extremism have taken hold in most sectors of society, especially governments, but including many churches. Conservative people, including Christians, seem to be frightened to speak up lest they be singled out as scabs on the body politic. Bible-believing Christians need as much a wake-up call as did the church(es) to whom Jude wrote his letter. It is a time for action!

A wake-up call to individuals (and eventually a nation) can have profound effects—for good or bad. In the 1930s, the Nazi Party had the swastika emblazoned on its banners, along with the words *Deutschland Ewache* (*Germany, Wake Up!*). Anyone who has seen films of the Nazi era saw hundreds of thousands of these banners. Germany responded to this message, giving the world the dreaded era of the Third Reich. That wake-up call had devastating effects on the world. The Letter of Jude is saying the same thing today. *Christians, Wake Up!*

If the Christian church takes heed of this call and responds as enthusiastically to the demands of Scripture as Germany did to Hitler, it will have a devastatingly good effect on their societies and the world. These things begin with individuals: people catching a dream (like Martin Luther King Jr.) and setting others' hearts on fire with its validity and truth. King's dream set ablaze a civil rights movement around the world. It has achieved much good. How much more should the dream of a Christ-centred world stir us to action *in a public manner!*

A recent article by an American Christian, entitled *Lord, Spare Our Land: How Revival Begins in America*, summarises the critical role of the church:

> Revival of a nation, should God be pleased to grant it, begins in the church.
>
> As we take thoughts captive to obey Christ, we must not forget to obey him ourselves. How easy it becomes to hate other men's sins more than our own; a nation's drift more than the church's. For the past two thousand years, it has been the 'time for judgment to begin at the household of God' (1 Pet. 4:7). And if God sees fit to begin at the household of God, so should we. Is this not the focus of all our New Testament letters?
>
> Our gaze should turn first within, on the vitality of Christ's church, and this can and will be a blessing for a nation. Our God has, in history, spared nations—or at least Zoars (Gen. 19:22)—for the sake of his righteous few.
>
> Isn't it amazing that God orchestrates his world, including the rise and fall of nations, with such a consideration for his people?
>
> The Christian church, even when abused or ignored, is the backbone of any land. God rules the world in

consideration of their good (even when their 'good' includes refining fires of persecution (1 Pet. 1:6–7). His curses and blessings, his ways and his mysterious acts of providence, all serve his own glory and the eternal benefit of his people—neither impeding the other. What might a praying, loving, waiting, expecting church do in a nation like ours?

Yet we can feel so small, so insignificant, so powerless. Perhaps we believe ourselves a dutiful afterthought of a God busily lording [it over] the world. We can look at the celebrities, the wealthy, the elite, and think that they hold all the influence

But while great men in expensive suits make great speeches about important decisions, the Monarch of mankind bends his ear to little children. He who holds the hearts of kings in his hand (Prov. 21:1) considers how all decisions will affect *them*.

Should we not rightfully believe that the command centre of this world, the place where real influence is wrought, is in the secret place of faithful Christian living? Even evil Queen Mary knew this when she confessed, 'I fear John Knox's prayers more than all the assembled armies of Europe'.

If God spared the lives of many for a few, if the heroic efforts of individual men, through faith, 'conquered kingdoms, enforced justice, obtained promises, stopped the mouths of lions, quenched the power of fire, escaped the edge of the sword, were made strong out of weakness, became mighty in war, put foreign armies to flight' (Heb. 11:33–34)— what might a praying, loving, waiting, expecting church do in a nation like ours?[324]

The Letter of Jude is clear: the most important priority is to contend for the gospel once for all time entrusted to the saints.

---

[324] . G. Morse, Lord, *Spare Our Land: How Revival Begins in America*, in https://www.desiringgod.org/articles/lord-spare-our-land. (Accessed 12 July 2021.)

Let us concentrate on that first in our homes, churches, places of work and social activities. The difference that makes might surprise you!

Greek Text of the Letter of Jude

1. Ἰούδας Ἰησοῦ Χριστοῦ δοῦλος, ἀδελφὸς δὲ Ἰακώβου, τοῖς ἐν θεῷ πατρὶ ἠγαπημένοις καὶ Ἰησοῦ Χριστῷ τετηρημένοις κλητοῖς:

2. ἔλεος ὑμῖν καὶ εἰρήνη καὶ ἀγάπη πληθυνθείη.

3. Ἀγαπητοί, πᾶσαν σπουδὴν ποιούμενος γράφειν ὑμῖν περὶ τῆς κοινῆς ἡμῶν σωτηρίας ἀνάγκην ἔσχον γράψαι ὑμῖν παρακαλῶν ἐπαγωνίζεσθαι τῇ ἅπαξ παραδοθείσῃ τοῖς ἁγίοις πίστει.

4. παρεισέδυσαν γάρ τινες ἄνθρωποι, οἱ πάλαι προγεγραμμένοι εἰς τοῦτο τὸ κρίμα, ἀσεβεῖς, τὴν τοῦ θεοῦ ἡμῶν χάριτα μετατιθέντες εἰς ἀσέλγειαν καὶ τὸν μόνον δεσπότην καὶ κύριον ἡμῶν Ἰησοῦν Χριστὸν ἀρνούμενοι.

5. Ὑπομνῆσαι δὲ ὑμᾶς βούλομαι, εἰδότας [ὑμᾶς] πάντα, ὅτι [ὁ] κύριος ἅπαξ λαὸν ἐκ γῆς Αἰγύπτου σώσας τὸ δεύτερον τοὺς μὴ πιστεύσαντας ἀπώλεσεν,

6. ἀγγέλους τε τοὺς μὴ τηρήσαντας τὴν ἑαυτῶν ἀρχὴν ἀλλὰ ἀπολιπόντας τὸ ἴδιον οἰκητήριον εἰς κρίσιν μεγάλης ἡμέρας δεσμοῖς ἀϊδίοις ὑπὸ ζόφον τετήρηκεν:

7. ὡς Σόδομα καὶ Γόμορρα καὶ αἱ περὶ αὐτὰς πόλεις, τὸν ὅμοιον τρόπον τούτοις ἐκπορνεύσασαι καὶ ἀπελθοῦσαι ὀπίσω σαρκὸς ἑτέρας, πρόκεινται δεῖγμα πυρὸς αἰωνίου δίκην ὑπέχουσαι.

8. Ὁμοίως μέντοι καὶ οὗτοι ἐνυπνιαζόμενοι σάρκα μὲν μιαίνουσιν, κυριότητα δὲ ἀθετοῦσιν, δόξας δὲ βλασφημοῦσιν.

9. ὁ δὲ Μιχαὴλ ὁ ἀρχάγγελος, ὅτε τῷ διαβόλῳ διακρινόμενος διελέγετο περὶ τοῦ Μωϋσέως σώματος, οὐκ ἐτόλμησεν κρίσιν ἐπενεγκεῖν βλασφημίας, ἀλλὰ εἶπεν, Ἐπιτιμήσαι σοι κύριος.

10. οὗτοι δὲ ὅσα μὲν οὐκ οἴδασιν βλασφημοῦσιν, ὅσα δὲ φυσικῶς ὡς τὰ ἄλογα ζῷα ἐπίστανται, ἐν τούτοις φθείρονται.

11. οὐαὶ αὐτοῖς, ὅτι τῇ ὁδῷ τοῦ Κάϊν ἐπορεύθησαν, καὶ τῇ πλάνῃ τοῦ Βαλαὰμ μισθοῦ ἐξεχύθησαν, καὶ τῇ ἀντιλογίᾳ τοῦ Κόρε ἀπώλοντο.

12. οὗτοί εἰσιν οἱ ἐν ταῖς ἀγάπαις ὑμῶν σπιλάδες συνευωχούμενοι ἀφόβως, ἑαυτοὺς ποιμαίνοντες, νεφέλαι ἄνυδροι ὑπὸ ἀνέμων παραφερόμεναι, δένδρα φθινοπωρινὰ ἄκαρπα δὶς ἀποθανόντα ἐκριζωθέντα,

13. κύματα ἄγρια θαλάσσης ἐπαφρίζοντα τὰς ἑαυτῶν αἰσχύνας, ἀστέρες πλανῆται οἷς ὁ ζόφος τοῦ σκότους εἰς αἰῶνα τετήρηται.

14. Προεφήτευσεν δὲ καὶ τούτοις ἕβδομος ἀπὸ Ἀδὰμ Ἐνὼχ λέγων, Ἰδοὺ ἦλθεν κύριος ἐν ἁγίαις μυριάσιν αὐτοῦ,

15. ποιῆσαι κρίσιν κατὰ πάντων καὶ ἐλέγξαι πᾶσαν ψυχὴν περὶ πάντων τῶν ἔργων ἀσεβείας αὐτῶν ὧν ἠσέβησαν καὶ περὶ πάντων τῶν σκληρῶν ὧν ἐλάλησαν κατ᾽ αὐτοῦ ἁμαρτωλοὶ ἀσεβεῖς.

16. Οὗτοί εἰσιν γογγυσταί, μεμψίμοιροι, κατὰ τὰς ἐπιθυμίας ἑαυτῶν πορευόμενοι, καὶ τὸ στόμα αὐτῶν λαλεῖ ὑπέρογκα, θαυμάζοντες πρόσωπα ὠφελείας χάριν.

17. Ὑμεῖς δέ, ἀγαπητοί, μνήσθητε τῶν ῥημάτων τῶν προειρημένων ὑπὸ τῶν ἀποστόλων τοῦ κυρίου ἡμῶν Ἰησοῦ Χριστοῦ:

18. ὅτι ἔλεγον ὑμῖν [ὅτι] Ἐπ᾽ ἐσχάτου [τοῦ] χρόνου ἔσονται ἐμπαῖκται κατὰ τὰς ἑαυτῶν ἐπιθυμίας πορευόμενοι τῶν ἀσεβειῶν.

19. Οὗτοί εἰσιν οἱ ἀποδιορίζοντες, ψυχικοί, πνεῦμα μὴ ἔχοντες.

20. ὑμεῖς δέ, ἀγαπητοί, ἐποικοδομοῦντες ἑαυτοὺς τῇ ἁγιωτάτῃ ὑμῶν πίστει, ἐν πνεύματι ἁγίῳ προσευχόμενοι,

21. ἑαυτοὺς ἐν ἀγάπῃ θεοῦ τηρήσατε, προσδεχόμενοι τὸ ἔλεος τοῦ κυρίου ἡμῶν Ἰησοῦ Χριστοῦ εἰς ζωὴν αἰώνιον

22. καὶ οὓς μὲν ἐλεᾶτε διακρινομένους,

23. οὓς δὲ σῴζετε ἐκ πυρὸς ἁρπάζοντες, οὓς δὲ ἐλεᾶτε ἐν φόβῳ, μισοῦντες καὶ τὸν ἀπὸ τῆς σαρκὸς ἐσπιλωμένον χιτῶνα.

24. Τῷ δὲ δυναμένῳ φυλάξαι ὑμᾶς ἀπταίστους καὶ στῆσαι κατενώπιον τῆς δόξης αὐτοῦ ἀμώμους ἐν ἀγαλλιάσει,

25. μόνῳ θεῷ σωτῆρι ἡμῶν διὰ Ἰησοῦ Χριστοῦ τοῦ κυρίου ἡμῶν δόξα μεγαλωσύνη κράτος καὶ ἐξουσία πρὸ παντὸς τοῦ αἰῶνος καὶ νῦν καὶ εἰς πάντας τοὺς αἰῶνας· ἀμήν.

Transliteration of Greek into English Letters

The normal form of pronunciation for *koine* Greek is called 'Erasmian pronunciation'. It is used for its pedagogical value, not for historical purposes. Some form of Erasmian pronunciation is fairly standard in academic circles. It is not what Greek sounded like in the first century ad, but it has the pedagogical advantage of distinguishing vowel sounds, many of which have similar pronunciations in other systems.[1]

Miniscule Form	Uncial Form	Greek Name	English Pronoun
α	A	ἀλφα	a (father
β	B	βετα	(bat) g
γ	Γ	γαμμα	(gave) d
δ	Δ	δελτα	(dog) e
ε	E	ἐψιλον	(met) z/dz
ζ	Z	ζητα	(adze) e
η	H	ἠτα	(their) th
θ	Θ	θητα	(thin) i
ι	I	ἰωτα	(machine)
κ	K	καππα	k (king) l
λ	Λ	λαμδα	(lake)
μ	M	μυ νυ	m (man
ν	N	ξι	n (noon
ξ	Ξ		x/ks (ax

---

1. For further information, see
https://academic.logos.com/2015/11/25/how– should–κοινῆ–greek–be–pronounced/.

όμικρον	*o (log) p*	omicron
πι	*(pea) r/hro*	pi rho
ρω	*(throw) s*	sigma
σιγμα	*(sing)*	tau
ταυ	*t (to) u*	upsilon
ύψιλον	*(cartoon)*	phi chi
φι χι	*ph (phone)*	
	ch/kh, ch	psi
ψι	*(Bach)*	omega
ώμεγα	*ps (lips)*	
	o (tone)	

Biography

A Prayer Book for Australia, The Anglican Church of Australia. Mulgrave, Victoria: Broughton Books, 1999.

Abrams, M. H. *A Glossary of Literary Terms.* 8th ed. Boston: Thomson Wadsworth, 2005.

Aichele, G. *The Letters of Jude and Second Peter: Paranoia and the Slaves of Christ.* Sheffield, UK: Sheffield Phoenix Press, 2012.

Andersen, F. I. 'Yahweh, the Kind and Sensitive God' in *God Who Is Rich in Mercy: Essays Presented to Dr D. B. Knox.* Edited by P. T. O'Brien and D. G. Peterson. Homebush West, NSW: Lancer Books, 1986.

Atkinson, D. *The Message of Genesis 1–11.* The Bible Speaks Today. Leicester, UK: Inter-Varsity Press, 1990.

Barclay, W. *The Letters of John and Jude.* Daily Study Bible Series, 2nd ed. Edinburgh: Saint Andrew Press, 1960.

Bauckham, R. J. *Jude, 2 Peter.* Word Biblical Commentary. Waco, TX: Word Books, 1983.

———, *Jude and the Relatives of Jesus in the Early Church.* London: T. and T. Clark, 1990.

Belleville, L. Ἰουνιαν ... ἐπίσημοι ἐν τοίς ἀποστόλοις: A Re-examination of Romans 16:7 in Light of Primary Source Materials,' *New Testament Studies* 51:2 (2005): 231–249.

Berkhof, L. *Systematic Theology.* Edinburgh: Banner of Truth, 1976.

Betz, H. D. *Galatians: A Commentary on Paul's Letter to the Churches in Galatia.* Philadelphia, PA: Fortress Press, 1979.

———, *2 Corinthians 8 and 9: A Commentary on Two Administrative Letters of the Apostle Paul.* Philadelphia, PA: Fortress Press, 1985.

Bigg, C. *A Critical and Exegetical Commentary on the Epistles of St Peter and St Jude.* The International Critical Commentary. New York: C. Scribner's Sons, 1901.

Black, M. 'The Maranatha Invocation and Jude 14, 15 (1 Enoch 1:9)' in *Christ and the Spirit in the New Testament: Studies in Honour of C. F. D. Moule*. Edited by B. Lindars and S. S. Smalley. London: Cambridge University Press, 1973.

Blaiklock, E. M. *Commentary on the New Testament*. London: Hodder and Stoughton, 1977.

Bray, G. L. (ed.) 'James, 1–2 Peter, 1–3 John, Jude,' *Ancient Christian Commentary on Scripture*, vol. 11. Downers Grove, IL: Inter-Varsity Press, 2000.

Brosend, W. F. ii. 'The Letter of Jude: A Rhetoric of Excess or an Excess of Rhetoric?', *Interpretation* 60:3 (2006): 292–305.

———, *James and Jude*. The New Cambridge Bible Commentary. Cambridge: Cambridge University Press, 2006.

Brown, M. J. 'Paul's Use of ΔΟΥΛΟΣ ΧΡΙΣΤΟΥ ΙΗΣΟΥ in Romans 1:1,' *Journal of Biblical Literature* 120:4 (2001): 723-737.

Bruce, F. F. *The Defence of the Gospel in the New Testament*. Grand Rapids, MI: Wm. B. Eerdmans Publishing Company, 1959.

———, *The Epistle to the Hebrews*. The New International Commentary on the New Testament. Grand Rapids, MI: Wm. B. Eerdmans Publishing Company, 1964.

———, *The Book of the Acts*. The New International Commentary on the New Testament. Grand Rapids, MI: Wm. B. Eerdmans Publishing Company, 1988.

Calvin, J. *Institutes of the Christian Religion* in *The Library of Christian Classics Series*, vols. 20, 21. Edited by J. T. McNeill and translated by F. L. Battles. Philadelphia: Westminster Press, 1960.

———, *Commentaries on the Catholic Epistles*. Edited and translated by J. Owen. Edinburgh: Calvin Translation Society. See *www.ccel.org*.

Charles, J. D. 'Those and These: The Use of the OT in Jude,' *Journal for the Study of the New Testament* 38:12 (1990): 109–124.

———, 'Jude's Use of Pseudepigraphical Source Material as Part of a Literary Strategy,' *New Testament Studies* 37:1 (1991): 130–145.

———, 'Polemic and Persuasion: Typological and Rhetorical Perspectives on the Letter of Jude,' in *Reading Jude with New Eyes:*

Methodological Reassessments of the Letter of Jude. Edited by R. L. Webb and P. H. Davids. London: T. & T. Clark, 2007, 89.

Charles, R. H. (ed.) *The Apocrypha and Pseudepigrapha of the Old Testament.* Oxford: Clarendon Press, 1913.

Charlesworth, J. H. and L. M. McDonald (eds). *The Function of 'Canonical' and 'Non-Canonical' Religious Texts.* London: T. and T. Clark, 2010.

Clarke, A. D. *Secular and Christian Leadership in Corinth: A Socio-Historical and Exegetical Study of 1 Cor 1–6.* Leiden: E. J. Brill, 1993.

Coleman-Norton, P. R. *Studies in Roman Economic and Social History.* Princeton, NJ: Princeton University Press, 1951.

Collins, J. J. 'The Assumption of Moses' in M. de Jonge (ed.) *Outside the Old Testament.* Cambridge: Cambridge University Press, 1986.

Constable, T. L. *Notes on Jude 2021 Edition,* in *https://www.planobiblechapel.org/con/notes /html/nt/jude/ jude.htm.*

Cranfield, C. E. B. *1 and 2 Peter and Jude.* Torch Bible Commentaries. London: SCM Press, 1960.

———, *The Epistle to the Romans,* vol. 1. The International Critical Commentary. Edinburgh: T and T Clark, 1975.

———, *The Epistle to the Romans,* vol. 2. The International Critical Commentary. Edinburgh: T and T Clark, 1979.

Davids, P. H. *The Letters of 2 Peter and Jude.* The Pillar New Testament Commentary. Grand Rapids, MI: Wm. B. Eerdmans Publishing Company, 2006.

———, *2 Peter and Jude: A Handbook on the Greek Text.* Baylor Handbook on the Greek New Testament. Waco, TX: Baylor University Press, 2011.

———, *A Theology of James, Peter and Jude.* Biblical Theology of the New Testament. Grand Rapids, MI: Zondervan Publishing House, 2014.

Deichgräber, R. *Gotteshymnus und Christushymnus in der frühen Christenheit.* Göttingen: Vandenhoeck and Ruprecht, 1967.

Dumbrell, W. *Covenant and Creation: An Old Testament Covenantal Theology.* Homebush West, NSW: Lancer Books, 1984.

Dunn, J. D. G. *Jesus and the Spirit.* London: SCM Press, 1975.

Dutcher, R. 'An Unorthodox Argument and Jude's Non-Canonical Sources,' *Asian Journal of Pentecostal Studies* 11:1–2 (2008): 33–43.

Ellis, E. E. *Prophecy and Hermeneutic in the Early Church.* Grand Rapids, MI: Wm. B. Eerdmans Publishing Company, 1978.

Ferguson, S. B. and D. F. Wright (eds), *New Dictionary of Theology.* Leicester, UK: Inter-Varsity Press, 1988.

Filson, F. V. 'The Significance of the Early House Churches,' *Journal of Biblical Literature* 58:2 (1939): 105–112.

Fiorenza, E. S. 'Rhetorical Situation and Historical Reconstruction in 1 Corinthians,' *New Testament Studies* 33:3 (1987): 386–403.

Friberg, T., B. Friberg and N. F. Miller, *Analytical Lexicon of the Greek New Testament.* Grand Rapids, MI: Baker Books, 2000.

Garnsey, P. and R. Saller, *The Roman Empire: Economy, Society and Culture.* Berkeley, CA: California University Press, 1987.

Goldsworthy, G. *According to Plan.* Leicester, UK: Inter-Varsity Press, 1991.

Goodman, M. *Rome and Jerusalem: The Clash of Ancient Civilizations.* New York: Vintage Books, 2007.

Green, E. M. G. *2 Peter and Jude.* Tyndale New Testament Commentaries. Grand Rapids, MI: Wm. B. Eerdmans Publishing Company, 1968.

Green, G. L. *Jude and 2 Peter.* Baker Exegetical Commentary on the New Testament. Grand Rapids, MI: Baker Academic, 2008.

Gunther, J. J. 'The Alexandrian Epistle of Jude,' *New Testament Studies* 30:4 (1984): 549–562.

Guthrie, D. *New Testament Introduction.* Downers Grove, IL: Inter-Varsity Press, 1970.

Hamann, H. P. *Chi Rho Commentary on James–Jude.* Adelaide, SA: Lutheran Publishing House, 1980.

Harman, A. M. *Isaiah: A Covenant to be Kept for the Sake of the Church.* Focus on the Bible. Fearn: Christian Focus, 2005.

Harner, P. B. *What Are They Saying About the Catholic Epistles?* Mahwah, NJ: Paulist Press, 2004.

Harris, M. J. *Slave of Christ: A New Testament Metaphor for Total Devotion to Christ.* New Studies in Biblical Theology 8. Downers Grove, IL: Inter-Varsity Press, 1999.

Hattersley, R. *The Life of John Wesley: A Brand From the Burning.* New York: Doubleday, 2003.

Hengel, M. *The Pre-Christian Paul.* London: SCM Press, 1991.

Hiebert, D. E. *Second Peter and Jude: An Expositional Commentary.* Greenville, SC: Unusual Publications, 1989.

Horrell, D. A. *The Social Ethos of the Corinthian Correspondence: Interests and Ideology from 1 Corinthians to 1 Clement.* Edinburgh: A. and C. Black, 1996.

Hultin, J. 'Jude's Citation of 1 Enoch' in *The Function of 'Canonical' and 'Non-Canonical' Religious Texts.* Edited by J. H. Charlesworth and L. M. McDonald. London: T. and T. Clark, 2010.

Huxley, T. H. in *The Oxford Dictionary of Quotations.* Oxford: Oxford University Press, 1999.

Isaac, E. '1 Enoch' in *The Old Testament Pseudepigrapha.* Edited by J. H. Charlesworth. Oxford: Clarendon, 1983.

Jeremias, J. *Jerusalem in the Time of Jesus.* London: SCM Press, 1969.

Jobes, K. H. *Letters to the Church: A Survey of Hebrews and the General Epistles.* Grand Rapids, MI: Zondervan Publishing House, 2011.

Josephus, Flavius *The Antiquities of the Jews.* Translated by L. H. Feldman. Loeb Classical Library. London: Heinemann, 1969.

Jurgens, B. A. 'Is It Pesher? Readdressing the Relationship between the Epistle of Jude and the Qumran Pesharim,' *Journal of Biblical Literature* 136:2 (2017): 491–510.

Keats, J. *To Autumn* (1820), *The Oxford Dictionary of Quotations* (Oxford: Oxford University Press, 1999.

Kelly, J. N. D. *A Commentary on the Epistles of Peter and of Jude.* Black's New Testament Commentary. London: Adam and Charles Black, 1969.

Kistemaker, S. J. *Exposition of the Epistles of Peter and the Epistle of Jude*. New Testament Commentary. Grand Rapids, MI: Baker Books, 1987.

Kittel, G. (ed.) *Theological Dictionary of the New Testament,* vol. 2. Grand Rapids, MI: Wm. B. Eerdmans Publishing Company, 1964.

Koester, H. *Introduction to the New Testament, vol. 2: History and Literature of Early Christianity*, 2nd ed. New York: Walter de Gruyter, 2000.

Kohlenberger J. R. III, E. W. Goodrick and J. A. Swanson, *The Greek English Concordance to the New Testament with the New International Version*. Grand Rapids, MI: Zondervan Publishing House, 1997.

Köstenberger, A. J. *Handbook on Hebrews through Revelation*. Grand Rapids: Baker Academic, 2020.

Lawlor, G. L. *Translation and Exposition of the Epistle of Jude*. Nutley, NJ: Presbyterian and Reformed Publishing, 1972.

Lenski, R. C. H. *The Interpretation of the Epistles of St Peter, St John and St Jude.* Minneapolis, MN: Augsburg Publishing House, 1966.

Letham, R. W. A. 'Calling' in *New Dictionary of Theology*. Edited by S. B. Ferguson and D. F. Wright. Leicester, UK: Inter-Varsity Press, 1988.

Lockett, D. 'Objects of Mercy in Jude: The Prophetic Background of Jude 22–23,' *Catholic Biblical Quarterly* 77:2 (2015): 322–336.

———, 'Purity and Polemic: A Reassessment of Jude's Theological World' in *Reading Jude With New Eyes: Methodological Reassessments of the Letter of Jude*. Edited by R. L. Webb and P. H. Davids. London: T. and T. Clark, 2008.

Lockyer, H. Sr (ed.) 'Seven, Seventh' in *The Hodder and Stoughton Illustrated Bible Dictionary*. Nashville: Thomas Nelson Publishers, 1986.

MacArthur, J. *2 Peter and Jude*. The MacArthur New Testament Commentary. Chicago: Moody Publishers, 2005.

———, *Slaves of Christ* in *https://www.gty.org/library/sermons-library/GTY112/slaves-of-christ*.

Manson, T. W. *A Companion to the Bible*. Edinburgh: T and T Clark, 1949.

Manuell, G. *Floating Down Under: Foreign Exchange in Australia.* Sydney: Law Book Company, 1986.

———, *Gender Wars in Christianity.* Brisbane, Queensland: Connor Court, 2018.

Marshall, I. H. *The Epistles of John.* The New International Commentary on the New Testament. Grand Rapids, MI: Wm. B. Eerdmans Publishing Company, 1981.

Marshall, P. 'Enmity in Corinth: Social Conventions in Paul's Relations with the Corinthians,' *Wissenschaftliche Untersuchungen zum Neuen Testament* 2 Reihe 23, 1987.

Martin, R. P. 'The Theology of Jude, 1 Peter, and 2 Peter' in *The Theology of the Letters of James, Peter and Jude.* Edited by A. Chester and R. P. Martin. Cambridge: Cambridge University Press, 1994.

Mayor, J. B. *The Epistle of St Jude and the Second Epistle of St Peter.* London: Macmillan, 1907.

Mbuvi, A. M. *Jude and 2 Peter.* A New Covenant Commentary. Eugene, OR: Cascade Books, 2015.

McGee, J. V. *The General Epistle of Jude*, vol 5. of *Thru the Bible with J. Vernon McGee.* Pasadena, CA: Thru the Bible Radio, 1983.

Milavec, A. *The Didache: Text, Translation, Analysis, and Commentary.* Collegeville, MN: Liturgical Press, 2003.

Mitchell, M. M. *Paul and the Rhetoric of Reconciliation: An Exegetical Investigation of the Language and Composition of 1 Corinthians.* Louisville: Westminster/John Knox Press, 1992.

Moffatt, J. *The First Epistle of Paul to the Corinthians.* The Moffatt New Testament Commentary. London: Hodder and Stoughton, 1947.

Morris, L. L. *The First Epistle of Paul to the Corinthians.* Tyndale New Testament Series. Leicester, UK: Inter-Varsity Press, 1983.

———, *The Gospel According to John.* The New International Commentary on the New Testament. Grand Rapids, MI: Wm. B. Eerdmans Publishing Company, 1995.

Morse, G. *Lord, Spare Our Land: How Revival Begins in America*, in *https://www.desiringgod. org/articles/lord-spare-our-land.*

Muilenburg, J. 'Form Criticism and Beyond,' *Journal of Biblical Literature* 88:1 (1969): 1–18.

NetBible Commentary on Jude, in *https://bible.org/netbible*.

New American Standard Bible. La Habra, CA: Foundation Press Publications, 1995.

Neyrey, J. H. *2 Peter, Jude*. New York: Doubleday, 1993.

Nobbs, A. "'Beloved Brothers" in the New Testament and Early Christian World' in *The New Testament in its First Century Setting: Essays on Context and Background in Honour of B. W. Winter on His 65th Birthday*. Edited by P. J. Williams. Grand Rapids, MI: Wm. B. Eerdmans Publishing Company, 2004.

Norden, E. *Die antike Kunstprosa vom VI Jahrhundert v Chr Bis in die Zeit der Renaissance 2* in Hengel, M. *The Pre-Christian Paul*. London: SCM Press, 1991.

O'Brien, P. T. 'Introductory Thanksgivings in the Letters of Paul'. *Novum Testamentum* Supplement 49. Leiden: E. J. Brill, 1977.

O'Brien, P. T. and D. G. Peterson (eds) *God Who Is Rich in Mercy: Essays Presented to Dr D. B. Knox*. Homebush West, NSW: Lancer Books, 1986.

Osburn, C. D. 'Text of Jude 22–23,' *Zeitschrift fur die neutestamentliche Wissenschaft* 63:1–2 (1972): 139–144.

———, 'The Christological Use of 1 Enoch 1:9 in Jude 14, 15,' *New Testament Studies* 23:3 (1977): 334–341.

Oswalt, J. N. *The Book of Isaiah, Chapters 1–39*. The New International Commentary on the Old Testament. Grand Rapids, MI: Wm. B. Eerdmans Publishing Company, 1986.

Owen, J. *The Holy Spirit: His Gifts and Power*. Grand Rapids, MI: Kregel Publications, rep. 1973.

Packer, J. I. 'Theism for Our Time' in *God Who Is Rich in Mercy: Essays Presented to Dr D. B. Knox*. Edited by P. T. O'Brien and D. G. Peterson. Homebush West, NSW: Lancer Books, 1986.

———, 'The Glory of God,' in *New Dictionary of Theology*. Edited by S. B. Ferguson and D. F. Wright. Leicester, UK: Inter-Varsity Press, 1988.

Perdue, L. G. and W. Carter, *Israel and Empire: A Postcolonial History of Israel and Early Judaism*. London: Bloomsbury T. and T. Clark, 2015.

Pfitzner, V. C. 'Paul and the *Agon* Motif,' *Novum Testamentum* Supplement 16. Leiden: E. J. Brill, 1967.

Plummer, A. *The Epistle of St Jude*. Ellicott's Commentary, vol. 8. Grand Rapids, MI: Zondervan Publishing House, 1943.

Plumptre, E. H. *The General Epistles of St Peter and St Jude*. Cambridge Bible for Schools and Colleges. Cambridge: Cambridge University Press, 1879.

Priest, J. 'Testament of Moses' in *The Old Testament Pseudepigrapha*. Edited by J. H. Charlesworth. Oxford: Clarendon, 1983.

Reese, R. A. *2 Peter and Jude*. The Two Horizons New Testament Commentary Series. Grand Rapids, MI: Wm. B. Eerdmans Publishing Company, 2007.

Reicke, B. *The Epistles of James, Peter and Jude*. The Anchor Bible. New York: Doubleday, 1964.

Rengstorf, K. H. 'δοῦλος' in *Theological Dictionary of the New Testament,* vol. 2. Edited by G. Kittel. Grand Rapids, MI: Wm. B. Eerdmans Publishing Company, 1964.

Richard, E. J. *Reading 1 Peter, Jude and 2 Peter*. Macon, GA: Smyth and Helwys, 2000.

Rist, J. M. *Human Value: A Study in Ancient Philosophical Ethics*. Leiden: E. J. Brill, 1982.

Robinson, A., S. Llewelyn and B. Wassell 'Showing Mercy to the Ungodly and the Inversion of Invective in Jude,' *New Testament Studies* 64:2 (2018): 194-212.

Robinson, J. A. T. *Redating the New Testament*. London: SCM Press, 1976.

Salmond, S. D. F. *The General Epistle of Jude*. The Pulpit Commentary. New York: Funk and Wagnalls, 1944.

Schaeffer, F. A. *The Great Evangelical Disaster.* Westchester, IL: Crossway Books, 1984.

Schelkle, K. H. 'Spätapostolische Briefe als frühkatholisches Zeugnis,' *Neutestamentliche Aufsätze fur J Schmidt,* edited by J. Blinzler, O. Kuss and F. Mussner. Regensburg: Verlag Friedrich Pustet, 1963.

Schreiner, T. R. *1, 2 Peter, Jude.* The New American Commentary. Nashville, TN: Broadman and Holman, 2003.

Smallwood, E. M. *The Jews Under Roman Rule.* Leiden: E. J. Brill, 1976.

Stewart, J. S. *A Man in Christ.* London: Hodder and Stoughton, 1935.

Stokes, R. E. 'Not Over Moses' Dead Body: Jude 9, 22–24 and the Assumption of Moses in Their Early Jewish Context,' *Journal for the Study of the New Testament* 40:2 (2017) 192–213.

Strong, J. *Greek Dictionary of the New Testament* in *The Exhaustive Concordance of the Bible.* 1890. 29th reprint, London: Hodder and Stoughton, 1970.

The Book of Common Prayer.

The Oxford English Reference Dictionary. Oxford: Oxford University Press, 1996.

Towner, P. H. *The Letters to Timothy and Titus.* The New International Commentary on the New Testament. Grand Rapids, MI: Wm. B. Eerdmans Publishing Company, 2006.

Travis, S. H. 'Hope,' in *New Dictionary of Theology.* Edited by S. B. Ferguson and D. F. Wright. Leicester, UK: Inter-Varsity Press, 1988.

Turner, N. *Grammatical Insights into the New Testament.* Edinburgh: T and T Clark, 1965.

van Unnik, W. C. 'Tarsus or Jerusalem: The City of Paul's Youth' in Sparsa Collecta 1, *Novum Testamentum* Supplement 29. Leiden: E. J. Brill, 1973.

Walck, L. W. 'Response to Jeremy Hultin's "Jude's Citation of 1 Enoch",' in *The Function of 'Canonical' and 'Non-Canonical' Religious Texts.* Edited by J. H. Charlesworth and L. M. McDonald. London: T. and T. Clark, 2010.

Wallace, D. B. *Greek Grammar Beyond the Basics.* Grand Rapids, MI: Zondervan Publishing House, 1966.

Wand, J. W. C. *The General Epistles of St Peter and St Jude*. Westminster Commentaries Series. London: Methuen, 1934.

Watson, D. F. *Invention, Arrangement and Style: Rhetorical Criticism of Jude and 2 Peter*. SBL Dissertation Series 104. Atlanta, GA: Scholars Press, 1988.

———, 'The Letter of Jude' in The New Interpreters Bible, 12 vols. Nashville, TN: Abingdon, 1994–2004.

Webb, R. L. "The Eschatology of the Epistle of Jude and Its Rhetorical and Social Functions," *Bulletin for Biblical Research* 6 (1996): 139-51.

———, 'The Use of "Story" in the Letter of Jude: Rhetorical Strategies of Jude's Narrative Episodes,' *Journal for the Study of the New Testament* 31:1 (2008): 53–87.

Webb, R. L. and P. H. Davids (eds), *Reading Jude With New Eyes: Methodological Reassessments of the Letter of Jude*. London: T. and T. Clark, 2008.

Welborn, L. L. 'A Conciliatory Principle in 1 Cor 4:6,' *Novum Testamentum* 29:4 (1987): 320–346.

———, *Politics and Rhetoric in the Corinthian Epistles*. Macon, GA: Mercer University Press, 1997.

Westermann, W. L. 'The Slave Systems of Greek and Roman Antiquity,' *Memoirs of the American Philosophical Society* 40. New York: Noble Offset Printers, 1955.

Williams, N. M. *Commentary on the Epistle of Jude*. An American Commentary on the New Testament. Philadelphia, PA: American Baptist Publication Society, 1888.

Windisch, H. 'Die Katholischen Briefe,' in *Handbuch num Neuen Testament 15*, edited by H. Preisker. Tübingen: J. C. B. Mohr, 1951.

Winter, B. W. *Philo and Paul Among the Sophists*. Grand Rapids, MI: Wm. B. Eerdmans Publishing Company, 2002.

Woudstra, M. W. *The Book of Joshua*. The New International Commentary on the Old Testament. Grand Rapids, MI: Wm. B. Eerdmans Publishing Company, 1981.

Zerwick, M. and M. Grosvenor, *A Grammatical Analysis of the Greek New Testament,* vol. 2. Rome: Biblical Institute Press, 1979.

General Index

Scripture Index

Non-Canonical Index

Author Index

About the Author

Guy's employment involved finance in a wide range of activities: the Reserve Bank of Australia (including personal assistant to the Governor), commercial and investment banks in economics and foreign exchange, as treasurer of large companies in Australia and New Zealand, an independent financial consultant to major Australian corporations and in financial regulation at the Australian Securities and Investments Commission. He authored the university textbook *Floating Down Under: Foreign Exchange in Australia in 1986*.

His academic qualifications include a BA in economics (Macquarie University), MCom (University of New South Wales), LLM (JD) (Monash University) and a Graduate Diploma in Legal Practice (College of Law). Reflecting his longstanding interest in early Christianity, he gained an MA in Early Christian and Jewish Studies from Macquarie University in 2000. Now retired from active employment, he has more time to undertake research and writing on biblical themes. He authored *Gender Wars in Christianity* in 2018, which 'provides a strong voice to declare a biblical understanding of what it means to bear God's image as male and female, and to reveal that image by how we live and relate.' (Dr. Larry Crabb)

Jude wrote his letter to Christians who were under pressure from ungodly practices and beliefs. This commentary updates an earlier edition. It is unique in its connection of the behaviour denounced by Jude with the same errors that had previously occurred in the Corinthian church. Guy believes that it is long overdue for Christians to wake up to the accommodation of much of the Western church to the same errors that Jude denounced. Like Jude, he is encouraging Christians in the modern church to promote biblical principles in a world where the gospel of Jesus Christ is being marginalised.

Guy lives in Curlewis on the Bellarine Peninsula, Australia with his wife, Bernice. They are members of Bellarine Presbyterian Church and have three adult children. His interests include history and theology and he is a keen fan of Australian Rules Football and US college basketball.